The United States and the Americas

Lester D. Langley, General Editor

This series is dedicated to a broader understanding of the political, economic, and especially cultural forces and issues that have shaped the Western hemispheric experience— its governments and its peoples. Individual volumes assess relations between the United States and its neighbors to the south and north: Mexico, Central America, Cuba, the Dominican Republic, Haiti, Panama, Colombia, Venezuela, the Andean Republics (Peru, Ecuador, and Bolivia), Brazil, Uruguay and Paraguay, Argentina, Chile, and Canada.

D0976543

The United States and the Americas

Mexico and the United States

W. Dirk Raat

Mexico and the United States: Ambivalent Vistas, Second Edition

The University of Georgia Press
Athens and London

© 1992, 1996 by the University of Georgia Press
Athens, Georgia 30602
All rights reserved

Set in 10 on 14 Palatino by Tseng Information Systems, Inc.
Printed and bound by McNaughton & Gunn

The paper in this book meets the guidelines
for permanence and durability of the Committee on
Production Guidelines for Book Longevity of the
Council on Library Resources.

Printed in the United States of America

00 99 98 97 96 P 5 4 3 2 1

Library of Congress Cataloging in Publication Data

Raat, W. Dirk (William Dirk), 1939–
    Mexico and the United States : ambivalent
    vistas / W. Dirk Raat.—2nd ed.
        p. cm.
    Includes bibliographical references (p.   ) and index.
    ISBN 0-8203-1812-4 (pbk. : alk. paper)
        1. United States—Relations—Mexico.   2. Mexico—
    Relations—United States.   3. Mexico—History—1810–
    I. Title.
    E183.8.M6R29   1996
    303.48'273072—dc20   95-24752

British Library Cataloging in Publication Data available

To Gerry, Kelly, David . . .
and Gizmo

Contents

Illustrations

Preface

This is a history of Mexico. Not an ordinary history, but one that views Mexico in the context of its relationship with the United States and the world-economy. The emphasis is on the manner in which the United States affected Mexican history, shaped its values, attitudes, and conditions, and vice versa. At times Mexico affected the United States tremendously; during the Mexican Revolution the United States was used as a source of materiel, recruits, and funds for Mexico, which resulted in social change and commercial growth for the American Southwest.

This is also an account of the growth of Mexico's economy vis-à-vis the United States. Part of that story can be found in the demographics of Mexico, the comparative resource base of Mexico and the United States, and the geopolitics of the international community. Spain's imperial rule bequeathed a heritage that resulted in an economic gap between Mexico and the United States, a gap that was widened by the wars of independence and the mid-nineteenth century Mexican war with the United States. Since 1870, Mexico's economy has been subordinate to that of the creditor nations in the world-economy, first Great Britain, and after 1900, the United States. In other words, Mexico's modern economy has been conditioned by the development and expansion of the North American economy.

Moreover, this is a study in comparative civilizations—the western culture of Protestant North America and the Native American-Hispanic society of Catholic Mexico. Mexico's Indian and Spanish background has made it a very different society from that of the democratic and capitalistic United States. A comparative methodology has also been used to demonstrate significant trends or solve particular historical problems. For example, a comparative approach can illustrate the differences between British and Spanish imperial policies relating to the frontier and Indian matters or explain why Mexico,

xiii

which along with Argentina underwent radical modernization upon entering the industrial world-economy of the early twentieth century, followed a violent path and Argentina did not.

This is also a diplomatic history, but not in the traditional sense of a study of the formal political and military relations between states. In analyzing formal relations, the "underground" history of U.S. intelligence and covert operations has been considered, as have the domestic dimensions of foreign policy in both the United States and Mexico.

Mexico's relationship with the United States is important if only because Mexico's history is unique in at least two ways. First, of all the countries of Latin America, only Mexico shares a common border with the industrialized and militaristic United States. This proximity has dictated that the relationship be asymmetrical: an economically and militarily powerful United States that views Mexico in terms of strategic and commercial interests and geopolitical concerns, and an underdeveloped Mexico that seeks to protect its cultural integrity and national identity while promoting economic growth in the face of the Colossus of the North. On those rare occasions when U.S. and Mexican interests converge, such as during the Juárista era or World War II, Mexico has been able to use the international situation to promote its own identity concerns.

Second, a shared border means that Mexico and the United States participate in the common history of a borderlands area, a region that is called Mexamerica today and was known historically as the Gran Chichimeca. The history of Mexico-U.S. relations must include this area; a society with a frontier past that is bilingual and bicultural but is neither Mexican nor American, yet of primary importance for policymakers on both sides of the border.

This work has been dependent on many authors for the macroeconomical theory found herein. The ideas of a world-economy have been developed before in the historical works of Fernand Braudel and the sociological studies of Immanuel Wallerstein. Eric Wolf's ideas on modes of production have also shaped my thinking, as has the notion of "incorporation" developed by Thomas D. Hall in his work on social change in the Southwest. University of Chicago historian John Coatsworth has noted the need for plausible macro-historical studies to substitute for dependency theory, modes of production analysis, and world-system models. Yet in the absence of suitable alternatives, what must be emphasized is that the important idea contained in Wallerstein and others is that nations are part of a dynamic world-system; that underdevelopment in one area and development in another are mutually contingent aspects of a transnational system. One can agree with Braudel and Wallerstein concerning the dynamics of interdependency without accepting all of their theoretical arguments. Needless to say, the interpretations and conclusions of this study are ultimately the responsibility of the author.

Acknowledgments

A Scholarly Incentive Award from the office of the Academic Vice President at the State University of New York at Fredonia and two New York State/United University Professions Faculty Travel Grants allowed me to do fieldwork in Chihuahua and along the border between Texas and Tamaulipas during the summers of 1987–89, as well as library work at the Nettie Lee Benson Latin American Collection of the University of Texas at Austin. This research, while related to other activities, aided in the development of this one.

A special thanks to individuals who assisted in this project, including the following who read portions of the manuscript: William Graebner, William T. Hagan, John Coatsworth, James Lockhart, David Weber, John Hart, Friedrich Katz, John Womack, Jr., David LaFrance, and Colin MacLachlan. Oscar Martínez assisted me in understanding the borderlands. Don Bush guided me through the Sierra Tarahumar, while Clemente Figueroa shared his Tarahumara lifestyle. B. W. Wolfe, a past Trico executive, contributed ideas about *maquiladoras*. At the State University of New York at Fredonia, Gary Barber and Deborah Lanni assisted me. I am in the debt of Charlotte Morse, Instructional Resources Center, SUNY Fredonia, for producing the illustrations. Over the years several students, too numerous to mention, inspired much of the thought and content of this work. At the University of Georgia, Lester D. Langley suggested the project and assisted in its development, while Karen Orchard provided valuable editorial guidance.

1   "Gringos" and "Greasers"

> The feeling of solitude, which is a nostalgic longing for the body
> from which we were cast out, is a longing for a place. According
> to an ancient belief, held by virtually all peoples, that place is the
> center of the world, the navel of the universe.
>
> Octavio Paz, *The Labyrinth of Solitude*

Most of humanity tends to perceive the world from an ego-
centric or ethnocentric point of view. Egocentrism is the habit of order-
ing the world so that components away from "self" diminish in value.
Because as individuals we are dependent on others for biological comfort and psychological security, egocentrism can only be realized in
part. Ethnocentrism (collective egocentrism), however, or at least the
delusion of group self-sufficiency, can be easier to obtain. As members of societies, individuals learn to differentiate between "we" and
"they," between real striking workers and "scabs," between our native
home and alien territory. "We" are at the center, and as people are
perceived as moving away from the center they are proportionally
dehumanized.[1]

The illusion of centrality and superiority is typical of most peoples.
The ancient Egyptians believed themselves superior to the nations
beyond the Nile. Eskimos thought their habitat was the world's geographical center and that early twentieth-century Europeans had come
to Greenland to learn good manners. Britain in the nineteenth century, and the United States until recently, each saw itself as the hub of
the world.[2]

In the northwestern part of New Mexico, five cultures maintain
their own flattering self-images in spite of geographical proximity to
each other and social intercourse between groups. When asked by an
interviewer in the 1950s as to the kind of community they would set
up after a hypothetical drought, their responses were as follows: The
typical Navajo said that "if I was a Holy People, I would first build
a good hogan." A Zuni informant indicated that he would ask the

1

Zunis to return "because a long time ago there *was* a drought . . . but the Zunis worshiped and prayed for rain and made the country good again." The Hispano said that he would make a community with *la gente,* "with Catholic religion, raising livestock . . . and [with] the *costumbres* [customs]." The Mormons responded that the newly made community would be "under the United Order [of the Church of Jesus Christ of Latter-Day Saints]; . . . their would be just one people, all of one belief . . . [and] this one belief would be Mormonism." The typical Texan response was to talk of a community of families, ranches, cows, Protestants, and "movie houses."[3]

With the age of exploration and navigation in the fifteenth and sixteenth centuries, the idea of Europe expanded in meaning. The style of ethnocentrism that dominated may be called Eurocentrism, a view that gave Europe the symbolic status as being the world's center. Europe was synonymous with history, race, religion (Christendom), language, and culture; Asia simply was not Europe and had no unity. Thus the European spoke of the Near East, the Middle East, and the Far East. Of course the Egyptians, Arabs, East Indians, and Chinese did not know they were all Asians. Nor did the Aztecs and Incas know that they were inhabitants of the East Indies, that is, Asiatic Indians without history, race, religion, language, and culture.[4]

The ancient Mexicano, a member of the Mexica or Aztec tribe, was a proud person. He or she was an urban dweller of Mexico-Tenochtitlán; the etymology of "Mexico" coming from *metztli* and *xictli,* meaning "the town in the navel or center of the moon." As descendants of the Toltecs (according to their official history), they were a civilized people whose symbol was Quetzalcoatl, the giver of the arts and sciences and all knowledge. The inhabitants outside the center were uncivilized. "We" are Mexicans, people of Quetzalcoatl. "They," the nomads of the north, are "sons of the dog," Chichimecas or "barbarians." "They" are the Otomí, rustics immediately outside the center. "They" are the Tenime, "a barbarous people, very unskillful, stupid and rude." To the northeast are the wretched Huaxtecs who stain their teeth black and red, and whose men wear no loin cloth, a fact certain to scandalize the Mexicans of the center.[5]

In the meantime many of the so-called Chichimecas had developed their own cultural characteristics, and had no knowledge of being "outsiders." Some were Anasazi Pueblos who lived in northeastern Arizona and northwestern New Mexico; others, like the Pima, were of the Hohokam culture of Arizona; and then there were the Mogollon occupying the broken highlands that separate New Mexico and Arizona; and finally a host of others, including Hakatayas, Salados, Yaquis, and Mayos. The descendants of these people, especially the Anasazi, include the modern-day Pueblos like the Zuni, Hopi, and Acoma.[6]

Zuni Indians trace their history back to the Anasazi Pueblos of A.D. 1100 and after. It is likely that their heritage even spans the earlier Basket Maker period. In the 1540s the Zuni pueblos discovered by Francisco Coronado became known as Cíbola. At that time there were six villages, but following the Pueblo Revolt of 1680, fear of Spanish and Apache reprisals led them to abandon their villages and reconsolidate into one village by 1705. This is the modern Zuni pueblo about forty miles west of El Morro National Monument in New Mexico.[7]

Zunis have a well developed sense of place. The earth is the center and principal object of the cosmos. Within the earth the compact settlement of the Zunis is the Middle Place. All the universe is oriented to the Middle Place, and their origin myths are preoccupied with ascertaining the correctness of the location of the center.[8]

From outside the Middle Place have come alien forces, first the conquering Spaniards and then the Athapaskan of the seventeenth century, including Apaches and Navajos. This early feeling of hostility seems to be the historical root of the current Zuni prohibition that prevents Spanish and Mexican Americans from witnessing any Zuni religious ceremonials (a prohibition that does not extend to other non-Native Americans) and explains why the Zuni word "apachu," meaning enemies, applies to all Apaches and Navajos.[9]

During pioneer times explorers and settlers came to the Middle Place from two directions. From the south came Spanish conquistadores with their Tarascan Indian allies, who were followed later by Catholic missionaries and colonists. From the east, at a much later time, came Anglo-American explorers, scientists, military men, and settlers. Although a geography textbook might describe New Mexico as a semiarid country, the early visitors perceived it differently, with eyes that had adapted to other values.

The Spaniards, motivated by glory to God and king, did not pay much attention to a land that was not all that different from Old Spain. When Coronado took note of the climate it was to mark the drop in temperature. In reporting to the viceroy in 1540 he wrote that the people of Cíbola "do not raise cotton because the country is exceedingly cold." So too did Don Juan de Oñate speak of the "rigorous winter" of 1599; and Bishop Tamaron, who visited New Mexico in 1760, referred to the ice-covered stream at Taos and the "freezing at dawn."[10] Spaniards and Mexicans, when moving north into New Mexico, always spoke of the presence of streams. They did not find the country barren—it was cold and wet.

In contrast to the Latins, the Anglos moved into the Middle Place from the humid east. In 1849 Lieutenant J. H. Simpson described the "almost universal barrenness which pervades this [Navajo] country." J. R. Bartlett, United States Commissioner of the U.S.-Mexico Boundary Commission, called the plains of New Mexico "barren and uninteresting in the extreme." Traveler Albert Pike, who entered New Mexico in 1831, spoke of this different world with prairies appearing as "bleak, black and barren wastes undulating in gloomy loneliness" and settlers "peculiarly blessed with ugliness." From boundary commissioners to historians, from W. H. Emory to Walter Prescott Webb, the Great Plains west of the one hundredth meridian was hot, barren, and arid.[11] In any case, like the Spanish pioneers these Anglo-Americans saw environment and place in terms of their own notions of centrality and superiority.

By the second quarter of the nineteenth century successful independence movements in America against England and Spain had led to the emergence of two young nations that shared a common yet undefined border. The attitudes and opinions of the Americans and Mexicans toward each other were naturally unfavorable. As contacts between the two nations increased these attitudes became important elements in producing what one author has called "culture conflict."[12]

A number of Texas narratives reveal opinions that are racist, big-oted, and prejudicial. The major traits of Mexicans as reported by these sources are ignorance, indolence, and cowardliness. For ex-ample, Mary Austin Holley's descriptions as published in her work *Texas* (1833) record that Mexicans in Texas "are very ignorant and de-graded, and generally speaking, timid and irresolute; and a more bru-tal and, at the same time, more cowardly set of men does not exist than the Mexican soldiery. They are held in great contempt by the Ameri-can settlers, who assert that five Indians will chase twenty Mexicans, but five Anglo-Americans will chase twenty Indians. . . . The Mexi-cans are commonly very indolent, of loose morals, and, if not infidels of which there are many, involved in the grossest superstition."[13] It is interesting to note that in this passage Holley constructed a hierarchy of bravery in Texas—first Anglos, then Indians, and finally Mexicans. Even today many Zunis and Navajos view Anglos as superior to Span-ish and Mexican Americans in terms of both power and prestige.[14]

When Texans declared their independence from Mexico in 1836, conflict between the two groups erupted openly. The battles of the Alamo and Goliad dispelled any doubts of Mexican cruelty to the Tex-ans, and the later success of Texas patriots at San Jacinto confirmed for Americans the ineptitude of the Mexicans. As one popular fantasy described the scene after the battle of San Jacinto, the buzzards and coyotes refused to touch the dead Mexicans "because of the peppery constitution of the flesh."[15] Here one can see the beginnings of cur-rent border usage in which Mexicans are called "chile peppers" and "greasers."

Spanish and Mexican attitudes toward Americans are reflected in much of the governmental literature. These works are filled with adjec-tives characterizing Americans as "presumptious," "ambitious," and "aggressive." Luis de Onís, the Spaniard who negotiated the Adams-Onís Treaty of 1819, is typical in his comments. He noted that the Americans were "arrogant and audacious," thought "themselves su-perior to all the nations of Europe," and believed "that their dominion is destined to extend, now, to the isthmus of Panama, and hereafter, over all the regions of the New World."[16] This indeed was the idea of Manifest Destiny that came to control American policy. While the

Americans talked of "expanding the realm of liberty," Mexicans complained of empire building and imperialism.

Raymund Paredes, after surveying travel literature in the United States between 1831 and 1869, noted that Americans from different regions had remarkably similar attitudes about Mexicans. These were generally negative and reflected anti-Catholic sentiment, racial prejudice, and hispanophobia. They were also ethnocentric.

> This last quality [ethnocentrism] was pervasive among Yanqui [used here to denote simply a citizen of the United States] travelers and thus especially pernicious. Frequently, travelers denigrated Mexicans essentially because they were unlike themselves. The Americans were not satisfied simply to describe the Mexicans, but, secure in their feeling of superiority, wished to stand in moral judgment of them. Yanqui writers seldom understood that it was one thing to suggest that Mexicans did not esteem work as much as Americans, and quite another to label them simply indolent.[17]

It should also be noted that this ethnocentrism came at a time when Americans were unabashedly undergoing a surge of nativism, a major characteristic of the age of Jacksonian Democracy.

Modern Mexico was born during the last quarter of the nineteenth century under the direction of Porfirio Díaz, dictator and president for over thirty years (1876–1911). This period (known as the *porfiriato*) was characterized by an influx of American capital that, when combined with domestic peace, paved the way to modernization. But there were social costs to this economic growth, and the Revolution of 1911 was one of them.

Campesinos in the northern high country joined *serrano* revolts that sought to protect municipal autonomy in the face of a burgeoning, bureaucratic state, while agrarians and peasants in the south, typified by Emiliano Zapata, fought the advances of commercial haciendas.[18] After 1913 urban labor, small scale artisans and merchants, and middle-class professionals entered the fray. An early result was the establishment of the nationalistic constitution of 1917, a document that guaranteed the rights of labor, agriculture, and management and restricted foreign ownership of property.

To implement the constitution, Lázaro Cárdenas nationalized the British- and American-owned oil fields on 18 March 1938. This expropriation decree thrilled Mexicans and angered Americans. The event immediately became a day of celebration for Mexicans; editorial opinion in most American newspapers was harsh and unforgiving.

In 1939 Burt McConnell surveyed the western press concerning the expropriation, and although his sources were skewed, his study did give a representative sample of corporate America's concern. Quoting from the *Beaumont* (Tex.) *Enterprise*, he noted that "this seizure of property in Mexico presents a new and novel political philosophy hitherto unknown to democratic nations. *It is the greatest blanket seizure of foreign properties since the Russian Revolution.*" The *Denison* (Tex.) *Herald* was quoted to the effect that "Leon Trotsky recently informed the Communists of the world that President Cárdenas was a 'better, brainer Communist than Stalin'." And the editors of the *Topeka State Journal* were convinced that "communism is confiscating the property of citizens of the United States and getting ready to build on our border a 'hell's kitchen' which will invite the 'red' element of the world and challenge us with problems that will become very real."[19] The Red Scare of 1919 had left its imprint on the American mind, and this would surface again with McCarthyism of the 1950s.

Meanwhile, John Merrill, while a graduate student at State University of Iowa, sampled the opinions of journalists and intellectuals in Mexico during the last year of the Eisenhower administration. In his work, which was eventually published, Merrill found that of twelve main themes appearing in the Mexican dailies, ten were unfavorable.[20] Included was the notion that the United States needed to improve its Latin American policy, was overly concerned with communism in the Americas, should try harder not to interfere in the internal affairs of Latin America, and was too concerned with money and possessions. When asked to rank characteristics of the typical North American, the most frequently checked by the informants were unfavorable: materialistic, discourteous, prejudiced, cynical, paternalistic, and imperialistic. When these journalists gave their opinions in essay form, their remarks noted that Americans were superficial, domineering, materialistic, incapable of understanding others, misled by their own propaganda, and had a national psychosis of the dangers of communism.[21] In other words, the American was a "gringo," an outsider with a displeasing personality.[22]

Among the many derogatory labels and ethnic insults that the American uses to describe the Mexican is the word "greaser." This is used along with "wetback," "spic," and "pepper belly" to describe the Mexican. Greaser, as a Texan epithet for Mexican, has been applied since at least 1836, while many mid-nineteenth century Anglo writers referred to northern Mexico as "Greaserdom." Greaser describes both the individual Mexican and Mexicans as a group. It is possible the word originated when nineteenth-century Anglos first encountered Mexican edibles in the Nueces-Río Grande area and were struck by the greasiness of the food. Later use focused on the appearance of the Mexican, especially the color and demeanor of the skin and hair. As in most racial insults, this epithet makes reference to physical appearance, diet, and customs that form a stereotyped image of the outgroup. It is another example of ethnocentrism.[23]

Not only do Mexicans and Americans suffer from ethnocentrism, they also tend to view reality differently. For example, several instances can be cited that exemplify the different meaning that Anglos and Mexicans assign to the same word or concept. For illustrative purposes only, three examples will be depicted: "smuggling," "democracy," and "national security."

To smuggle means to move illegal goods across a border, bypassing duties and taxes in the process. Relative to the U.S.-Mexico border, some goods are considered contraband by both countries, others only by one of the countries. Smuggling liquor into the United States is an infraction of U.S. laws, while bringing electronic goods from the United States into Mexico violates Mexican law.

Both Mexicans and Americans disapprove of the illegal trade in drugs, but Mexicans generally tend to idealize the smuggler, especially the *tequilero* (individuals who smuggled tequila into Texas during the twenties). The person who disregards customs and immigration laws is not a figure of reproach in Mexico; however, the individual who historically represents law and order on the frontier and fought smugglers, the Texas Ranger for example, is idealized by Texans. And, of course, rangers were notorious for their revenge killings of Mexicans.[24]

One must look at the nineteenth-century history of the east Texas border area to understand the Mexican attitude toward smuggling. Before the Mexican War this area was the province of Nuevo Santander and included the southern part of Texas and what is the Mexican state of Tamaulipas today. When the international line was drawn along the Río Grande, it cut through the middle of what had been Nuevo Santander, separating Mexicans on both sides. People who had been neighbors, friends, and relatives were now in different countries.

The pre-boundary social and economic patterns prevailed, and Mexicans continued to carry farm products, manufactured goods, and laborers back and forth across the border. Legally this was smuggling. Folk attitudes eventually developed and idealized the action of smuggling, especially when the smuggler was in conflict with the hated rangers, those upholders of American law. A *corrido* (ballad) tradition glorified the heroic smuggler in his struggle with rangers, border patrolmen, customs officials, and other *rinches* (lawmen).[25] So it is that the *bandido* and the lawman evoke very different images to the American and the Mexican.

The same can be said for the concept of democracy. Contemporary North American political traditions resulted from the liberalism of the Protestant Reformation and a colonial experience of religious tolerance, as well as the nineteenth-century background of Jeffersonian and Jacksonian democracy. For Hispanics the experience was different, derived from a colonial tradition of authoritarian hierarchism in church and state.

In the nineteenth and twentieth centuries, when Mexicans created their constitutional governments, they imitated North American values by superimposing ideas of federalism and liberty on top of personalism and authoritarianism. Today, when the Mexican speaks of democracy one does not know if he is referring to the written or the unwritten tradition. The first, as in the constitution of 1917, establishes Montesquieu's separation of powers between the executive and the legislative and judicial branches of government. The second is unwritten and reflects the real politics of history in Mexico and orders the concentration of power in the hands of the president.[26]

As for national security, the example of U.S. and Mexican policies vis-à-vis Nicaragua between 1979 and 1988 can be cited. Official U.S. strategy under the Reagan administration was to oppose the Sandinista revolution by contributing guns, munitions, and CIA aid to the contras, or "freedom fighters" as they were known in Washington. In addition, American Green Berets provided specialized training for contra patrol commanders. America's fears were based on the belief that Soviet and Cuban troops were establishing a beachhead in Nicaragua, which would eventually lead to revolution in El Salvador, Guatemala, and Mexico. In general, American policy reflected the traditional concern with the spread of communism in the Americas.

It is no secret that the policy failed. American public opinion, weary over another involvement in a Vietnam situation, refused to support the president. Congress was divided as well. Perhaps the most telling reason for the American failure came from a senior U.S. diplomat in Central America who oversaw contra policy. At the height of the conflict, he noted that it was a miracle that the contras survived at all. "I seriously doubt the United States Government has the capacity to organize and manage a successful guerrilla war. We don't understand revolutions, the CIA lacks political vision and the Pentagon doesn't want to touch it with a stick." And as Eden Pastora, the former Sandinista, noted, "You Americans don't know how to manage a revolution that depends on the masses. You want to solve everything quickly with dollars."[27]

To understand the Mexican point of view, one must know about Mexico's recent history. The first social revolution in the twentieth century in Latin America occurred in Mexico. It began before the Russian Revolution, lasted during its violent stage from 1910 to 1917, and was initially nationalistic, popular, and socialist. It is important to remember that sympathy for revolutions in Latin America is an outstanding feature of Mexico's foreign policy, and that Mexico's experience has been similar in many respects to that in Cuba and Nicaragua.

After World War I, Mexico was not allowed into the League of

Nations because it was considered a rebel nation. Mexico was opposed to American involvement in Guatemala in 1954 and objected to the imposition of sanctions against Castro's Cuba. At a later date it was supportive of Salvador Allende's Chile, and after the United States aided in Allende's fall, Mexico opened its doors to Chilean exiles. Recently Mexico gave technical and financial aid to Nicaragua.[28]

Obviously national security is defined differently in Mexico than in the United States. As Olga Pellicer de Brody notes, "national security in Mexico acquires connotations different from those frequently encountered in other Latin American countries and from those that prevail in U.S. political thinking. It is defined not in terms of the 'danger of aggression' but rather in terms of the fulfillment or non-fulfillment of the great objectives in the Constitution of 1917."[29] For Mexicans, national security is grounded in social security. This means protection of national resources, creation of wealth, and the equitable division of income.

Having said all of this, perhaps it is time for the American people and their government to realize the limits of ethnocentrism when it comes to shaping attitudes, opinions, and policies. As Immanuel Wallerstein has observed, a decline of the United States in the capitalist world-economy has occurred recently, and since 1967 North America no longer dominates the world military arena and political economy.[30] Perhaps American thinking can no longer assume a U.S. supremacy in all matters.

Although thinking in terms of centrality and superiority may be the natural thing to do, it no longer is either realistic or pragmatic to do so. Mexicans should realize that there are many facets to a gringo personality, not all of them harmful to Mexico. Americans should not conceive of Mexicans as greasers but as fellow members of an international community. The public health of nations might be improved if we would only acknowledge that we are all further from the center than we care to admit.

2   Space/Time in the Tierra de la Mexica

> Plains, valleys, mountains: the accidents of terrain become mean-
> ingful as soon as they enter history. Each history is a geography
> and each geography is a geometry of symbols.
>
> Octavio Paz, *The Other Mexico*

The 1990 census indicated that there were over 240 million persons residing in the United States, a country lying adjacent to
Mexico with perhaps as many as 80 million inhabitants. While the rate
of population growth in the United States had been relatively high
during the "baby boom" years of the 1950s, a decline set in after 1960.
During the 1970s the population of the United States slowly increased
from 203 million to 226 million. Mexico's citizenry grew from 26 million in 1950 to today's 80 million and had an annual growth rate of
over 3 percent. While the Colossus of the North had an aging society growing more slowly than its older neighbor to the south, Mexico
had a relatively young and aggressive population at its neighbor's
doorstep.[1]

By 1988, over 19 million North Americans indicated that they were
of Hispanic origin (mostly Mexican), and Mexico was the major country from which legal immigrants came to the United States. This figure
does not take into account the eight or nine thousand Mexicans who
enter illicitly on a daily basis or a possible illegal alien population in
the United States between 4.5 million and 8 million. It is no wonder
that Californians joke about Los Angeles being the second largest city
of Mexico.[2]

The Mexico of yesterday and today is part of a larger geographical
and cultural context known as Middle America. At first appearance
Middle America looks like a jumble of mountains, valleys, deserts,
and jungles. Yet underneath this surface one can see a cultural map of
heartlands and frontiers.

12

The heartland territories consist of the densely populated highlands of central Mexico and Guatemala and their adjacent lowlands. This was the home of the "civilized" Mesoamerican Indians—the Mexica (Aztecs), Tarascans, and Mayas. Historically the heartlands have been bounded on the north and southeast by sparsely settled frontiers. The southeastern frontier includes the tropical forests and savannahs of the lowland country and extends from eastern Honduras through Panama. The northern frontier region ranges from the current U.S.-Mexico boundary to the basins of central Mexico and is a vast semi-desert plateau that grows increasingly more arid as one travels from south to north (see figure 1).[3]

Economically and politically the most important of these areas has always been the central highland of Mexico. It is often likened to one of the pyramids built by its early inhabitants. As the Mexican essayist Octavio Paz has noted, "The geography of Mexico spreads out in a pyramidal form as if there existed a secret but evident relation between natural space and symbolic geometry and between the latter and what I have called our invisible history."[4] These mountains have massive walls on all sides—an eastern and western escarpment, and a southern face that has been cut by the Papaloapan and Balsas rivers. On the northern side the pyramid is bounded by the westward flowing Lerma-Santiago River, and the Pánuco River that winds its way into the Gulf of Mexico. The apex of this pyramidal form, at seven thousand feet above sea level, is the five thousand square miles of tableland known as the valley of Mexico.[5]

Just as the central highland has typically overshadowed the periphery, so the valley of Mexico has traditionally dominated the highland. Here waters were trapped, lakes were formed, and agriculture flourished. Around the five lakes the Aztecs built their city of Tenochtitlán, a "second Venice" from the Spanish point of view. Then the Spaniards erected their new Jerusalem on the Mexica ruins, and la ciudad de México became the viceregal center of the colony of New Spain. And in 1990, the megalopolis of Mexico City, teeming with over 21.3 million souls, remains the political, financial, and educational center of Mexico.[6]

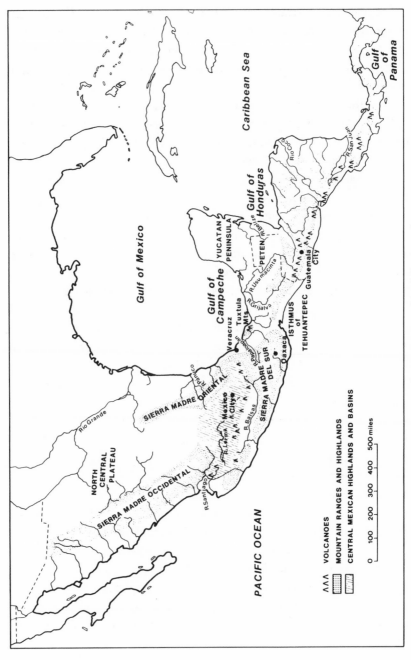

Fig. 1. Physiography of Middle America

This mountainous environment shaped the civilizations that developed. Although preservation of water was important and a variety of irrigation projects evolved, the lay of the land inhibited the growth of large-scale irrigation. With no great bodies of water and intramontane basins that shut off open spaces that could be saturated with water, the hydraulic state, so important in the history of Peru and Egypt, did not mature. These same mountains also turned the country into a mosaic of climates, with some areas experiencing the warmth of sun and excessive rains while neighboring valleys were left cold and arid.[7]

Yet this environmental diversity actually made for social cohesion. Each valley was a separate ecological system producing its own variety of products. For example, in Texcoco in the valley of Mexico, the high ground provided beer and charcoal, the piedmont fruit, and the lake shore maize. Similarly, goods flowed from lowland to highland, from villages to towns, and from valley towns to regional capitals. The most important nodal point was, of course, the valley of Mexico. Here, from ancient times to the present, the population has clustered around this fertile expanse in a country of marginal land.[8]

The pyramid shaped the politics and mind-set of the Mexican people. From the pyramidal apex Mexico has been ruled in turn by the Aztec *tlatoani*, the Spanish Viceroy, the nineteenth-century *caudillo*, and the Institutional Revolutionary Party of recent history. In spite of the personalism of the *caudillo*, it is a despotic tradition, hierarchic and bureaucratic. It is something quite different from the political traditions of North Americans.[9]

The mind-set of the Aztec ruler who controlled the people of Mexico from the top of the pyramid, like those he controlled, was not one that separated space and time as in the western world. Ruler and ruled thought in terms of space/time. The Aztec calendar had several combinations of "space/time." As Octavio Paz has noted, "to be born on a certain day was to pertain to a place, a time, a color and a destiny."[10] This space/time consciousness is part of the mental luggage of every Mexican today, a heritage of the Indian past and part of what Paz calls the invisible history.

When Mexico is placed in the larger context of North America, some interesting geographical comparisons can be made between Mexico and the United States. Concerning climate, one notes immediately that most of southeastern Canada and the eastern United States fall under the forest category, while much of the central United States is in the grassland climatic region. Yet most of Mexico is either steppe or desert country, with the obvious exception of the Yucatán peninsula. This means that the temperature, precipitation, and vegetation patterns of Mexico are more akin to the semiarid plains and mountain country of the western United States than that of the humid area east of the hundredth meridian.[11]

To use the language of the layman, the north central and eastern United States experiences a moist, cold winter, while the southeastern and south central area is moist and mild. In this respect central Mexico is like the southeastern United States, while northern Mexico and the western United States is dry. Only southern Florida and the Pacific and Gulf coastal regions of Mexico are tropical areas. The eastern United States and central Mexico are areas of moderate to heavy rainfall. Northern Mexico and the western United States receive only light rains, less than ten inches annually in many places.[12]

Like Mexico, geography and resources shaped the industries of British America. Abundant rainfall and good soil nourished agriculture, so the common English grains (wheat, oats, barley, and rye) were developed. However, rocky land, short summers, and long winters made New England an inferior farming country (although soil was good in New Jersey and Pennsylvania and suitable for raising tobacco in the southern colonies). Because of its slender farming base, New England very quickly developed other resources, especially timber and seafood.[13]

As a productive resource, wood was to colonial New England what coal and iron ore were to the nineteenth-century northeast, and copper and oil are to twentieth-century America. Wood, the virgin forests of oak and pine, was the raw material for ships, potash, and dyes. It was the source of pitch, tar, and resin, which made vessels seaworthy, and the fuel for iron and glass manufactures.[14]

The coastline provided the settlers with inlets and harbors, and rivers linked the coastal plain with the seaports, and through them with Europe and European goods. Coastal mountains, while retarding western expansion, provided rivers and falls, a source of transportation and water power for the people of the coast. As for seafood, there were oysters, crabs, bass, cod, sturgeon, lobsters, eels, shad, catfish, herring, trout, and salmon—all to be used locally or in trade.[15] It is little wonder that the children of New England eventually outproduced old England and by 1776 had declared their own independence from the mother country.

In spite of their many differences, British North America and Spanish Mexico did have one thing in common. They shared the same frontier zone of the southwestern United States and northern Mexico. It was in this zonal region that Mesoamerica first made commercial contact with the higher Indian cultures of the American Southwest. It was here that Anglos first confronted Spain in America. This was the frontier culture that produced the Tejano-Mexicano conflict. In 1848 a political boundary was created through this area that separated the United States from Mexico. By 1900 modernization and the growth of the state had changed this frontier zone into a border region; a boundary line protected by armies, immigration officers, and the customs agents of two nations. Today this is the United States' gateway to Latin America.

Geographers and ethnologists refer to this territory as the Gran Chichimeca. The well-known anthropologist Charles Di Peso says that the Gran Chichimeca may be defined as comprehending all of that part of Mexico that is situated north of the Tropic of Cancer up to 38 degrees north latitude, including Baja and Alta California, New Mexico, southern Utah and Colorado, and western Texas. The northern limits would extend from San Francisco (124 degrees west longitude) to Wichita Falls, Kansas (97 degrees west longitude). Mesoamericans called the "barbaric" inhabitants of this area *chichimecas*, a Nahuatl word that translates into the Spanish *hijos del perro* ("sons of the dog"), and the land was the Gran or Great Chichimeca (see figure 2).[16]

In general, this borderlands country is a craggy, dry land. The Rocky Mountains and Sierra Madres are its spine. One major extension of

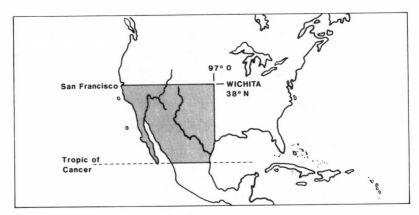

Fig. 2. Gran Chichimeca

the Rocky Mountains is the high Sangre de Cristo range of south central Colorado and north central New Mexico, which leads discontinuously through western Texas and emerges eventually as the Sierra Madre Oriental of Coahuila and Nuevo León. Another extension of the Rockies is the San Juan range of southwestern Colorado. These mountains reappear in northwestern New Mexico and southeastern Arizona to become the Sierra Madre Occidental of Chihuahua and eastern Sonora. This spinal ridge forms a continental divide separating the two major watersheds of the borderlands—the Río Grande del Norte that flows into the Gulf of Mexico, and the Colorado River that drains into the Gulf of California.[17]

All of these mountains serve as impediments to moisture-laden air, which comes mostly from the Gulf of Mexico. The dryest conditions prevail west of the Sierra Madre Occidental, a region that includes the Sonoran Desert and its various components (see figure 3). Throughout northwestern Mexico precipitation is basically seasonal, with winter rains being the more variable; summer storms are often intense, causing local floods. Inadequate rainfall, in combination with hot winds, contributes to the aridity of the borderlands and makes deserts of certain areas.[18]

In the annals of Western Americana the Gran Chichimeca was known as the Great American Desert. As American pioneers learned that corn could be grown in Kansas and sheep raised in Colorado, the Great American Desert retreated toward the west and southwest, shrinking as it went.[19] Today only two true desert areas are to be found in North America. One starts at the Laguna district of Chihuahua and Coahuila and spreads throughout western Texas and New Mexico up the Río Grande beyond Albuquerque. The other is the Sonoran Desert, a region that includes both coasts along the Gulf of California (including most of Baja) and about half of western Sonora, the southwestern third of Arizona, the Mojave portion of California, and about half of Nevada.[20] If a quest for fertile land has been the historical focus of the central Mexican highlands, then the struggle for water was and is the main theme of the Gran Chichimeca.

Many of the myths about Mexico's legendary wealth—the Aztec gold and Spanish silver—explode in the face of stubborn geographic fact. A comparative look at agriculture and natural resources in the United States and Mexico illustrates the limits of Mexican growth.

In Mexico land is marginal with only 10 percent of the total land mass potentially usable. Illinois counts on more arable land than all of Mexico, as do Minnesota, Iowa, and Kansas. In 1960 the farmers of Iowa harvested more land than all Mexican farmers combined, even though Iowa had only 8 percent of Mexico's population. In California, farmers irrigate more land than all Mexican farmers together. Marginal land has dictated settlement patterns throughout Mexico's history, explaining why over 50 percent of Mexico's population has always lived in the fertile core and metropolitan area of central Mexico.[21]

The rich endowment of North America with natural resources explains in large part the rapid economic development of the United States. Nowhere in Mexico is there a natural navigable system of water transportation akin to the Ohio and Mississippi rivers, nor is there an internal waterway like that of the Great Lakes. One cannot find iron ore and coal in abundance, and in close proximity to one another, the way that iron ore in the Masabi Range is linked to the coal fields of Pennsylvania by the Great Lakes. A supply of petro-

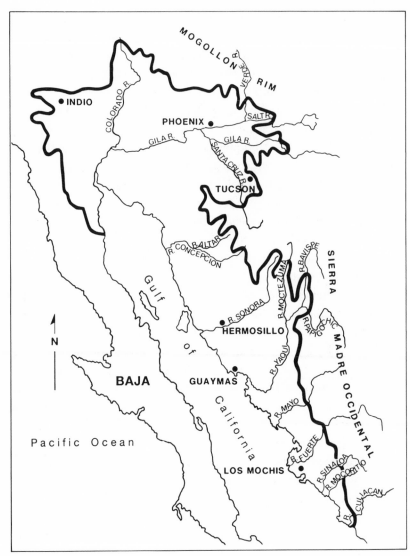

Fig. 3. Sonoran Desert

leum has made the United States one of the largest world producers of oil. Great resources of gold, silver, copper, uranium, and other metals have aided in making the United States a major industrial and technological power.[22]

Regarding Mexico's loss of over half its national territory to the United States after the Mexican War of 1845, historian Joe B. Frantz notes:

> While the historian's role is not to indulge in *cantina* conjecture, one can't help wondering what the history of the Borderlands would have been if in 1849 gold had been discovered at Sutter's Mill *in Mexico!* Or if all the copper in Arizona and Utah, the uranium in New Mexico, the California timber, lettuce, grapes, and climate and the silver in Nevada had been left under Mexican sovereignty. These resources . . . made it [the United States] a power in the world. Mexico in turn has been fragmented by mountains and dried by desert. . . . It has had to rescue its mineral resources from foreign hands. . . . In many ways the two countries were about equal in the 1840s, but the United States wound up holding a winning lottery ticket which it could cash in for investment and aggrandizement.[23]

Poor Mexico, the *lotería* is as much a natural part of the Mexican scene as *mariache* bands and *sombreros*.

While geography and resources have shaped the histories of the United States and Mexico and account for some of the many differences between the two peoples, it is, perhaps, the Indian factor that best distinguishes Americans from Mexicans. While the Indians left only a minority legacy in the United States, indigenism and *indianismo* have been dominant themes in Mexican history. In Mexico today the Native American component constantly reappears—here in the form of Moctezuma, there in the actions of Benito Juárez; yesterday in the cries of Malinche, tomorrow in the hopes of Emiliano Zapata. The Indian, the oriental, the Easterner—all have been an enigma for the western mind.[24]

Although figures vary greatly, the best estimate of the size of America's aboriginal population in 1492 was 57 million of which 4 million were in Canada and the continental United States, and 21 million were in Mexico. Of that total, the Gran Chichimeca may have contained about 813,000 Native Americans. The discovery of America was followed by a demographic disaster, primarily due to epidemics of smallpox that reduced Mexico's Indians from 21 million in 1521 to 3.5 million by 1570. The contemporary Native American population (considered racially, not culturally) of Latin America is estimated at 18 million, of which 5 to 6 million can be found in Mexico. In 1980 the Native American population of the United States was between 1.3 and 1.4 million (and had grown to 2 million by the 1990 census).[25]

The early "red men," as the settlers called them, were physically diverse people. In skin color they were not red but ranged from yellowish white to light brown, from bronze to copper. The Utes had squat, powerful frames, as did the Maya of Mesoamerica, a small people with broad heads and faces. The Crows were known for their height, as were the long-legged Yaqui, Pima, and Tarahumara of the Gran Chichimeca. Although most Native Americans are related to the Asian Mongoloids, the Otomí of highland Mexico displayed negroid characteristics.[26]

These physical variations then combined with hundreds of different spoken dialects and languages. The seminomadic Utes of eastern Utah, so different from the "civilized" Mexica (Aztecs) of central Mexico, shared the same parent language of the Nahuatl speaking Aztecs. The Mayan language of the lowlands was similar to the Huaxtec spoken along the eastern coast of the Gulf of Mexico, but radically different from the Zapotecan languages of southern Mexico or the Nahuat of central Mexico. The Tarascans, a civilized group living next to the Aztecs, spoke a language of unsure origins not related to any other Middle American group.[27]

Most band and village people were patrilineal, practiced polygamy, and waged war. There were some who practiced little or no war, like the California-Nevada Shoshoni or the Mission Indians of California. The Papagos regarded war as a form of insanity; however, the Iroquois, a matrilineal and monogamous people, were very warlike and cannibalistic and treated their prisoners mercilessly. The Aztecs prac-

Fig. 4. The Americas on the Eve of Conquest

ticed human sacrifice and, according to some scholars, cannibalism to an extent unheard of or unknown in other Native American societies.[28]

The Native Americans of America can be generally categorized as sedentary, semisedentary, and nonsedentary (see figure 4). The so-called higher civilizations of the Aztecs and Mayas were imperial, sedentary societies, while the Pueblos, some of the Ohio Mound Builders, the Chibcha of Colombia, and the Caribbean Arawaks were nonimperial, sedentary Native Americans. In the sedentary societies intensive agricultural techniques were interwoven with hamlet life. Men shared fully in planting and harvesting the land. The central social-political unit (in central Mexico the *calpulli*) was a hamlet group that held the land communally, but alloted plots on an individual or family basis.[29]

The two most important groups in these societies were tax-paying commoners or agriculturalists and a directing corps of nobles. In addition, there were craft specialists and a class of people who were auxiliaries outside the normal protection of the hamlet group. The auxiliaries were often serfs who worked the land of others. And, of course, in Aztec and Maya society there were slaves. In highland Mexico these societies developed a complex civilization that was state oriented, urban, and imperial. All of these classes or groups would eventually be used by Spain in developing its own Latin American empire.[30]

Many preconquest peoples had societies that were intermediate between farming and hunting and gathering. These were the semisedentary Native Americans. Predominantly forest peoples, they had villages and cultivated fields; however, these villages and fields shifted frequently. Hunting and fishing were important pursuits. Unlike the sedentary groups, the men in these societies left most of the farming and gathering to the women and children, while they pursued the hunting and warfare. There were no specialized social classes, and all trading was done on a kinship basis (unlike the tributary system of the Aztecs). One large block of semisedentary Indians lived in the woodlands of eastern North America, another was spread through the tropical rain forest region of South America. Europeans would find it difficult to make permanent contacts with these Native Americans, given the lack of surplus produce, permanent lands, and groups to administer, produce, and channel goods.[31]

Finally, there were the nonsedentary people of Northern Mexico and the American Southwest. These were the Chichimecas, known to the Aztecs as "barbarians" and "sons of dogs." They had no cultivation skills and no permanent settlements. A hunting and gathering people on the move, they excelled at warfare and made ready use of the dreaded bow and arrow. Their population densities were low. With no surplus or economic modes to exploit, the Europeans had very little social interaction with these peoples. They were either defeated and destroyed in battle, forced into missions where they often died, or sold into slavery. Interestingly enough, messianic movements, which were the reaction of societies facing extermination, appeared more often among nonsedentary groups than of any other kind.[32]

To reiterate, the nonsedentary groups lived mostly in the area of the Gran Chichimeca, between the high cultures of the American Southwest and the higher civilizations of central Mexico. The semi-sedentaries were woodland peoples who occupied the humid forests of the northeast. The Pueblos of New Mexico, Colorado, and Arizona were a nonimperial, sedentary group. Finally, the Mexica of the central highlands of Mexico and the Mayas of the lowlands were fully developed, sedentary Indians. Urbanism was more fully developed in the highlands, with the Aztecs having their own political empire, or at least hegemony.

One of the first true urban centers in the Americas was Teotihuacán, a preindustrial city with a population of about 120,000 between A.D. 450 and 650. The city, laid out in a grid pattern and extending over nine square miles, was located twenty-five miles north of the present site of Mexico City. At this time there were more than four thousand single-story apartment houses throughout the city, many of them home factories producing featherwork, obsidian items, stone objects, and several kinds of pottery. The Teotihuacanos traded throughout Mesoamerica, including Oaxaca and Chiapas in southern Mexico and the highlands of Guatemala. There were also cultural outposts in northern Mexico designed to protect Teotihuacán from the incursions of the Chichimecas. A Nahua-speaking people who engaged in irrigation, food production, industry, and commerce, the Teotihuacanos were Mexico's first genuinely urban people.[33]

With the collapse of Teotihuacán after A.D. 750, the Toltecs settled Tula (or Tollán) in what is southern Hidalgo today, about 50 miles north of present-day Mexico City. Having earlier been influenced by Teotihuacán, the Toltecs adopted irrigation and terracing, developed a municipal and state organization, and evolved an empire that spread both north and eastward, to Chihuahua in northern Mexico and the Yucatán peninsula in the east. By so doing they pushed the Mesoamerican frontier into the border zone, defending their imperial interests with fiscal and trading colonies. A Nahuat-speaking people, they participated fully in Mesoamerican culture—religion based on common deities like Tlaloc the rain god, Quetzalcoatl the feathered serpent, and Tezcatlipoca the god of the night sky; measurement based on mathematics and calendrics; and an urban lifestyle based on intensive agriculture and the art of writing. When Tula fell after A.D. 1150, this heritage was passed on to the Mexica, or Aztecs.[34]

The agricultural frontier of northern Mesoamerica now contracted southward, and several pretender "Toltec" groups developed in the central plateau area. One of these bands competing for a place in the Basin of Mexico was the Mexica. A Nahuatl-speaking, semiagricultural group who were originally mercenaries to more powerful tribes, the Mexica eventually emerged to a position of power by the mid-fifteenth century.[35]

Their capital city, Tenochtitlán, was built in the former marshes of Lake Texcoco and stretched some twenty-five hundred acres. After a century and a half of labor it had been transformed into a geometric network of canals, earthworks, causeways, dikes, residences, marketplaces, workshops, temples, pyramids, centers, and quarters. It was the home of over 130,000 inhabitants (akin to Venice in the Old World). The urban center to suburban towns of over a million people, and the headquarters of thirty-eight tributary provinces, the empire spread from the Huaxteca country in the northeast to Oaxaca in southern Mexico. When the trading ports of western Mexico, coastal Guatemala, and the Gulf of Honduras are included, the Aztec hegemony probably affected the lives of 10 to 15 million inhabitants.[36]

The locus of sovereignty was the main plaza in the central part of town in which was located the royal residences of the *tlatoani* (the emperor), his advisers, and the ruling class of nobles (*pilli*). North of the plaza was the great marketplace of Tlatelolco where goods from near and far were traded. The *pochteca* were a special class of traders who traveled to the fringe of the empire to exchange goods, collect tribute, and provide intelligence for the *tlatoani*. Raw materials like gold and cotton were collected as tribute and then manufactured into jewelry and cloth by a special class of craftsmen.[37]

Supporting this society were the plebeians, members of the local provincial unit (*calpulli*) who acted as farmers, fishermen, porters, gatherers, and workmen. In addition, there were slaves, serfs, and auxiliary servants (*naboría*), whose labor was used by individuals and the state. Of the slaves, the most important were prisoners of war who were the primary source of sacrificial victims.[38]

A deadly pantheon of bloodthirsty divinities—Tlaloc, the water god; Xipe Totec, "our lord the flayed one," god of goldsmiths; and Huitzilopochtli, the war god, to name a few—demanded that the life-giving force be donated by man so that the eternal cycles could be sustained. And, as evidenced by the skull racks of Tenochtitlán, the Mexica practiced human sacrifice far in excess of other peoples and often in conjunction with cannibalism. The victim, a reluctant god-incarnate, could award his captor with the prize of immortality. So the victory party partook of the body and flesh of the god, leaving only the torso for the hungry animals of the emperor's zoo.[39] This then was Tenochtitlán, a New World martial state and a New World Venice, home for fanatical priests and warriors and the dwelling of poets and artists.

At the conquest the Spaniards built Mexico City on the ruins of Tenochtitlán—the Aztec capital erected in the likeness of Tula, the Toltec city modeled after Teotihuacán, the first true city on the American continent. Mexico today is a land of superimposed pasts, with every Mexican carrying within his soul the legends and superstitions of a two-thousand year history.

One remarkable feature of modern Mexico is the contemporary Maya Indian of the Yucatán—perhaps as many as two million live there today. The Maya are one of the few peoples who have a continuous history from 9000 B.C. to the present. Their earliest ancestors were big game hunters. Between 5500 B.C. and 3300 B.C. they lived in great coastal villages along the Caribbean, dining on lobster and crab while their poorer neighbors ate beans and squash. After 3300 B.C., many Mayas migrated up river valleys and became farmers. By the classic era, A.D. 200 to A.D. 900, they had developed complex societies, intensive forms of agriculture (aided by irrigation systems and fertilizers), and ceremonial centers at sites like Palenque, Piedras Negras, Bonampak, Copan, and Tikal. A population numbering between twelve and sixteen million spread across one hundred thousand square miles of lowlands through present-day Mexico, Guatemala, Honduras, and Belize.[40]

For a long time scholars believed that the classic Mayas were a peaceful, intelligent, theological people. That they excelled intellectually cannot be denied in that they developed a highly accurate calendar, a style of glyph writing, and the science of mathematics. However, it is now known that they were anything but peaceful, engaging in dynastic quarrels and wars with each other. Warfare was accompanied by captive sacrifice and bloodletting ceremonies, which occurred in conjunction with the ritual of royal succession. Bloodletting, combined with drug taking (including drug enemas), induced visions and hallucinogenic experiences that blurred the lines between the supernatural and natural worlds.[41]

The mystery of the Maya collapse long haunted scholars. In deciphering the Maya calendar it was known that as many as nineteen different centers had erected dated monuments in A.D. 790, yet by A.D. 889 the last stelae had been carved. Most of the ceremonial centers were abandoned, some of them left in ruin, suggesting that the Maya collapse was as abrupt as it was complete. Several causes have been given to account for the suddenness of the decline, including catastrophic natural disasters, malnutrition and disease, warfare, population stresses, and the limits of *milpa* (slash-and-burn) agriculture.[42] However, it now appears that the collapse was not so sudden or final. In fact, instead of decline one should talk about transition. Instead of studying society from the top down, one should look at it from the bottom up; in other words, instead of viewing Maya society from the point of view of the priest-king, one should look at it from the viewpoint of the peasant and merchant.

After the fall of Teotihuacán in the Mexican highlands, a new Maya group emerged from the gulf coast lowlands that are the states of Tabasco and Campeche today. These people were the Putún, a seafaring merchant group that spoke Chontal Maya, a Mexicanized dialect unknown to the Mayas of the interior. The Putún wanderings southward may have aided the collapse of cities like Tikal by interrupting trade along the Usumacinta river, while their travels into and across the northern lowlands contributed to a flowering of that area.[43]

With the fall of the Toltecs and their Toltec city of Chichén Itzá in the thirteenth century, the Putún stepped in to facilitate long-range trade around the Yucatán. Headquartered in Cozumel, they founded Mayapán in A.D. 1250 to replace Chichén Itzá and then developed trade between the Gulf of Honduras and the Bay of Campeche. Cacao, cotton, honey, and salt went from Campeche and the northern Yucatán to the Gulf of Honduras and were exchanged for obsidian, jade, copper, quetzal plumes, and other items from the southern mountains.[44]

As pioneers in the mass production of simple shapes, the Putún manufactured standardized ceramics that were designed for stacking and transporting. Their kind of mercantile pragmatism not only meant a rise in the standard of living for non-elites but also reflected the ascendancy of a merchant class at the expense of the old theocracy. Just as the classic era saw the dominance of priest-kings and ceremonial centers, the post-classic period witnessed a flowering of mercantilism. The Putún were the traders that Christopher Columbus first encountered in 1502 off the coast of Honduras on his fourth and final voyage.[45]

During the colonial era the Maya of the Yucatán continued to maintain their indigenous traditions. They were less westernized than their highland counterparts and were very rarely affected by modernization. The military conquest started later here and was more prolonged than in central Mexico. The hacienda (a large, private estate), when it finally did emerge, was never tied to a local market and had a rather brief history in the Yucatán. During the bloody fighting of 1847 and 1855, the Maya rebels of eastern and southern Yucatán governed themselves. They called their culture the Cruzob, a Native American folkway society that was an alternative to Europeanization. The Cruzob tailored Christianity and westernization to their own values and principles and were no less Maya as they adjusted to colonial and postcolonial rule. They simply became a colonial, and later postcolonial, Maya.[46]

During the preconquest era, Mesoamerican culture was influencing that of the Gran Chichimeca. Over the years the Mesoamerican border advanced and receded as ecology, geography, and trade relations changed. Around the time of Christ the Mesoamerican border extended from the central highlands eastward to the Gulf of Mexico and the Huaxteca country. Seven centuries later Mesoamerican culture expanded into the Gran Chichimeca during the Pax Teotihuacano period to include parts of Sinaloa, Jalisco, Zacatecas, and Durango. With the rise of the Toltecs of Tula, Mesoamerica broadened in the west to include all of Sinaloa and parts of Sonora. However, after the fall of Tula, by A.D. 1200, the Mesoamerican border receded, while the Chichimecas increased their territory.[47]

Perhaps the most important center of cultural diffusion in the preconquest period was Casas Grandes, a trading post in Chihuahua. Around A.D. 1060 Toltec merchant families arrived in Casas Grandes, Guasave, and Pueblo Bonito. They were probably financed by their families in the hope that the exchange of seashells and parrot feathers for turquoise, peyote, wild animal skins, herbs, and slaves would prove profitable. Obtaining jurisdiction over the lands and people, the *pochteca* developed drainage and irrigation systems that permitted higher crop yields. Multistoried apartments, patios, plazas, ball courts, and marketplaces were erected. Craftsmen fashioned rings, necklaces, and mosaics. Scarlet macaws were brought in from Veracruz for their bright plumage, and turkey pens were raised in the plazas. Religion was also imported, including the cults of Quetzalcoatl, Tezcatlipoca, and Xipe Totec.[48]

The relationship of Casas Grandes to the Toltec core was an unequal one, with raw materials and manufactured articles flowing southward from the Chichimecan periphery to the Mesoamerican center. At times, a semiperipherial trading nucleus like Casas Grandes would send finished articles both to the various nonstate, seminomadic groups in the Great Chichimeca, as well as to the Toltec core.

All of this came to an end after A.D. 1340. A Chichimecan revolt spread throughout the region, and there is some evidence that Casas Grandes was burned. In addition, there is also evidence of a climatic shift and overuse of lands and water. Some towns were abandoned, new sites were created and others reverted to nomadism. The Hohokam of Arizona declined. Some Anasazi Chichimecans regrouped into what became the historically recognized Hopi, Zuni, Acoma, and Río Grande Pueblos. Other Pueblos increased their influence in the Great Plains. When the Spaniards arrived in the sixteenth century, they introduced European diseases to the Native American survivors. Perhaps as many as 90 percent of the populace suffered death in the Chichimecan villages.[49]

The dominance in central Mexico of the Gran Chichimeca continued under the Spaniards. The conquest of the northern fringe was spurred by the discovery, development, and continued expansion of silver mining. The Spanish military had to adapt their techniques to the Chichimeca frontier, where most Indians were excellent bowmen, skilled in sneak attacks, and made efficient use of the horse. As in the conquest of the Aztecs, the Spaniards often used their Native American allies to take the brunt of the fighting. In this case it was the Otomí who were drafted into the Spanish armies. Forts or presidios, manned by *castas* (mixed breeds) or Hispanicized Indians (like the Tlaxcalans), were used to pacify the area. Many Native Americans were killed or enslaved.[50]

The primary instrument of pacification was the mission—the creation of Native American settlements under the auspices of one of the orders. The Franciscans went into the north central area, including New Mexico. In the seventeenth century they were followed by the Jesuits who moved into Sonora, Arizona, and the western coastal areas. Lay Spaniards followed, attracted by the lure of instant wealth coming from the mining camps. Haciendas and ranches soon developed to support the mines, and the "cowboy" industry eventually extended into what is now the American Southwest.[51]

The other tool of civilization was the Spanish town. This could have been a political and administrative center like Mexico City, a commercial town like Veracruz, a mining camp like Guanajuato or Durango, or an army garrison on the frontier. Civil authorities insisted on the direct integration of the Native American into Spanish life. The Indian was to be under the control of the local town council (*cabildo*), forced to develop European work habits in the factories (*obrajes*), mines, and estates, and fused through intermarriage into the community.[52] Yet the reality was often slave labor in the factories, segregated neighborhoods, and death by disease or exploitation. If the Native American survived, he or she was Hispanicized.

Generally speaking, the nonsedentaries perished. In missions and towns, or as slaves, they either died from disease or became indistinguishable from other Hispanicized Indians. In the mining towns they lost all identity. If they retained their own societies, or fled to rugged pockets in the mountains (like the Tarahumara), they might survive, taking what they needed from the Spaniards such as weapons, horses, cattle, and Spanish as a lingua franca. To this day the Indians of the Gran Chichimeca show less European influence than do their counterparts in central Mexico.[53]

The degree of acculturation and miscegenation that the Native American society underwent in its relationship with Europeans was dependent on its own cultural development and style. As has been suggested earlier, the sedentary Indians provided the Europeans with the most opportunity for contact and conquest. The invading and occupying group required commoners for tribute labor and to deliver goods; the Native American nobles could be used as intermediaries between conquerors and conquered, and the dependent groups could become servants and auxiliaries. The Mexica and Maya and their neighbors met these needs, as did the Pueblos of New Mexico. The eastern woodland Indians and the Chichimecas did not; they had no compact core territory, very little surplus produce, and no mechanisms capable of delivering and channeling produce and labor.[54]

In the Mexica countryside the Indian village endured. The Spaniard, whether cleric, statesman, or colonist, wanted tribute, labor, and land. The Spaniard transformed Indian elite culture, but popular culture survived. In fact, the tributary system established by the Spaniards was not so different from that of the pre-Columbian world. Provincial hamlets (usually a *cabecera*, or head town, with several kinship groups, or *calpultin*) and their surrounding villages (*sujetos* of one *calpulli* each) simply transferred their allegiance from a Native American noble to the Spanish overlord, often channeling goods and labor through the same Native American intermediaries. Spanish institutions like the *cofradía* (parishioners' association) and the fiesta were enlisted to support the village.[55] While it is true that by the end of the colonial era many villages had been partially Hispanicized, with Spaniards and mestizos living in and around the village, they still retained an essential Native American character. In spite of reduced populations, shrinking lands, the racism of outsiders, and the outrageous demands for tribute by the state, the community survived.

The raison d'être of the Spanish conquest was the obligation to civilize the Native American. Duty to God and king required that the Indian be converted to Christianity. Idolatry was wholly evil. The setting for civilization must be town life, governed by Spanish law and authority. The first missionaries were the conquistadores, who, as *encomenderos*, received the right to Native American labor and tribute and the obligation to look after the spiritual welfare of their Indian charges. Many *encomenderos* hired priests and friars who lived in the villages of the *encomienda* (allocation). Sometimes the major Indian town in an area would become the site of the church, while surrounding villages or *visitas* would be subject to the authority of the church in the head town (the entire entity being known as a *cabecera de doctrina*). Franciscans, Dominicans, Jesuits, and other orders soon established missions in towns and on the frontier, and the result of this missionary work was a Native American population that practiced syncretic religion, a blending of paganism and Christianity.[56]

The first generation of Spaniards took what was originally a Native American provincial unit of a *cabecera* surrounded by *sujetos*, and transformed it into an *encomienda*. Usually a mestizo steward (*majordomo*) would live in the area of the *encomienda* and manage it for the *encomendero*. Thus goods and labor would flow to the city where the *encomendero* had his townhouse. By the mid-seventeenth century, the *encomienda* would be phased out (unless it was on the frontier) and the original provincial unit would now become a Native American municipality.[57]

At the same time, several *cabecera-sujeto* units would be incorporated into a *corregimiento* under the supervision of a *corregidor* and his staff who would live in a central Indian town. The towns would have their own Indian *cabildos* and officials, and tribute would flow from the *corregidor* to the city.

It was also at this time that the hacienda appeared, and by the end of the colonial period it made some encroachments on the lands of the villages. Yet *hacendados* always needed extra labor, especially at peak times of harvesting, and community Indians were a necessary source of that labor. It was only in the late nineteenth century and early twentieth that haciendas developed at the expense of villages, and community Native Americans became peons, unskilled rural laborers, and small sharecroppers. Commercial agriculture then replaced traditional farming, and capitalism entered the countryside (see figure 5).[58]

The Spanish conquest was also a sexual conquest. Hernán Cortés, the first *macho* of Mexico, violated *la chingada*, the Indian mistress, Malinche.[59] The Spaniards came without their women and hoped to find enough gold so that they could return to Spain as wealthy men of status. As has been indicated, when all the booty had been divided and there was no more gold, they were given an allocation of Indian labor known as *encomiendas*. Through this arrangement many female servants became sex slaves and concubines of their Spanish masters. At times Native American chieftains would seek favors from the Spanish captains by providing them with women as tokens of friendship. The result was a new generation of mixed breeds, mestizos, the offspring of a Spanish father and a Native American mother. By 1650 Mexico had over 150,000 mestizos, a figure that increased to over a million by 1800, 11 percent of the population. Today, of course, Mexico is a mestizo country with every mestizo a living testimony to his Native American past.[60]

In British North America, Native American relations were different. As the North Americans pushed west, they carried with them stereo-

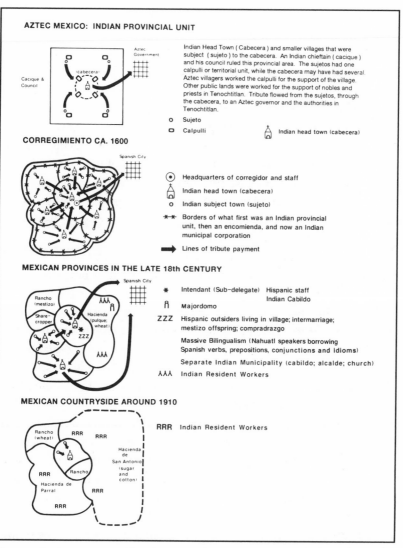

AZTEC MEXICO: INDIAN PROVINCIAL UNIT

Cacique & Council

(cabecera)

Aztec Government

Indian Head Town (Cabecera) and smaller villages that were subject (sujeto) to the cabecera. An Indian chieftain (cacique) and his council ruled this provincial area. The sujetos had one calpulli or territorial unit, while the cabecera may have had several. Aztec villagers worked the calpulli for the support of the village. Other public lands were worked for the support of nobles and priests in Tenochtitlan. Tribute flowed from the sujetos, through the cabecera, to an Aztec governor and the authorities in Tenochtitlan.

o   Sujeto

◻   Calpulli   Indian head town (cabecera)

CORREGIMIENTO CA. 1600

Spanish City

⊙   Headquarters of corregidor and staff

   Indian head town (cabecera)

o   Indian subject town (sujeto)

✻—✻   Borders of what first was an Indian provincial unit, then an encomienda, and now an Indian municipal corporation

➡   Lines of tribute payment

MEXICAN PROVINCES IN THE LATE 18th CENTURY

Spanish City

Rancho (mestizo)

Share-cropper

Hacienda (pulque; wheat)

ZZZ

✻   Intendant (Sub-delegate)   Hispanic staff

                             Indian Cabildo

   Majordomo

ZZZ   Hispanic outsiders living in village; intermarriage; mestizo offspring; compradrazgo

      Massive Bilingualism (Nahuatl speakers borrowing Spanish verbs, prepositions, conjunctions and Idioms)

      Separate Indian Municipality (cabildo; alcalde; church)

ⴙⴙⴙ   Indian Resident Workers

MEXICAN COUNTRYSIDE AROUND 1910

Rancho (wheat)

RRR   RRR

Hacienda de San Antonio (sugar and cotton)

RRR   Rancho

Hacienda de Parral   RRR

RRR

RRR   Indian Resident Workers

Fig. 5. The Mexican Countryside. Source: Adapted from schemata in James Lockhart and Stuart B. Schwartz, *Early Latin America* (Cambridge, 1983), pp. 40, 170.

types of Indians as "wild savages," wanderers who were addicted to warfare. Part of this mind-set was inherited from their Puritan past. The Puritans came to New England to escape the tyranny of Old England, and to create a City of God in the wilderness. Their pre-occupation with purity and their doctrines of providence, grace, and special election, meant that Satan's sinners would be excluded from their holy community. The indigenous inhabitants of New England were viewed as "devils in the devil's den," some of Lucifer's fallen angels placed in the wilderness by God as a test of their faithfulness. As devils they were to be cast out from the City of God, excluded and exterminated. After the Pequot War of 1637, Increase Mather called upon his congregation to thank God, "that on this day we have sent six hundred heathen souls to hell."[61]

In contrast with Spain, colonial Americans not only had no sense of mission to pacify the Native Americans, but no settled policy for "civi-lizing" the Indians. The British failed to conceive of a colonial empire in America that included the Indians as an integral part of its citizenry. Initially, the early Americans simply attempted to push and drive the Indians westward, not unlike the British practice in New Zealand that allowed for an uneasy coexistence between Maori and whites.[62]

In general, the American settlers thought in terms of extermination, removal, or forcible isolation—rather than Christian conversion. This idea of isolating the Indian, so different from Spanish policy, soon led to the concept of the reservation. After 1850 the practice of the settlers was one of isolating Indians on the reservation. On the plains, where limited land could not support the Indian habit of hunting and gather-ing, the U.S. government came to support the Native Americans on a ration basis, and with the Dawes Act of 1887, the reservations were administered to by an agent of the Bureau of Indian Affairs. The entire system was testimony to the Anglo belief that Native Americans were incapable of governing themselves.[63]

Thus, there were many differences between Spain's Indian policy in the Spanish Borderlands and that of Anglo-America in the North American frontier. The unified church and mission system so promi-nent in New Spain was lacking among Anglo-American institutions.

The demography was also different. In central Mexico large numbers of Native Americans faced a small number of Spaniards, and the *encomienda*, an institution that would allow a few Spaniards to coerce a large number of Native Americans, was the solution. In the United States, large numbers of white settlers faced relatively small numbers of Native Americans. Greater resources in manpower and technology allowed the United States to grow without Indian labor. Assimilation was the ideal, but isolation and extermination was the reality.[64]

When the Mexican Amerindians confronted the Spaniards, an uneasy coexistence developed between Mesoamerican civilization and occidental civilization, between what scholar Guillermo Batalla refers to as "México profundo" and "México imaginario."[65] Profound Mexico is the Mexico of today's Native American population, its popular culture, and those indigenous values that have been partly assimilated by the mestizo masses—fatalism, communalism, cooperativeness, reciprocity, vitalism, sexual equality, and the cyclical, organic and harmonious nature of Nature. The imaginary Mexico that exists in the minds of Mexico's elites is the product of western civilization and the colonial past. Its values are those of individual freedom, competition, materialism (consumerism), science, technology, and a belief in linear progress.

The indigenous and colonial mix has created a mestizo culture in which the values of both societies are less than realized. The Mexico of today is an imperfect imitation of western democracy and development. In terms of the western model, its modernization has been limited and partial, with a traditional economy subordinate to the superpowers, an underdeveloped working class, a middle sector of entrepreneurs who look to state patrons for protection and support, and a corporate form of government that is both patrimonial and autocratic. This was and is the heritage of the Native American and colonial past, a tradition shaped by the space/time dimensions of Mexica life.

3   Up and Down from Colonialism

> Since the uprising of Hidalgo, and more especially since inde-
> pendence, Mexico has been perennially agitated by revolutions,
> and the Mint had declined considerably. Instead of finding that
> immense quantity of gold and silver which used to arrive from
> every direction, today one only finds copper in that place where,
> according to Baron Humboldt, there was minted in fifteen days a
> larger amount of precious metals than could have been extracted
> from all the mines of Europe put together, and from which has
> emerged a total of 2 billion hard piastres.
>
> Jean Louis Berlandier
> *Journey to Mexico* (ca. 1825)

The productivity gap that exists between Mexico and the
United States today is the result of the late colonial era and the early
years of the national period, roughly between 1770 and 1870. From
its colonial base, the economy of the United States "took off," while
the Mexican economic spiraled downward after 1770. In effect, the
United States went up from colonialism, while Mexico went down. To
grasp the differences between the overdeveloped United States and
the underdeveloped Mexico of today, it is necessary to understand
this heritage.[1]

The differences between New Spain and English North America
were partly the result of ecology and climate. The historian Clarence
Haring has divided the European colonies of the Americas into two
groups: farm colonies and exploitation colonies. The former were
generally established in temperate zones and produced commodities
similar to those of Europe. Immigration to these colonies tended to
come from the middle classes at home: small farmers, artisans, and
the like. Those who were not middle class, such as indentured servants, became, if they survived, sharecroppers, tenant farmers, and
smallholders.[2]

38

The so-called exploitation colonies were usually settled in the tropics and produced and exported staple articles such as sugar, cotton, indigo, and gold (and in the highlands of Mexico and Peru, silver). Labor was usually compulsory, and since immigrants were not attracted to an area of servile workers, a community of landlords and serfs developed. Obviously, under Haring's scheme, the northern colonies of English North America were farm colonies, while New Spain (and the American South for that matter) were exploitation colonies.[3]

Timing, as well as place, conditioned the differences between the two societies. Colonial Mexico was born of a different order and time than English America. Mexico City was founded by Hernán Cortés in 1521, a hundred years before William Bradford led the pilgrims to Plymouth on their historic voyage in the *Mayflower*. New Spain was an older fragment of Europe, a quasi-feudalistic and traditional society quite unlike the bourgeois and liberal republic that emerged in North America. From Old Spain the Middle Ages were carried outward by conquerors and colonizers to New Spain.[4]

The epic of Spain in Mexico began before the Reformation and developed in part as a reaction to Protestantism. An absolutist Spanish state imposed a religious, linguistic, and political unity upon the diversity of pre-Columbian Mexico. This patrimonial state fostered a cult of hierarchy in government and religion. In terms of the world-economy, New Spain's relationship to the core would always be through the semiperipheral area of Spain, an economic satellite of western Europe after 1600 (unlike English North America with its direct ties to the central commercial zone of Europe).[5]

In the Spanish Indies, colonization occurred precisely when the power of the Castilian Cortes (parliament) was declining. It was in Castile that the king had his most success in undermining any institutional opposition to royal absolutism. The conquistadores represented the Castilian king, not parliament (in fact, the Cortes never developed in colonial Mexico). The conquerors, because of the medieval tradition of *reconquista* (reconquest), had the aristocratic ethos of military adventurers, the Catholic faith of crusaders, and the submissive habits of loyal servants. Even the merchants, craftsmen, and professionals took their place in a social system in which values were determined by that earlier generation of *encomenderos*, friars, and public servants.[6]

The exploration and early development of Mexico came in the sixteenth century when the Mediterranean region with its Italian city-states *was* the world-economy. It is important to know that Aragon and other provinces of Mediterranean Spain were oriented toward Italy during the late medieval period. In addition, a major theme of Spain's medieval history was the Reconquista—the reconquering of areas lost to the Muslims after A.D. 711. These two legacies, that of Mediterranean mercantile capitalism and Iberian territorial conquest, were twin aspects of the revival of Europe. These traditions merged in the Spanish discovery of America.[7]

In the Mediterranean the basic unit of mercantilism was the *compañía* (company), a partnership between a home-based investor and a "factor" who would manage the company in the field and travel overseas. At times the backer providing the capital would be Genoese, while the field manager would be Spanish. Of course, the company was frequently composed of all Italians or Spaniards. Whatever the nationality of the members, their relationships were often familial, with the senior partner the father or older brother and the distant factors sons or cousins.[8]

Another characteristic of the Mediterranean world was that the company, if designed for commerce, was a factory (*factoría*) or trading fort, which provided the factors with a safe place to conduct trade with the local people. They were an excellent way in which a permanent commercial presence could be established without the cost of conquest and occupation. If the enterprise were agriculture, it would usually be a commercial activity designed to produce and distribute a staple luxury in demand, most often sugar. The Genoese took the initiative in establishing sugar mills and plantations in the Mediterranean, southern Iberia, the Atlantic colonies of Spain and Portugal, northeast Brazil, and the Caribbean. Three of the largest mills on Hispaniola in the 1540s were run by the Genoese. Their influence in the Caribbean did not begin to wane until after 1550.[9]

The Iberian tradition of Reconquista was based on military conquest and territorial occupation carried out by the *compaña*, or a band of men. Unlike the Genoese factory system staffed by employees, these men were risk-takers who held shares in the company. If the adventure was successful, like the conquest of Cajamarca and Cuzco in Peru, then the individuals were paid in accordance with their number of shares. For example, a knight might receive a share for himself and a share for his horse, while a foot soldier might only receive a fraction of a share. Generally speaking, the Genoese maritime-commercial *compaña* prevailed in the Caribbean, while the Iberian reconquest *compaña* predominated during the mainland phase of colonization.[10]

The two individuals who epitomize these merging traditions are Christopher Columbus (Colombo) and Hernán Cortés. Columbus was typically Genoese in most of his actions. When he left Italy he went west as an employee of a Genoese mercantile firm. While in Madeira he worked for a Genoese sugar company and married the daughter of an Italian who was donatary captain of the Portuguese island of Porto Santo, next to Madeira. His best friends were to be found among the Genoese merchant-exporters of Seville. When he came to the Caribbean he continued the Genoese maritime-commercial tradition.

Cortés was in the best traditions of the Reconquista, and when he left Cuba for Mexico he had ideas of conquest and occupation in mind. His hope was not to become a dirt farmer, or even an important merchant, but to become an aristocratic landlord with wealth and status matched only by loyalty to God and king.[11] Like Francisco Pizarro in Peru, his expedition was one of subjugation, and his followers were shareholders, not employees. This was the Iberian tradition of Reconquista.

Another basic entity of the Mediterranean world was the city-state, province, or town. Loyalty to the *patria chica* (home town) was second only to family. Provinciality loomed larger than nationality to both Genoese and Castilian. The Reconquista reinforced this basic attitude in that the reconquest took place on an urban frontier. The towns erected were military and religious centers that controlled the population of the countryside.[12]

This urbanity was transferred to the New World. The first political act of a conquistador was to erect a town (for example, when Cortés founded Veracruz). These New World cities were patterned after the Castilian experience with a layout that included a central plaza and a gridwork of streets forming square or rectangular blocks. The city, with its *cabildo* (town council), was the center of political authority. Here resided the civil and religious authorities, and their jurisprudence spread into the intervening countryside. A Spaniard in the countryside was there doing business for the city. In the Americas, the Spaniards established in less than a century an urban frontier that ran from north central Mexico to the Río de la Plata.[13]

Once the initial conquest was over, the Habsburg kings sought to extend their royal authority over a frontier society. The patrimony and patriarchy of Spanish society was reflected in the Spanish state. In this neo-medieval world, all parts of society were related through a patrimonial or symbolic center rather than to one another. King and church were united, and any group or corporation (church, bureaucracy, family estates, for example) formed a hierarchy of graded ranks in which the senior figure was protector and disciplinarian. In government the patriarchal and patrimonial symbol was the king, personified in colonial Mexico by the king's agent, the viceroy (and the royal court or *audiencia*; both viceroy and *audiencia* were established in Mexico by 1535). Even if regional loyalties and institutional rivalries developed, as they did in Mexico, still the ideal was Habsburg absolutism.[14]

The church in colonial Mexico was under the immediate control of the crown in all matters outside of religious doctrine and discipline. The Mexican church paid homage to the Council of the Indies in Castile, not to the Roman papacy. The crown aided in the financial support of the church, gathering tithes and constructing churches and monasteries. In effect, the Catholic church in Mexico was the imperial branch of health, education, and welfare: the monasteries and convents established hospitals; the orders dominated scholastic education in the universities and vocational training in the Indian schools; and the clergy instituted charities and orphanages.[15]

The secular hierarchy, from parish priest to cathedral chapter, was distinct from the regular orders of missionary friars and monks. The missionary orders included Franciscans, Dominicans, and Jesuits and were an important part of the frontier landscape. The Inquisition, which dealt mainly with blasphemy, sorcery, and bigamy, although manned by ecclesiastics, was only another councillor arm of government. Its main targets were English Protestants, New Christians, Jews, and the secular and regular clergy. In most of its activity, in Mexico City or on the frontier, the church realized the spiritual needs of the populace and the imperial objectives of the crown.[16]

As has been mentioned in a previous chapter, conquest culture in Mexico meant that duty to God and king required that the conquered be converted to Christianity. The conquest was legitimized by conversion. Thus the Native American, with his indigenous religious traditions, was greeted by the Catholicism of Rome and the Counter Reformation. The result was a syncretic religion, pagan and Christian, a blending that one writer described as "idols behind the altars." It is best exemplified today by the cult surrounding the Virgin of Guadalupe, a Native American fertility goddess (Tonantzin) in medieval Christian garb ("the most holy Virgin Mary, Mother of Orphans").[17]

Although pre-Columbian Mexico was a mosaic of tribes and languages, the Spaniard succeeded in incorporating the Native American into a unique cultural mix. Originally the Hispanic world in Mexico consisted of European Spaniards and Africans, while the Indian world included the indigenous population living separately in rural villages. Soon, however, acculturation and miscegenation complicated the three-category system.

This resulted in a multidimensional web consisting of Spaniards, community Indians, Indians-among-Spaniards, and *castas*—blacks, mulattoes, and mestizos (anyone not a Native American or European). In a social sense blacks, because of their cultural resemblance to Spaniards, were ranked higher than Native Americans. Yet, because Indians looked more like Spaniards, the Native Americans had the edge as to phenotype. In any case, the Native American was usually subordinate to all other groups in any given situation. After three hundred years of colonial rule Mexico was racially (although not culturally) a homogeneous society, with most individuals being Euro-mestizos, Afro-mestizos, or Indo-mestizos.[18]

The economy of New Spain was both domestic and foreign. The domestic economy consisted primarily of agricultural and ranching estates and *obrajes,* or factories. These produced the foodstuffs and woolen clothing for the colonists, both conquerors and conquered, and supplemented the trade from Europe. The *estancias,* or ranches, also served the needs of the mining towns. The international or transatlantic economy included silver mining, the economic motor of New Spain—silver was the chief export product. As a currency, it was the medium of exchange for international merchants who supplied European goods to the colony, including the mining centers.

Mexico's estates came in a variety of sizes and shapes. A hacienda in northern Mexico might have twenty-two thousand acres and be devoted to livestock raising, while an estate in the valley of Puebla might only amount to twenty-five hundred acres. Yet the Puebla estate might actually be of greater worth because of water access, suitability of soil, and nearness of market. Thus, a hacienda is defined as an estate engaged in agriculture or ranching and is considered large by local standards. And it may not be a contiguous unit, with *ranchos* (small one-owner farms) and Indian villages interspersed within the hacienda vicinity.[19]

The *hacendado* of the seventeenth century, like the *encomendero* of the sixteenth, was an urban dweller. He may have had his manor house (*casa grande*) on the hacienda and his economic base in the country, but his social, political, and religious concerns were found in his townhouse, the local city, and Europe. *Casta* stewards (*majordomos*) managed his country estate, and he and his family only went there on visits or during times of economic trouble.

Haciendas furnished European goods for the colonists, such as cereals (wheat, barley, oats), olives, and fruits. They also produced for the Native American market such items as corn and pulque. If the nearby towns required wool for their factories, then the haciendas would raise sheep; if the slaughterhouses were in need, they would provide cattle, pigs, and lambs. In the mining districts haciendas, *ranchos,* and *estancias* raised horses, mules, burros, and oxen. Although usually diversified, the hacienda would at times specialize in one crop, such as sugar. Like the other products of the hacienda, Mexican sugar sold only in the markets of New Spain.[20]

As for the human side of estate history, three periods of labor procurement can be delineated. These are the *encomienda* of the early conquest period, the *repartimiento* from 1560 to 1620, and finally, with the rise of the hacienda, informal individual agreements. The *encomienda*, in which entire Native American villages were assigned to one Spaniard, allowed the *encomendero* to monopolize Native American labor for a lifetime. The succeeding *repartimiento* was a state allocation of temporary Indian labor to Spaniards for ad hoc purposes and for a limited duration. Finally, Indian laborers came individually to Spanish enterprises and worked out their own contracts. The overall trend was toward more flexible, individual arrangements; away from temporary to permanent labor; and from no pay for *encomienda* laborers to salaries for contract workers. As for debt peonage, it was neither as common or widespread as previous historians have believed.[21]

The end of the eighteenth century witnessed an increase in the profitability of large-scale agriculture. Demographic increases and migration from the country to the city caused the cities to grow, and the towns in turn demanded more foodstuffs from the country. This led to additional commercialization of agriculture and more profits for the landowner, while surplus labor brought about declining real wages for farm workers. In addition, peasants had less access to fertile lands. While *hacendados* worked their *demesne* farms, income from land rentals and sharecropping added to hacienda revenues. In effect, wealth was being transferred from the countryside to the city and from peasant to landlord. The result was agricultural growth, demographic increase, and a decrease in the living standards of the mass of the people. It was social philosopher Henry George's paradox, poverty in the midst of progress.[22]

A similar occurrence was happening in the international sector of the economy as well. After 1546 strikes were made in Zacatecas, Guanajuato, San Luis Potosí, Parral, and in other areas of the Gran Chichimeca. As time went by, different levels of ore were extracted: first, the outcroppings were exploited in the late sixteenth century; then, the darker ores below the surface until the late seventeenth century; and finally, the deep ores in the eighteenth century. Since Mexico's mines were located in the north, away from large populations of sedentary Native Americans, the majority of unskilled and skilled workers were, unlike in Peru, not the product of the *encomienda* or *repartimiento* but instead were permanently salaried employees. These individuals became acculturated over time into Spanish-speaking mestizos.[23]

With the discovery of the mercury amalgamation process in the sixteenth century (a process that used mercury and salt to separate out the silver from the ore), the fantastic bonanzas of northern Mexico provided Spain with the lion's share of silver coins and ingots then in circulation in the global economy. These, of course, went to Spain's foreign merchants—Genoese, French, Dutch, English, and even Mexican—and to western Europe. Much of the silver reached Europe through contraband dealings with the enemies of Spain—the Dutch West Indies Company and the English sea traders. Almost all the silver in circulation in the Far East at this time came either directly across the Pacific from Acapulco to Manila in the Philippines or from Europe by way of America, that is, Mexico and Peru.[24]

Not only did mining maintain the metropolitan economy and Spain's not-too-certain international position in western Europe, it also provided for the administrative costs of an empire, including the financing of Habsburg foreign wars. One cannot overlook the fact that colonial Mexico functioned as a peripheral segment of the expanding western European economy, financing British, Dutch, and French growth, while at the same time underwriting the costs of Spain's inflated imperial commitments and military involvements.[25]

By the late colonial period the decay that characterized the rural population was affecting the mining sector as well. Even though silver mining production boomed during the first quarter of the eighteenth century, and again in the early 1740s and the decades of the 1770s and 1790s, the late colonial mining industry was in decline by the early 1800s, and definitely ill by 1810. Between 1780 and 1810, the industry faced rising costs due to the poor quality of ore, the depth of mine shafts, and the high costs of labor. By 1810 a scarcity of mercury added to the industry's problems. Collapse came in 1810 when the Spanish government could no longer afford to provide subsidies to support the industry. The wars of independence only prolonged the colonial heritage into the late nineteenth century.[26] All of this, of course, was quite different from the condition of the British colonies of North America.

The year 1607 looms large in the history of the Americas. As is well known, the English made their first permanent settlement on the American mainland with the founding of Jamestown. What is not so well known is that 1607 was the year Spain declared national bankruptcy, an event that soon led to the failure of the Bank of Genoa. This was the beginning of the end of the Mediterranean economy. Meanwhile, the British success at colonization indicated that the world-economy was entering a new phase.

Englishmen brought to the New World two traditions from the Old World that were critical to the success of the North American experiment. First, there was the experience of the English (and European) Reformation. Secondly, there was the inheritance of a 250-year commercial revolution that took place in England between A.D. 1350 and 1600.

In France, Holland, England, and Germany the Reformation established the principle that secular power should preside over the national church. Opponents of these established state churches were exposed to persecution and were more than willing to solve their situation through emigration. So the first to colonize America were the French Huguenots who settled Florida in the 1560s. Scrooby Separatists from Holland migrated to Plymouth. British Calvinists, whether Scottish Presbyterians or English Puritans (including Congregationalists), later joined English Quakers and settled in northern colonies. German peasants—Mennonites, Amish, Dunkers, to name a few— went to Pennsylvania. Anglicans settled in Virginia, and Catholics settled in Maryland.

Most of these people were farmers, artisans, and traders. Because they usually could not settle in the Catholic colonies of Spain and

France, they sought refuge in the American colonies of England. Thus was laid the foundations of a Protestant society inclined to assert individual rights over external authority and proclaim the rights of the humble to be free from royal and priestly dominance.[27]

The dominant Protestant tradition in the United States came from the Puritans of New England, and Puritanism affected all phases of American life. While Catholic aristocrats in Mexico were indulging themselves in the cult of the festival and the passion for spending, the Puritans in Massachusetts were living simple and "plaine" lifestyles in accordance with the maxim that "God's altar needs not our polishing." This was purification, not communion.[28]

The Calvinist beliefs of providence, grace, and special election, when shorn of their religious aspects, translated into the doctrines of contract, fundamental law, representative government, and the right of resistance. The economic views of Calvin sanctified productive labor, while private property enjoyed a divine sanction. In general the Calvinists approved of business, trade, and profit making.[29] It is not surprising that ministers, lawyers, and merchants in New England all adhered to the same religious and economic credos. "Healthy, wealthy, and wise" Benjamin Franklin, the ultimate capitalist, was just an eighteenth-century secular version of John Winthrop and other Puritan leaders of seventeenth-century Massachusetts.

The popular and familiar procedures practiced by the commercial companies were later extended into the political realm as colonial assemblies.[30] A classic example of this was the history of the General Court in Massachusetts.

Originally, in 1630, the charter of Massachusetts lodged all power over the colony in the general court of the company, which in turn consisted of shareholders (or freemen). Since very few freemen came to the colony with John Winthrop, several settlers demanded that they be admitted as freemen of the Massachusetts Bay Company. In 1631 some of the settlers were made freemen of the company, but only those who were members of an approved Puritan church. By 1634 a representative plan was adopted in which the towns selected deputies to represent them, and by 1644 the General Court had split into two houses: the court of deputies and the court of assistants, each with a power of veto over the other. Through these developments the Massachusetts Bay Company, originally a trading corporation, was transformed into a governing body.[31]

Building on the heritage of the Reformation and the English economic revolution of 1350–1600 (a process that witnessed the liberation of serfs; the growth of towns, trade, and merchants; the development of the wool industry; and the rise of commercial companies), Europeans found in America an underpopulated virgin land endowed with extraordinary resources directly facing Europe with a similar climate.

This land of opportunity was exploited by the Puritans and their descendants. The New Englanders made money first from fishing and then industry and trade. Shipbuilding, textiles, cast iron, rum distilleries, and other manufacturing developed. Before 1776, New York and Philadelphia merchants were found along the entire North Atlantic, through Madeira to the African coast. As Fernand Braudel notes, "America undoubtedly appeared as a rival from the start and her growing prosperity dented Britain's own prosperity and worried the great merchant houses of London."[32]

In the late eighteenth century both royal dynasties—England's House of Hanover (George III) and Spain's Bourbons (Charles III)—attempted to extend the rule of the metropolis over the colonies. After 1763, at the conclusion of the French and Indian War, Britain's thirteen colonies were faced with a series of regulatory acts: the Proclamation of 1763; the Sugar Act of 1764; the Stamp Act of 1765; the Quartering Act; the Townshend Duties of 1767; and so on. Collectively these policies meant that Great Britain was abandoning its earlier tradition of neglect and insisting that the colonists forsake their investments west of the Appalachians to pay for the costs of the empire. These policies principally affected the interests of the colonial elite, such as land speculators, merchants, property owners, lawyers, journalists, and other professionals. These were the groups that filled the ranks of the rebels in Boston and elsewhere. By 1776 independence had been declared.

While the British Parliament was passing the Stamp Act, Bourbon

Spain was naming José de Gálvez *visitador* (inspector) to New Spain. He was charged with implementing a new policy of tax control and making recommendations for reforming the mining sector of the economy. This was the "enclave" economy of miners and exporters whose profits were derived from exports to the metropolis. Although the reforms that resulted from his recommendations (from administrative decentralization through remodeling of the military to freer trade) had many effects, the most lasting was the Bourbon decision to modernize and upgrade the mining sector. To seek additional revenue, the crown issued a royal decree in 1804 nationalizing church properties and forcing the sale of estates. Many *hacendados* who had mortgaged their properties to the church were now faced with ruin. Thus, in Mexico, Spain's policy affected that part of the elite, primarily landowners and industrialists (and the lesser clergy), who were not a direct part of the favored enclave economy. These disaffected would follow Father Miguel Hidalgo in 1810.[33]

Of great significance for the advancement of the United States after 1783 was the growth of trade with the ex-metropolis, a development that took off after the War of 1812. English investment soon followed trade. In the meantime, Hamiltonian principles were creating a banking system and a capital market for George Washington's America.

In the United States, the years 1793 through 1807 were extraordinarily prosperous ones characterized by increases in employment, the domestic market, imports, and prices for foodstuffs. International conflict between 1793 and 1814 allowed the United States to enter the Atlantic trade as neutrals. When the carrying trade slumped during the War of 1812, idle resources were applied to textile manufacture. With the revival of an external demand for cotton and rising prices for foodstuffs, the New South and the New West attracted more immigrants. The North was not only able to become a financial center for southern and western agriculture but also developed its manufacturing base in flour, cotton goods, lumber, textiles, iron, leather, woolen goods, liquors, and machinery. Although the Civil War interrupted the process, in the long run that war was simply a catalyst for America's industrial revolution.[34]

At the outset of Mexican independence in 1821, a large portion of the Mexican population was unable to read or write, thought of politics only in a local context, and spoke little if any Spanish. Mexico had none of the cultural homogeneity of the United States and emerged from independence a weak debtor nation, intimidated by powerful creditor nations like Great Britain. Unlike the optimists in the thirteen colonies, where independence was an assertion of economic freedom and political democracy, Mexico's elites looked backward by declaring independence at Iguala to preserve the traditional privileges of the church and landholding aristocracy, only to be threatened by Spanish reformers and Indian revolutionists. Unlike the emerging United States, Mexico was born affirming the past. While making a legal break from the Spanish state, institutions, customs, and beliefs (when not Native American) were still medieval, Spanish, and Catholic. Independence had only fostered the integration of Mexico into the European world-economy dominated by London.[35]

Throughout the colonial era, Mexico, along with Eastern Europe, the southern colonies of British North America, and the rest of Latin America, had been on the periphery of the world-economy. In these peripheral areas, Mexico engaged in agriculture or mining through highly coercive forms of labor control (forced cash-crop labor, slavery, *mita* labor in Peru, *desagüe* or flood control work in New Spain or colonial Mexico,), the profits of which accrued to groups in the core area, international trading groups, and local supervisory personnel (such as civil servants and *hacendados* in colonial Mexico). Agriculture tended toward monoculture, political entities were weak, and population densities were low. All social relations became organized around the constraints of the world-economy. Overall, surpluses from the periphery went to meet the needs of the population of the core.[36]

The core of the world-economy at this time was the region of northwestern Europe. Its organization was more complex than the periphery. Population densities were high, agriculture was diversified and intensive, and labor was more skilled. Although agriculture remained a majority activity, cereals and bullion from the periphery liberated some labor for specialization in other tasks. This resulted in the monetization of rural work relationships, with wage labor and money rents becoming the means of labor control. A stratum of independent small farmers developed. In addition, towns flourished, industries were born, and merchants became an important economic force. In the political sphere, strong nation-states appeared. Generally, the continual cumulation of advantages at the core continued to expand the disparities of the whole.[37]

Midway on a continuum running from the core to the periphery was the semiperiphery (Spain, North Italy, the northern colonies of British North America). The dominant form of labor in this third zone was something in between the free labor of the core and the forced labor of the periphery, usually indentured servitude, tenant farming, or sharecropping. Population density was higher than in the periphery, and this affected the type of labor. As sociologist Immanuel Wallerstein argues, "when labor is plentiful sharecropping is probably more profitable than coerced cash-cropping."[38]

In the case of late medieval and early modern Spain, there developed a typically colonial infrastructure dependent upon the sale in foreign markets of a single product—wool. Such a society, colonial in structure and undercommercialized, invited exploitation by more developed centers of trade; thus, the temptation for Italian merchants and bankers to enter the peninsula.[39] As Braudel has pointed out, the "simplest, if not the best criterion [for determining the level of societies outside the central area], is the presence in a given region of colonies of *foreign* merchants." After the New World was discovered, much of its mineral wealth went through the semiperiphery of Spain to the developing economies of England, France, and northwestern Europe.[40]

When the core demand for sugar and tobacco increased, new peripheral areas evolved in tropical America: first sugar in sixteenth century Brazil and, in the seventeenth century, the Caribbean, especially Barbados and Jamaica; then, the tobacco and indigo plantations of the southern mainland of British North America.[41]

At the same time the semiperipheral areas were changing. With declining revenues from the New World and increasing expenditures of warfare in Europe, the Spanish state attempted to fill the gap with increased taxes in Mexico and Peru. This was a self-defeating activity that only led to further plunder, fraud, contraband, and parasitism, and further semiperipheralization of Spain.[42]

Yet while Spain was declining, the semiperipheral northern colonies of British North America (New England and the Middle Atlantic colonies) were gaining ground. By 1700 the northern colonies were making great strides as shipbuilders and commercial middlemen. The various triangular trades were flourishing, the industry of naval stores was thriving. Conditions were being created whereby the northern colonies could first share in the prosperity of the core and by the mid-nineteenth century, as an independent republic, move into the central-world zone of industrial and commercial powers.[43]

The early post-independence histories of the United States and Mexico continued the trend. While the United States emerged in the nineteenth century with a prosperous economy characterized by full employment, growing imports, developing cotton and foodstuff trades, and an established industrial and financial base, the Mexicans, as a poor debtor nation, entered a European world-economy dominated by London fads and Parisian customs. Civil anarchy during the battles of independence forced capital out of Mexico. In addition, Mexico's mines were flooded, its lands scorched and abandoned, and a large underclass wandered the backstreets of the cities. With independence, the colonial heritage of inadequate transport and inefficient economic structure was now encumbering Mexico with the costs of warfare.[44]

In concluding, it is informative to compare the economies of Mexico and the United States during the nineteenth century. In 1800, Mexico's per capita income was about half that of the United States. By 1877, Mexico's per capita income had dropped to a little over one-tenth that of the industrial United States. In 1800, Mexico produced a little over half the goods and services of the United States. By 1877, Mexico only had 2 percent of the production that came from the farms and plants of the United States.[45]

In 1821, the Mexican Republic was the largest in this hemisphere, nearly twice that of the newly independent United States of America. By 1853, at a little less than two million square kilometers, Mexico fell to one-fourth the size of her northern neighbor. At the same time, the landed area of the United States more than tripled. In 1800, Mexico's population of six million, many of whom were citizens of cities, exceeded that of the mostly rural United States (just over five million). By 1854, Mexico only had eight million inhabitants; the Colossus of the North had twenty-three million. In 1911, at the end of the *porfiriato*, Mexico's population was fifteen million while the United States had grown to ninety-two million.[46]

The Mexico of 1800, although beginning to decline and with many economic problems, was still Spain's richest colony in the New World. It had an advanced mining industry exporting huge quantities of processed metals and a significant and diverse internal market based on agriculture and manufacturing. It also had urban areas. For example, Mexico City had over 150,000 inhabitants, second only to Madrid in the empire. New York, the largest of the cities of the newly independent United States, only had sixty thousand people. In 1800, the United States was still a predominantly agrarian country decades away from its industrial revolution. Yet half of a century later the economic (and later military) gap that distinguished the developed United States from the underdeveloped Mexico was a reality.

Post-independence Mexico was a weak, disunited community dependent on foreign loans and goods. Nearby was the United States ever eager to expand its own economy at Mexico's expense. Yankee adolescents had moved up from their semiperipheral past, and the would-be giant was now playing in Mexico's backyard. The outcome of war between the two peoples was initially uncertain. But defeat for Mexico would make the social and economic gap real. In 1835 the future looked bleak. Yet Mexico had taken one faltering step—down and away from Spanish colonialism.

4 Texas and a Collision of Cultures

> The invaders were all men who, moved by the desire of conquest, with rights less apparent and plausible than those of Cortés and Pizarro, wished to take possession of that vast territory extending from Béxar to the Sabine belonging to Mexico. What can we call them? All the existing laws marked them as pirates and outlaws.
>
> Antonio López de Santa Anna

> After reiterated menaces, Mexico has passed the boundary of the United States, has invaded our territory, and shed American blood on American soil.
>
> James K. Polk

While 1846 may have been a momentous year for Bernard De Voto in his western narrative *The Year of Decision*, it was 1848 that proved to be epochal in world history. For Europe it was a year of revolt in Paris, Vienna, Berlin, Milan, and Rome.` Across the oceans from the Old World, armies were on the move. British frontiersmen were arriving in New Zealand, and Texas Rangers were returning from central Mexico. The Mexican-U.S. war had ended in February, and by October the Treaty of Guadalupe Hidalgo was ratified. The United States had acquired a vast domain at Mexico's expense.

Mexico's loss of territory in 1848 signified the end of any likelihood that Mexico, rather than the former thirteen colonies of British North America, would become the predominant power in North America. The initial unpreparedness of the American military establishment, characterized by divisiveness within the army and between civilian and military authorities or by inadequate medical services,[1] was replaced in time by a highly efficient war machine and a trained officer corps capable of victory. The use of breech-loading rifled guns by the U.S. Army and the Texas Rangers during the Mexican War is only one example of the evolution of that machine. Territory lost by

Mexico to superior arms was used by the United States to launch its own industrial revolution. A militarized and industrialized America would extend its empire beyond the continent. Thus, 1848 marked the long beginning of the rise of the United States as a world power, a movement that would culminate after 1945 with hegemony in Latin America, the Pacific Basin, and Western Europe.

The area lost by Mexico to the United States consisted of the northern part of the Gran Chichimeca, primarily those provinces of late colonial Mexico known as Nueva (or Alta) California, northern Sonora, Nuevo México, Tejas, and northern Nuevo Santander (between the Nueces and the Río Grande). The Hispanic (Spanish and Mexican) frontier in the north was a separate region of Mexico, with its own geography, culture, and history. Its isolation from Mexico City fostered a distinctiveness that gave the area its peculiar character; a remoteness that led the Gran Chichimeca to evolve economic ties with the United States a quarter of a century before the military conflict erupted, and an isolation that prompted Mexico City's politicians to ignore its needs until it was too late.

The frontier and its indigenous peoples modified Hispanic society so that it never mimicked central Mexico. The marginal farmland, low population, and relative poverty of the frontier could not support the elaborate institutions and hierarchical practices of the center. By the late eighteenth century, the church and the military, guardians of tradition elsewhere, were too weak on the frontier to enforce the will of the central government. New Spain's far north was more democratic and self-reliant than the core. For example, after 1770 Sonora was populated with metropolitan and commercialized merchants, artisans, miners, and *hacendados* who created a regional society that was more urban, entrepreneurial, and self-reliant than the rural and semi-feudal world of central Mexico.[2]

Of the various institutional complexes that medieval Spain gave to the New World, ranching was one of the more important. By the mid-eighteenth century, the inheritance of the plainsman had spread through northern Mexico into Tejas (or Texas), especially the mesquite and plains country along the San Antonio and Guadalupe valleys, between the Nueces and the Brazos rivers—an area of luxuriant grasses, belts of timber, and ample water. Here Andalusian cattle, a hybridized offshoot of semi-wild, black Iberian bulls and all-purpose, lighter-colored European cows, ran wild and multiplied prodigiously. Eventually, in the nineteenth century, these animals would intermingle with meat cattle from the Carolina coast to produce the Texas longhorn so typical of the western Great Plains.[3]

Unlike Iberia, the British Isles, and West Africa, the type of ranching that evolved in Latin America, Australia, Anglo-America, and South Africa was, at least in the beginning, open range. Frontier conditions (such as labor shortages and inadequate fencing materials) necessitated letting the cattle run loose. On the periphery of the world-economy, where long distances separated farmers from markets, the rancher put more capital into transportation than into land or labor. Thus a less intensive form of agriculture, like livestock raising, developed. And although ranching on the American Great Plains was of mixed origins, the traditions from Spain and Mexico dominated.[4]

Cattle ranching on the open range involved a variety of activities. The skills of horsemanship included roping, branding, driving, skinning, building corrals, and rounding up cattle. The widespread use of corrupted Spanish vocabulary by Anglo and black cattlemen to identify tools and costumes reflected Hispanic traditions. Take the following words for example: lariat or lasso (*lazo*); chaps (short for *chaparajos*); bronc (*bronco*); corral (*corral*); ranch and rancher (*rancho* and *ranchero*); rodeo (*rodeo*); and buckaroo (a corruption of *vaquero*). Wild and ownerless horses were known as *mesteños,* from which "mustang" is derived. The Anglos did give one name to the trade, however, that was not from the Spanish. Unbranded stray cattle were known by Anglos in Texas as mavericks, named after San Antonio's most prominent lawyer, Samuel Maverick, the son of a wealthy Charleston, South Carolina merchant.[5]

The ranching industry of Spanish Texas was originally designed to support New Spain's mining communities, missions, and towns of central and northern Mexico. It was primarily restricted to hides and tallow. The most important communities of Spanish Texas were

Fig. 6. Mexico, 1821–1836

Nacogdoches, near the old presidio of Los Adaes on the edge of
French Louisiana and deep in the forests of East Texas away from the
prairie openings; La Bahía del Espíritu Santo (present-day Goliad) on
the lower San Antonio River; Béjar (or "Béxar," today's San Antonio,
named for the nearby mission), one hundred miles north and west of
La Bahía on the San Antonio River and the chief center of Texas with
a town, presidio, and several missions (see figure 6).[6]

Béjar was on the main trade route between Nacogdoches and Louisiana to the north and east, and Laredo and Monclova to the south and
southwest. Silver coins and bars and assorted supplies from San Luis
Potosí and Zacatecas moved north in exchange for hides from Texas,

either through Saltillo and Monclova to Béjar, or Monterrey and Mier (on the Río Grande) to La Bahía. From La Bahía the path continued in a northerly direction where it intersected the road from Béjar at the Trinity River. From there the trail led to Nacogdoches. Because of Spanish regulations there was little if any coastal trade.[7]

Béjar and La Bahía were in ideal ranching areas and had been settled by pioneers from the Canary Islands;[8] the northern provinces of Nuevo Santander, Nuevo León, and Coahuila; and central Mexico. Settlement patterns followed the traditions of the Spanish past, with the towns laid out in the standard grid pattern found throughout Spanish Latin America.

Nacogdoches, however, was on the edge of the empire, composed of squatters, smugglers, and Native American traders, with a population that was as much French and English as it was Spanish. In fact, since the late eighteenth century a contraband cattle trade had developed between East Texas and Louisiana in spite of royal prohibitions. In exchange for livestock, the inhabitants of Louisiana would trade silk shawls, ribbon, braid, and other luxury items, as well as once-scarce items like nails. For residents of Béjar, it was cheaper to acquire goods from the French colonists via New Orleans and Nacogdoches than to purchase items that came by way of the overland route from Spanish Veracruz. Thus, Béjar profited not only from the trade with Old Mexico, but with Louisiana, New Orleans, and the world at large. In this respect there is a direct historic link between the pre-1821 Texas cattle drive to Louisiana and the post-1821 mercantile invasion of northern Mexico by American entrepreneurs.[9]

The distinctive nature of the Gran Chichimeca, a sparsely settled and mostly semiarid area based on a trade in hides and tallow, not only made it remote in its relationship with Mexico City but pushed it toward the ever-expanding new nation of the United States of America after 1776. After 1821 Mexico's northern frontier underwent extensive Americanization.

Mexico's first national charter, the constitution of 1824, envisioned a federalist republic composed of autonomous states. The promise of political autonomy did not, however, extend to the north where California and New Mexico became territories under congressional control in Mexico City, and Texas was tied to its larger and more populous neighbor to the south, Coahuila, as the single state of Coahuila y Texas. To make matters worse, Mexico City was preoccupied with its own national, not regional, problems and was forced to deal with the multiple threats of fiscal instability, civil war, foreign invasions, army plots, and factious priests.[10]

In the mid-1830s, Mexico abandoned the federalist system, replacing it with a centralist government. This was the last straw for advocates of local autonomy. Revolts against the central government spread between 1835–38 from Texas and Sonora to New Mexico and Alta California. In the interior the federalist governor of Zacatecas was deposed by Santa Anna, and in Yucatán, a state that communicated more easily with New Orleans and New York than central Mexico, the autonomous movement intensified.

The Catholic church, represented on the frontier by Jesuits and Franciscans, began to decline in the late eighteenth century. In 1767 the Jesuits were expelled, and after the wars of independence against Spain, many Spaniards were forced to leave the Republic, including several Franciscans. Weakened by a lack of funds and clergy, the bishops of the secular church could not fill the void left by the departing Franciscans. Most of the empty parishes that existed in Mexico in 1828 were located on the frontier. As historian David Weber has noted, "the once-powerful church on the Mexican frontier had become a paper tiger, its temporal and ecclesiastical power greatly diminished by the time of the United States invasion."[11]

At the same time Mexico's political and ecclesiastical authority was weakening, her military supremacy over the frontier was declining. The decades after independence saw relations worsen between Mexican frontiersmen and *indios bárbaros*, those autonomous tribes of semi-nomadic Native Americans who rejected Christianity and Hispanic culture. By the mid-1830s, Comanches kept the province of Mexican Texas in a state of constant agitation, while Apaches raided farms and ranches in southern New Mexico, northern Chihuahua, and the Gila Basin in Sonora. In 1845, the Navajos ravaged those *nuevomexicanos*

(New Mexico's Mexicans) living in the upper Río Grande valley, while the Utes raided as far afield as Alta California to gather mules and cattle for their American backers.[12]

Much of the breakdown of relations between Mexican frontiersmen and *indios bárbaros* was due to the activities of unscrupulous traders from the United States. These dealers furnished whiskey, guns, and powder to the Native Americans in exchange for stolen goods and captives. American encouragement and firearms permitted the Native Americans to raid and plunder the ranches, mining camps, and communities of northern Mexico. Indian raids multiplied Mexico's problems at a time when Texas, and then the United States, was presenting military threats to the far North. Mexico's underdeveloped military, with a demoralized soldiery and a politicized officer corps, had to face the United States on two fronts—the Native American and Anglo-American frontiers.[13]

Perhaps Mexico's greatest failure was its inability to integrate the frontier into the nation's economic system. Texas and the northern territories became dependent upon outsiders, especially Americans, for manufactured goods. After Mexico became independent of Spain in 1821, the Santa Fe Trail was inaugurated, linking St. Louis, Missouri, with northwestern New Mexico. Soon the Missouri trade extended into Chihuahua City, the mining center of north-central Mexico. In exchange for silver, mules, and wool, American merchants imported clothing, tools, and household items, often underselling their Mexican competitors.[14]

These venturesome merchants quickly found another source of wealth along the rivulets and streams of the high plateau country— the beaver—and the hunt for pelts and "hairy banknotes" eventually spread along the river valleys to Sonora and California. Meanwhile, New England maritime merchants made a similar thrust into California exchanging manufactured articles for otter skins, cowhides, and tallow. In Texas, the livestock trade with Louisiana continued. Eventually Texan cotton would also become an important export item.[15]

The results of all of this trade were many. Imports from the United States were expensive, and *californios, nuevomexicanos,* and *tejanos* (as

Mexicans living in those provinces were called) often bought on credit or bartered their goods. Specie remained in short supply. The value of manufactured imports always exceeded agricultural exports, resulting in a trade imbalance favoring American creditors. The pull of the American economy reached beyond U.S. borders and into the neighboring Mexican frontier, and American economic colonialism quickly supplanted the old Spanish structure after 1821. In general, the commercial orientation of Mexico's far North was shifting to the United States with Mexico's frontier gradually becoming part of the New South and the New West of the expanding American empire.[16]

The westward movement and dynamic expansionism of the United States during the nineteenth century is the other side of the story of why the Mexican North became the American Southwest. The incentives for American expansionism were many, but certainly the commercial and mercantile interests predominated. Merchants and land lawyers were found throughout the Gran Chichimeca, from San Antonio to San Diego. These were the capital-based and export-oriented elements of the frontier folk. Mercantile interests figured also in the thinking of Polk and his administrators who purposely sought trade outlets to the Pacific and had their eyes on the coasts, harbors, and bays of Oregon and California.[17] The British textile industry demanded cotton and stimulated the development of the New South, from Louisiana to East Texas. After the United States annexation in 1845, Texas, with its favorable climate and fertile soil, climbed rapidly in the list of cotton-producing states, ranking fifth by 1859.[18]

Anglo Texans had grandiose notions of international trade. The Río Grande with its headwaters in Colorado could connect the Chihuahua-Santa Fe trade with the Gulf of Mexico and the global market. In addition, the Río Grande contributed to the commerce of Matamoros on the lower end of the river. In the 1830s Matamoros was the largest town on the Mexican frontier, an entrepôt of silver, lead, wool, hides, and tallow from Saltillo and San Luis Potosí. It is not surprising that when Texas declared its independence in 1836 it asserted as its boundary with Mexico the entire Río Grande—a strategic claim that included a river that could rival the Mississippi as the most important trade route of the continent.[19]

The ideology that justified expansion for many Americans was Manifest Destiny, a mixture of natural rights, freedom of religion, democracy, republicanism, Anglo-Saxonism, geographical predestination, and other components. Americans believed that no nation had the right to hold soil virgin and rich yet unproducing. This doctrine was originally applied to Native Americans but was then expanded to include Mexicans and others. As was noted in the *U.S. Democratic Review* in 1858, "no race but our own can either cultivate or rule the western hemisphere."[20] Manifest Destiny was a racist doctrine that held that Anglo-Saxon Protestant culture was innately superior to all others and that republican forms of government and democracy must be expanded in order to "extend the area of freedom." Obviously, lazy, depraved, inferior, authoritarian, Catholic Mexicans must be outside of the destined realm. At least many Americans thought so.[21]

By 1824, when the first American settlers followed Stephen Austin into Texas, the United States was already pursuing a diplomacy of continental expansionism. The new U.S. minister, Joel R. Poinsett, proposed to the Mexicans that they relocate Mexico's boundary from the Sabine River to the Río Grande so as to be spared the problem of fighting the Native Americans of the area. In 1827, Secretary of State Henry Clay advised Poinsett to offer $1 million in compensation for territory up to the Río Grande. In 1830, the next U.S. minister, Anthony Butler, cunningly argued for a Río Grande border. After 1835 the United States again offered the Mexicans $1 million in exchange for moving the border from the forty-second to the thirty-seventh parallel. This would enable the United States to acquire San Francisco. All of these appeals fell on deaf ears as Lucas Alamán and his cohorts took steps to terminate Anglo colonization into Texas and contain the Americans.[22]

Before 1830, the influx of Americans into Texas increased. The state of Coahuila y Texas granted permits to developers, Mexican and foreign, and the colonists received their concessions from these *empresa-*

rios. Most of these permits restricted slavery and required the colonists to be Roman Catholic, but the colonists tended to ignore both requirements. Originally Austin's group settled San Felipe on the lower Brazos. Then Green DeWitt settled three hundred families in his city of Gonzales on the southwestern side of the Austin colony. Robert Leftwich was permitted to bring in two hundred families, while Hayden Edwards was allowed eight hundred. Martín de León settled about forty Mexican families just east of Goliad at Victoria. Further south Irish promoters established colonies at Refugio and San Patrico.[23]

While some Mexicans and Europeans settled in Texas, for the most part the immigrants came from the southern United States—Louisiana, Arkansas, Alabama, Kentucky, Tennessee, and Missouri—and they brought their slaves with them. Driving their cattle and hogs before them, the colonists came through Nacogdoches and down the old La Bahía road to San Felipe to file for riverine holdings. By 1835, the immigrant population was between twenty-five thousand and thirty thousand including slaves, while the Mexican population had barely passed seventy-eight hundred.[24]

In 1827, General Manuel Mier y Terán was commissioned to study the problems of the Texas border. To his superiors he expressed his fears that the growing influence of the North Americans would result in the loss of Texas. Noting the cultural, educational, and legal differences between the two peoples, he said, "Thus, I tell myself that it could not be otherwise than that from such a state of affairs [of mutual ignorance] should arise an antagonism between the Mexicans and the foreigners, which is not the least of the smoldering fires which I have discovered. Therefore, I am warning you to take timely measures. Texas could throw the whole nation into revolution." Mier went on to recommend the establishment of more presidios (forts and militias), the colonization of Texas by Mexicans and Europeans, and the creation of customhouses.[25]

After 1829, in part because of Mier's suggestions, a strategic plan to strengthen Mexico's hold on Texas was initiated. On 15 September 1829, all slavery was abolished throughout the Republic. In 1830, Lucas Alamán promulgated a new colonization law that prohibited the entrance of new U.S. settlers. Between 1830 and 1834, in spite of the clamor of the colonists, the state of Coahuila y Texas was maintained intact. However, Texas was divided into three departments, each with a pair of forts, one to be situated along the old Spanish axis, the other on the coast.[26]

East Texas became the Department of Nacogdoches, with a presidio at Nacogdoches and another at the new site of Anáhuac near the mouth of the Trinity River. The Department of Béxar, containing San Antonio de Béxar and Goliad, was created in the south. In between was the Department of Brazoria, centered around Austin's colony of San Felipe. Only Béxar was truly Mexican in both soil and culture. Nacogdoches, which stood on Mexican soil, was ethnically and culturally an extension of Anglo-America. The suspension of political autonomy to Texas by Santa Anna in 1835 provided the Texans with the pretext they needed, and in that year William B. Travis seized Anáhuac, and Sam Houston occupied Texas's most important city, San Antonio de Béxar. The military phase of the Texas Revolution had begun.[27]

In May of that year General Santa Anna, with a combination of deceit and valor, devastated the federalist stronghold of Zacatecas. Over two thousand civilians, including women and children, lost their lives in the rape and pillage of that city. The centralist victory over Zacatecas did not bode well for "Texicans," as Santa Anna, backed by an immense army of some six thousand troops and good generals, started to march north.

In February of 1836 Santa Anna, ahead of his troops, arrived at the Río Grande. The bulk of the Mexican army remained farther back, outside Monclova, when a blizzard struck, hitting a horde of pitiful Mayas from the Yucatán the worst. Without shoes, warm clothing, and blankets, these Mayas froze to death. At the rear of the army, *soladeras*, female camp followers, and their children huddled together— their frozen bodies found later. Mules and horses froze to death as well. The army had suffered a tremendous loss, perhaps as many as 90 percent of the original six thousand.[28]

In March of 1836, when Santa Anna finally started the siege of

San Antonio's former Franciscan mission, the Alamo, he had only six hundred men. Eventually the number that actually stormed the walls increased to more than eighteen hundred. Many of these were bedraggled Mayan conscripts who did not speak Spanish, had little fighting experience, and had smooth-bore muskets that were outclassed by the Alamo defenders with their rifles and artillery.[29]

As for the makeup of the Alamo garrison, very few of these 180 men were Texans. Excluding the few Mexicans in the ranks, most came from New York, Pennsylvania, and sixteen other states. But the technological advantage that the protectors of the Alamo had was eventually overcome by the force of numbers. Displaying the blood-red flag of No Surrender, with buglers sounding the *degüello* (the Moorish refrain that signaled no quarter be shown the enemy), the Mexican army attacked the walls of the adobe fortress for several days. Considered pirates and international outlaws by the Mexicans, most of those inside the Alamo were killed, either in the initial attack or in the executions that followed. A few escaped. It was a terrible loss for the Texans and their American backers.[30]

While the Alamo is famous in the annals and folklore of Texas, a more significant battle took place several weeks later outside Goliad. There Colonel James W. Fannin had to surrender an army of over 365 men to the soft-spoken General José de Urrea, the commander of 1,200 Mexican troops who had come thundering up from the south. Through mismanagement, Fannin had left his outfit defenseless—his soldiers and oxen without food and water. The prisoners, like those at the Alamo, were considered by Santa Anna to be pirates and therefore subject to the death penalty. Even though his orders were protested by his officers, the entire Texas force was executed. As word of Santa Anna's butchery spread, hundreds of volunteers ran away to help their fleeing families. In March, the Texas army had numbered 1,400 men; by the Battle of San Jacinto in mid-April it was down to 784.[31]

Good fortune and assistance from the United States finally came to the aid of the Texans. After the Alamo and Goliad, Santa Anna had the Texans on the run. Sam Houston spent this time both retreating and reorganizing. From New Orleans there came more volunteers and from the U.S. government semiofficial support in the form of arms and money. Santa Anna finally overextended himself, and on 21 April his troops were caught off guard near the San Jacinto River (near today's Houston) outside the Department of Béxar and inside the Anglo-American zone of influence. Two days later Santa Anna himself was captured by one of Houston's patrols. The defeat at San Jacinto and General Vicente Filisola's withdrawal made the loss of Texas final. The Lone Star Republic of Texas had been born. The Texans chose David Burnet as president and the Mexican populist and radical politician Lorenzo de Zavala vice-president (the latter choice symbolic of the role the *tejanos* took in fighting for Texas independence).[32]

For the Texans, the butchery at the Alamo and Goliad dispelled any lingering doubts of Mexican treachery and cowardliness. Now the Texas Rangers could justify their own violence toward Mexicans. "Santy Anny" became the favorite villain in Texas. One popular view, which dealt with a scene after the San Jacinto battle, appeared in several variations by a number of Texas writers. It was as follows:

> The dead Mexicans lay in piles, the survivors not even asking permission to bury them, thinking, perhaps, that in return for the butchery they had practiced, they would soon be lying dead themselves. The buzzards and coyotes were gathering to the feast, but it is a singular fact that they singled out the dead horses, refusing to touch the Mexicans, presumably because of the peppery constitution of the flesh. They lay there unmolested and dried up, the cattle got to chewing the bones, which so affected the milk that residents in the vicinity had to dig trenches and bury them.[33]

After Texas independence, during the period of the Lone Star Republic from 1836 to 1845, hostilities between "Texicans" and Mexicans would persist, and the forces of American expansion would continue.

During the last days of Andrew Jackson's administration, in March of 1837, the United States recognized the independence of Texas. Both the independence of Texas and American recognition were repudiated by Mexico. Although not all *norteamericanos* approved of expansionism, their voices were drowned out by those who would benefit from cheap grazing lands, fertile cotton-producing soil, free trade with Santa Fe, and commercial access to San Francisco, China, and Japan. Even the Texans were not immune as they claimed New Mexico as their territory and unsuccessfully sent their armies into Santa Fe and Matamoros in 1842. Likewise, between 1836 and 1845, Mexico invaded San Antonio on more than one occasion and attempted unsuccessfully to reconquer Texas. Finally, in the last days of President John Tyler's administration, a decree was signed annexing Texas to the United States. Mexico considered this annexation an act of aggression, and the Mexican minister in Washington, D.C., broke off negotiations and went home.[34]

With the expansionist James K. Polk in the White House, events soon got out of control. Polk was intent on defending the Texas frontier, even if it inadvertently led to war with Mexico. He also desired a west coast harbor. Secretary of the Navy George Bancroft ordered the U.S. fleet to keep the gulf ports under surveillance, and Commodore John D. Sloat had instructions to take both Monterey (in California) and San Francisco in case of war. At the same time, Polk's special envoy to Mexico, John Slidell, was given instructions to negotiate the Texas boundary at the Río Grande and to secure New Mexico and California. In January of 1846, President Polk ordered General Zachary Taylor to march into disputed territory between the Nueces and the Río Grande.

Taylor established himself on the north bank of the Río Grande and proceeded to construct Fort Texas (later renamed Fort Brown, and today's Brownsville). On 9 May, Taylor reported to Polk that a skirmish had broken out between his dragoons and the Mexican cavalry, resulting in the death of several American soldiers. Polk could report to Congress that American blood had been shed on American soil. A declaration of war was stampeded through Congress. Eventually, General Winfield Scott would be named commander-in-chief of the expeditionary forces. In Mexico City the view was different—not only had the United States taken Texas, but it had changed the traditional boundary to twice its size![35]

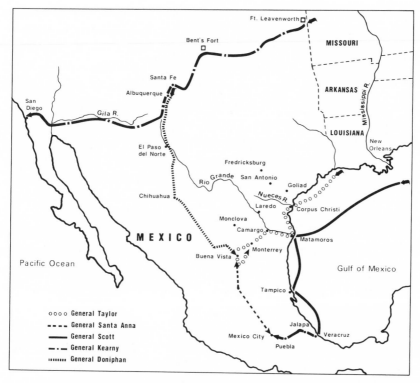

Fig. 7. U.S. Invasion, 1846–1848

U.S. strategy called for a three-pronged offense by the army with logistical support from the navy. The Army of the Center would take northern Mexico; the Army of the West would occupy New Mexico and California; the Army of Occupation would carry the war into Mexico City (see figure 7). The navy was to escort the transports of both Taylor and Scott, guard their bases from the sea, capture the coastal towns of Tampico and Monterey, maintain a blockade on the Gulf and Pacific sides, and assist the army at Veracruz. The manpower problem was solved by private recruiters who promised their inductees "roast beef, two dollars a day, plenty of whiskey, golden Jesuses, and pretty Mexican girls." Although the Mexican army in-

cluded about thirty thousand men against less than fifty-five hundred regulars in the American establishment, compared to the United
States, their artillery was outmoded, their officers corrupted by politics, and their men, although brave, were poorly trained.[36]

As the war proceeded, General Stephen W. Kearny, commanding
the Army of the West, left Ft. Leavenworth in June of 1846 with some
fifteen hundred men. Nine hundred miles later he arrived in Santa
Fe, initially taking the city without firing a shot, but later being harassed by Mexican and Pueblo Indian guerrillas. Then Kearny divided
his army. Alexander Doniphan led a contingent south to Chihuahua,
while Kearny joined Commodore Sloat in California. After defeating
the Mexicans in an artillery duel at Chihuahua, Doniphan's troops
joined Taylor at Buena Vista outside Saltillo.

Meanwhile, Taylor had moved from Matamoros to Camargo and
from there to Monterrey. Needing reliable scouts experienced in the
rugged terrain and thick chaparral of northern Mexico, Taylor reluc-
tantly accepted Texas Rangers who he thought "were too licentious to
do much good." Originally the Rangers were mounted riflemen created during the early days of the Lone Star Republic to capture and
kill Comanches and Mexican cattle rustlers operating beyond the Nueces. Eventually half of Taylor's army of six thousand was composed of
such volunteers, those whom the Mexican priests described as "van-
dals vomited from Hell." After a three day struggle and suffering
heavy losses, the city of Monterrey surrendered. From there Taylor
went to Buena Vista to face Santa Anna's twenty thousand men. After
an initial stalemate, Santa Anna withdrew from the battlefield to re-
solve a dispute between liberals and clerics in Mexico City, leaving
northern Mexico to the invaders.[37]

In December 1846, General Scott arrived at Brazos Santiago above
Matamoros. Infuriating Taylor, Scott reassigned several thousand of
Taylor's regulars and volunteers who were in Matamoros, Camargo,
and Buena Vista to the Army of Occupation. On 9 March 1847, Scott
and his ten thousand men made an amphibious landing south of the
harbor of Veracruz. For forty-eight hours Scott laid waste to the city,
killing over a thousand civilian inhabitants. From there Scott's forces

outmaneuvered Santa Anna at the mountain pass of Cerro Gordo, rested his troops at Puebla, and eventually fought for control of Mexico City in the battles of Contreras, Churubusco, and Chapultepec. On 15 September, despite heroic resistance from the capital's citizens, the stars and stripes waved over the National Palace.[38]

On 2 February 1848, at the Villa de Guadalupe, a treaty was signed ending the war and ceding Texas and the territories of New Mexico and California to the United States. The Río Grande and a California that included San Diego were part of the settlement. The United States paid Mexico an indemnity of $15 million and assumed over $3 million in claims that United States citizens had against the Mexican government. Mexico lost half of its territory (including Texas) but did manage to save Baja California and have it linked by land to Sonora. Articles 8 and 9 of the Treaty of Guadalupe Hidalgo guaranteed to the Mexicans in the ceded territory the protection of their property and the "free exercise of their religion," while Article 11 committed the United States to control the Native Americans in the ceded area. A few years later, Santa Anna would sell the Mesilla valley (today southern New Mexico and Arizona) to the United States for $10 million, and America's destiny would be made manifest (see figure 8).[39]

The Mesilla tract, known in U.S. history as the Gadsden Purchase, contained thirty thousand square miles of presumably barren Sonoran desert and included both the garrisoned presidio of Tucson and the new town of Mesilla. Around 1850, approximately two thousand *nuevomexicanos* who wanted to live in Mexico moved to Mesilla thinking that they were in Chihuahua. Because Article 5 of the Treaty of Guadalupe Hidalgo provided for surveying and marking of the boundary by commissions of the two nations, a line was surveyed from the lower Río Grande westward to San Diego. Although most of the boundary along Texas and California was not controversial, that section defining the Chihuahua-New Mexico area was disputed. Lacking precise information about the true location of Paso del Norte, the commissions placed the city north and east of its actual position. Eventually, due to the new terms of the Mesilla Treaty and the expertise, cooperation, and good work of both the Mexican commission

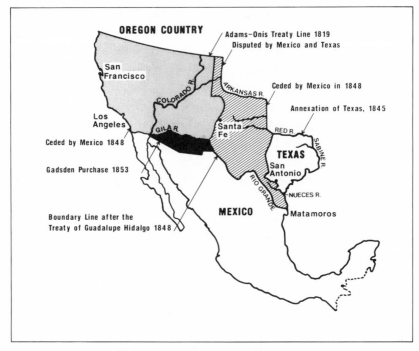

Fig. 8. U.S. Expansionism, 1845–1853

and the American engineers, a satisfactory boundary was established by 1857.[40]

A perplexing war was over, but its significance for the history of the two nations cannot be underestimated. The results were many and varied and affected the areas differently—whether that part of the Gran Chichimeca that was now "occupied" Mexico, the vanquished nation of Mexico, or the victorious United States.

The Spanish-speaking population of the vast area acquired from Mexico between 1845 and 1854 is estimated to be somewhere between 75,000 and 95,000: perhaps 60,000 *nuevomexicanos:* 7,500 *californios;* 1,000 Mexicans in and around Tucson and Tubac (in what would eventually be called Arizona); and as many as 25,000 *tejanos.* After the war, as many as 2,000 refugees left "occupied" Mexico and settled across the Río Grande in the older, established towns of Paso del Norte,

Mier, Camargo, Reynosa, and Matamoros; or they established themselves in new towns such as Mesilla, Guadalupe, or Nuevo Laredo. In addition, black slaves from East Texas escaped their situation by fleeing to the Mexican side of the Río Grande. Despite these refugee movements, Texas south and west of the Nueces remained predominantly Mexican, with as many as 18,000 Mexicans to 2,500 Anglos. In some places in southern Texas the ratio of Mexicanos to Gringos was twenty-five to one.[41]

Yet the other side of the coin was the rapidly growing Anglo population. In Texas it quadrupled from 30,000 in 1836 to 140,000 in 1846, an increase that was largely due to Anglo immigration into East Texas. While Hispanos were a majority in New Mexico, by 1850, Spanish-speaking Californians constituted only 15 percent of the state's population of 380,000. Yet "occupied" Mexico was still a frontier area with a low ratio of inhabitants to lands.[42]

For some parts of the American Southwest, the Mexican War marked the transition of the economy of the conquered provinces from subsistence cultivation to market production—a change that involved the displacement of a traditional landed elite by a new elite whose base was commercial capital. The freeing of the land from traditional, patrimonial Mexican claims was accompanied by increasing linkages with national and world markets. This transition took longer in New Mexico than in California or Texas, but the result was the same. Anglo-Americans introduced their own standards for the adjustment of land claims and the liberation of entailed property; and the Anglo merchant, lawyer, judge, and sheriff were the agents of this enormous land grab, legal or not.[43]

Mexicans in Texas, especially above the Nueces, lost much land through fraud and outright confiscation. In the south and west of the Nueces, however, a system of incorporation occurred. There an accommodation took place between the victorious Anglo elite and the defeated Mexican elite. Sometimes the American merchant, lawyer, or soldier would intermarry with members of the old elite. These Anglos would be "Mexicanized," becoming *patrones* and *compadres* who would sponsor baptisms and marriages. As powerful *hacendados* they would eventually rule over small landowners (*rancheros*), *vaqueros*, and *peones*. Legal mechanisms, such as taxation or court-ordered surveys, became the instrument for dispossessing both Mexican elites and *rancheros*. Eventually all of Texas would be integrated into the national market, and the most exportable item was, of course, the Mexican longhorn. Thus, the Mexican War created the basis for a powerful export-oriented upper class whose rules and regulations were enforced by the Texas Rangers.[44]

Another heritage of the Texas Revolution and the Mexican War was heightened animosity between Texans and Mexicans, especially between that "special breed of men" known as the Texas Rangers and *los fronterizos* (borderlanders). Anglo Texans developed a set of attitudes that may be called the Texan legend, in which the violence of the ranger is rationalized because of the barbarities of the Alamo; the racial superiority of the ranger is asserted; and the cowardly, degenerate character of the Mexican is affirmed.[45]

The most distinguished historian Texas has produced, Walter Prescott Webb, is himself a primary source of the legend. He says in his book, *The Texas Rangers* (originally published in 1935), "Without disparagement it may be said that there is a cruel streak in the Mexican nature, or so the history of Texas would lead one to believe. This cruelty may be a heritage from the Spanish of the Inquisition; it may, and doubtless should, be attributed partly to the Indian blood. Among the common class, ignorance and superstition prevail. . . . The Mexican warrior . . . was, on the whole, inferior to the Comanche and wholly unequal to the Texan."[46] And, of course, the Texas legend has its counterpart in the *corridos* or folk ballads of the border Mexicans.

The savage behavior of the wartime rangers in Camargo, Monterrey, and Mexico City established their reputation in Mexico as *los tejanos sangrientes* ("bloody Texans") and *los diablos tejanos* ("Texas devils"), and along the Río Grande as *los rinches de la Kineña* ("Rangers of the King Ranch," the personal strong-arm men of Richard King and other cattle barons). The *corridos* tell us that the ranger was a Mexican killer who shot first and asked questions later. Rather than a law enforcer, the ranger was believed to be a source of lawlessness, a lawman who shot innocent Mexicans in the back and raped their women. A common anecdote says that the Texas Ranger always carried a rusty old gun in his saddlebag to use when he killed a Mexican. He would drop the gun beside the dead Mexican in order to claim he killed in self-defense. Whatever, the *corridos* testify to a continuing heritage of deep hatred and mistrust of American authority along the border.[47]

As for Mexico proper, the war and the ensuing Treaty of Guadalupe Hidalgo brought in its wake the danger of social and political dissolution. Indian and peasant rebellions occurred in northern and central Mexico, in the Huaxteca region of Veracruz, and in the Yucatán peninsula. In 1847, following an attempt at independence by the sisal producers of Yucatán (who were simply imitating the behavior of their Anglo Texan brothers), the Mayan peons revolted. Soon a major caste war pitted Cruzob Mayas against their former masters. Only the money secured as part of the war indemnity (as well as funds received later from the Gadsden Purchase) enabled the government to restore social order after 1855.[48]

It was also no accident that Mexico's liberal reform of 1857 (known as La Reforma) and the Maximilian episode of 1863 followed hard upon the Treaty of Guadalupe Hidalgo. In Mexico City, liberals and conservatives viewed with alarm the impotence of their country in 1847, and both reasserted their national programs as solutions for the country's ills. Liberals believed that there had been no national resistance because there had been no nation—simply a confused and ineffective collection of Indian slaves, overly taxed and regulated merchants, foreign artisans, a poorly trained military, and greedy clerics. La Reforma, that is, the attack on the properties of clerical and military corporations and Indian communities, was the liberal bourgeoisie solution. As for the conservatives, they knew that Mexico's problems were due to its republican past. Only a return to a constitutional monarchy, such as that which was promised by the Austrian archduke, Ferdinand Maximilian of Habsburg, could lift Mexico out of its anarchy and sorrow. Maximilian and the French intervention lasted until 1867.[49]

Finally, there was the significance of the Mexican War for the United

States. With the exception of the Indian campaigns, this war was America's first major imperial adventure, and the result was the beginning of the militarization of American society. Part of this was facilitated by mechanization. In 1836, the inventor and engineer Samuel Colt registered in Hartford, Connecticut, the patent of the revolving pistol, and from Texas came the first order for shipment. By 1850 the manufacture of small arms was a major New England industry.[50]

Another factor was that the Mexican War was the proving ground for the U.S. Civil War, and the names of those who fought for Taylor and Scott amount to a roll call to military greatness: Robert E. Lee, Ulysses S. Grant, George Gordon Meade, William Tecumseh Sherman, and Stonewall Jackson, to name a few. From the navy came, among others, David G. Farragut and Franklin Buchanan. In fact, the decade following the war was a time of expansion for the U.S. Navy—in 1849 there were only seven ocean-going steamers; by 1860, twenty-six. Finally, the penchant that Americans have for electing military heroes to the presidency was renewed, with three of the U.S. officers in the Mexican War attaining that high office—Taylor, Grant, and Franklin Pierce. A fourth, Jefferson Davis, was elected president of the Confederacy.[51]

The Mexican War, like most wars in American history, was divisive. There were some who thought that Manifest Destiny meant that the United States should expand to the isthmus of Panama and take all of Mexico in the process. Some Whigs in Congress cursed the war and criticized the president, while voting for appropriations for the army and praising the bravery of the soldiers. Nicholas P. Trist, the American negotiator at Guadalupe, believed that continued occupation of Mexican soil could lead to the end of the "Jeffersonian vision" for America. Critics were also aware that imperial commitments could lead to the enhancement of executive authority at home. Polk, by provoking war, manipulating Congress, establishing a secret fund, and holding close personal control over the military establishment, did not fail his critics. As John C. Calhoun warned, "there is not an example on record of any free State ever having attempted the conquest of any territory approaching the extent of Mexico without disastrous consequences." The forbidden fruit of Mexico, when consumed, proved fatal to the body politic, as slavery in the newly acquired territories became the major constitutional and political issue leading up to the Civil War.[52]

In the nineteenth century, territorial expansion (including the Oregon territory acquired from the British in 1846) and the spoils of war added lands to the United States that amounted to almost 70 percent of the national domain, all of which were sparsely populated. Between 1790 and 1860, the landed area of the United States tripled in size, and population pressure changed from 4.5 persons per square mile in 1790 to 10.6 per square mile by 1860. The existence of abundant, accessible, fertile land drew off thousands of potential wage earners who might have crowded the cities of America. Scarce labor in the cities and limited immigration translated into higher wage costs that gave incentives to manufacturers to replace labor with machines. The application of capital-intensive technology to production, and the dual role of the West as a source of basic resources and a market for industrialized goods, led to the economic development of the post–Civil War United States. As economic historian Stuart Bruchey notes, "in the nineteenth century the American common market was to the United States what the European Common Market is to twentieth-century Europe."[53]

Material capital accumulations, that is, improved lands, amounted to three-tenths of the rise of the total GNP during the 1869–1914 period, or over one-fourth of the increase in output per man-hour. With improved lands and investments in health, skills, education, buildings, and machines, a sustained economic growth became the central feature of United States history between the Civil War and World War I. Cotton gins, steel plows, McCormick reapers, machine tools, locomotives, and so on were all evidences of the industrial revolution that was at hand.[54]

The loss of Texas, New Mexico, and California deprived Mexico of immense natural resources. The gold rush of 1849 was only the beginning, and within twenty years the lost area was producing more mineral wealth than all the fabled silver mountains of Old Mexico. By

1900, the mineral output alone of the lost territories amounted to more than the national income of the Mexican Republic. Unlike the United States, human capital stagnated, especially in education and health. The Mexican economy, half as productive as that of the United States in 1800, was only one-eighth as productive in 1867. The economic gap between the United States and Mexico, originating in the late colonial period, was now well developed and established.[55]

The capital that accumulated in the United States during the Gilded Age (1875–1900) needed an outlet. It was now time for the ever-expanding United States to invest in lands and resources in that part of the Gran Chichimeca lying south of the Río Grande, and to transform Mexico's remaining northern frontier into an international border.

5   From Pueblo to Global Village

> It was better that a little blood should be shed that much blood
> should be saved. The blood that was shed was bad blood; the
> blood that was saved was good blood.
>
> Porfirio Díaz

British historian Eric Hobsbawm interpreted the history of
what he called the "long nineteenth century" (1789–1914) in three
works. The first, *The Age of Revolution 1789–1848*, traced the double
breakthrough of the first industrial revolution in Britain and the
Franco-American political revolution. The former established the capitalist productive system that penetrated the globe and was rationalized by the ideas of classical political economy (economic liberalism
or the doctrine of free trade). The latter created the model for bourgeois society and the creed of utilitarianism (or political liberalism).
His second volume, *The Age of Capital*, covered the brief period between the 1848 revolutions and the onset of the 1870s depression. It
dealt with the themes introduced in the first book in a narration of
the conquest of the globe by the capitalist economy and the victories
of the bourgeoisie and their liberal ideology.[1]

The last work of the trilogy, *The Age of Empire 1875–1914*, recounted
the transformation of the economic and military supremacy of the
capitalist countries by the "new imperialism." This was an era when
most of the world was divided into the informal territories of a handful
of powerful states, primarily Great Britain, France, Germany, Italy, the
Netherlands, Belgium, Japan, and the United States. Although capital
investments propelled some of this colonial expansion, the most important motive was a search for markets abroad. The overproduction
of the 1870s and 1880s led to a widespread export drive throughout
the world.[2]

It was also during the Age of Empire when the United States (and to
a lesser extent Germany) was beginning to outproduce Great Britain in
terms of iron and steel, while Great Britain, with a slower rate of indus-

79

trial growth relative to the United States and Germany, was showing the first signs of a declining power. World trade patterns were changing too. In 1860, over half of the exports of Latin America, Asia, and Africa went to Great Britain. By 1900 the British share had dropped to one-quarter, and Third World exports to western Europe were already larger than those to Britain (31 percent). For North Americans, it was a time when the United States ceased to be on the semiperiphery of Europe.[3]

These global trends were an important backdrop to Mexico's "long nineteenth century" (1770–1911). The economic gap that developed from 1770 to 1870 between Mexico and the United States was a microcosm epitomizing the events of the world in general. In 1750 the per capita levels of industrialization in Europe and the Third World were roughly the same, but by 1900 the latter was only one-eighteenth of the former, and only one-fiftieth of the United Kingdom. The respective positions of Europe and the rest of the world, before 1800 and after the industrial revolution, indicate to us today the tremendous significance of industrialization for world history.[4]

The industrial revolution in Britain from 1770 to 1860 occurred in several economic sectors simultaneously. By 1820 the British population had increased to twelve million and was almost eighteen million by 1850. This massive demographic revival was caused in part by the utilization of intensive agriculture techniques in the countryside and the rise of industry. And industry was the outcome of technological innovations (for example, spinning mules, power looms, steam engines, coke-smelting, iron-refining) that were adopted when demand and prices were favorable. Steam power accelerated the manufacture of cotton textiles, the spread of an inland transport system involving turnpikes and iron rails, and a foreign market facilitated by steamships. Iron (eventually steel) and cotton were the bases of Great Britain's global commercial supremacy. The machine revolution was a worldwide phenomenon.[5]

Throughout the century, Britain remained Europe's foremost exporter of manufactured goods and exponent of free trade. Since British manufactures were not particularly competitive in the markets of the industrializing countries, it was of paramount importance that the United Kingdom preserve its privileged position vis-à-vis the non-European world. Without a peasantry at home, Britain relied on the non-European world for foodstuffs, including cereals, wheat, beef, cheese, and eggs and in return exchanged finished items. Britain also dominated the trade in primary goods like tea, cotton, wool, cane sugar, and rubber. Free trade was indispensible for maintaining the symbiosis between industrial Great Britain and the underdeveloped world on which British supremacy rested. However, the most important export for Britain was capital, especially of "invisible" financial and commercial services.[6]

Although most of Britain's foreign capital investments went to either settler colonies (Canada, Australia, New Zealand, South Africa) or the United States, the last quarter of the nineteenth century and the beginning of the twentieth witnessed a significant increase of British investments in Latin America. Between 1875 and 1914 British investments in Latin America rose from £85 million to £750 million; 50 percent of the total coming in the last decade.[7]

As for the British share of Mexico, its investments during the age of Porfirio Díaz (the *porfiriato,* 1876–1911) were primarily in government bonds, public utilities, banks, railways, tramways, rubber, cotton, silver, and nonferrous metals. After the turn of the century, when Britain's navy was converting from coal to oil, the petroleum sector became important, especially Sir Weetman Pearson's Compañía Mexicana de Petroleos El Aguila (1908).[8]

Yet as impressive as British global influence was in Mexico and elsewhere, in hindsight it is obvious that the Age of Empire would be a time when the United States, until then a secondary power, would enter the world stage as a major economic force and a potentially powerful military state. This all began after the Mexican War during the Gilded Age (1870–1890), when the territory acquired from Mexico, the so-called last frontier of the Great Plains and the intermountain West, would undergo, along with the rest of the nation, an industrial and modernizing revolution.

With the Civil War over, the United States was able to exploit its numerous natural advantages, including rich lands and raw materials. Because the land was vast, labor was always scarce and expensive (in spite of the increase in population). Thus entrepreneurs were motivated to develop labor-saving machines and technology to develop the country's resources. Meanwhile, foreign and domestic investment capital transformed the nation's economy at a stunning pace, and the manufacturing revolution took off. By the turn of the century, the United States was the leading manufacturing nation in the world.[9]

By 1914, with a national income of $37 billion and a population of ninety-eight million, the per capita income of the United States was $377, more than a third greater than Britain's $244. U.S. steel production, usually a measure of both industrialization and military potential, was 31.8 million tons a year, almost double that of Germany and over four times that of Britain. The United States led all industrial powers in energy consumption of fossil fuels (that is, coal, petroleum, and natural gas) and hydroelectricity.[10]

Industrialization also altered the traditional trade patterns. Prior to the Civil War, the United States had exported raw materials (like cotton) and imported finished manufactures, but post–Civil War America exported farm machinery, iron and steel goods, copper cable and wire, electrical supplies, machine tools, and other wares onto the world market. While wheat and other foodstuffs were still being exported, raw materials for America's industry were being imported in ever-larger numbers. At the same time, the northern industrialists' lobby was powerful enough to ensure that Congress would develop and retain a protectionist tariff policy. By 1910, the sale of manufactured goods was beginning to exceed exports of raw materials.[11]

After 1880, U.S. economic interests in the form of capital and industrial surpluses extended into Mexico and continued to expand during the administrations of Theodore Roosevelt, William Howard Taft, and Woodrow Wilson. In 1890, total U.S. investment was around $130 million. At the turn of the century, American capital invested in Mexican enterprises amounted to a little over $200 million. By 1910, according to figures published by the Mexican government, total foreign capital amounted to over 2 billion pesos, of which 1.2 billion pesos (or over $500 million U.S.) were American.[12]

Of the largest businesses in Mexico in 1910–11, seven were owned by American interests either outright or as joint enterprises with the Mexican government and other foreign nationals. Anglo-American interests dominated the express, mining, utilities, and petroleum industries, and the American Smelting and Refining Company and the Greene Cananea Copper Company were the second- and third-largest concerns in all of Mexico (only the multinational Ferrocarriles Nacionales de México was larger).[13]

By the end of the *porfiriato*, foreigners owned over 20 percent of Mexico's land surface and most of the eighty-largest industrial and commercial concerns. Of these, twenty-three were British and twenty-one were American. By 1911 the United States controlled nearly 38 percent of the aggregate foreign investment in Mexico, mostly in railroads, mining, and real estate. In all of Latin America, only in Mexico did U.S. finances, which constituted 45 percent of all U.S. investments in the Americas, exceed the British.[14]

The foundation for this capitalist invasion of Mexico and the *porfirian* economic miracle that followed was laid in the earlier part of the nineteenth century. If investments were to flow into Mexico from the United States, the tradition of violent intervention by foreigners, both citizens and states, had to be curtailed. Between 1821 and 1878, when the United States finally recognized the Díaz government, Mexico had endured foreign intervention, separatist movements, war with the United States, colonization by a European power, and unlimited filibustering attempts by citizens of the United States. The most notorious of these filibusters were active in the decade of the 1850s, beginning with William Walker and his unsuccessful endeavor to conquer Baja California and adjoining Sonora in 1853, continuing through the attempt by Henry A. Crabb to overthrow the governor of Sonora in 1857, and concluding with Sam Houston's immodest plan of 1859 to use thousands of Texas Rangers and Native Americans to establish a protectorate in northern Mexico. Filibustering was yet another part of the history of territorial aggression and expansion by the United States with Mexico.[15]

The impulse for foreigners to take Mexican land and resources by force was lessened considerably when Díaz agreed, as the price of diplomatic recognition in 1878, to grant generous concessions to American investors. This was a kind of payback to South Texas investors, especially Brownsville merchants, who had supported Don Porfirio's assault on the Sebastian Lerdo de Tejada government with rifles, pistols, knives, grenades, monies, and personnel in 1876. These same American investors (mostly Río Grande valley bankers and railroad men like James Stillman, and wealthy Texas ranchers like Richard King and Mifflin Kenedy) used their considerable influence to get the United States to recognize Mexico.[16]

Specifically, the agreement of 1878 allowed foreigners to purchase real estate in border areas and extended the duty-free zone westward from Tamaulipas to Baja California. This meant that northern Mexico and Tamaulipas would be opened to direct American economic penetration, and that U.S. railroad interests would soon be surveying routes from several border towns to central Mexico. Díaz also agreed to reciprocal border crossings by troops in pursuit of hostile Native Americans and cattle rustlers, and put an end to the attempt by Juan Cortina, the Mexican hero who was considered a cattle thief in Texas, to lay claim to lands north of the Río Bravo. Finally, the agreement provided indemnities for U.S. property owners for damages in previous conflicts. After 1880, the United States would substitute for its earlier strategy of physical conquest one of economic domination through expanded trade and investment.[17]

Throughout the nineteenth century, Mexican entrepreneurs paved the way for their foreign counterparts. After 1825, when the Mexican state had difficulty in attracting foreign loans, it turned to local merchants or money lenders (agiotistas). In time they took over many attributes of the state such as delivering mail, running mines, and purchasing army equipment. In effect, the agiotista was a member of modern Mexico's first governmental or public bourgeoisie. As they increased their state power, their investments became more diverse to include banking and industry. By the 1850s, these *empresarios* were an important part of the national economy—a group of entrepreneurs who turned commercial capital into financial capital and then took their loan profits and transformed them into industrial capital.[18] After the Reform era they were rewarded with nationalized church lands and concessions for Mexico's first railroad, connecting Veracruz and Mexico City. As historian Barbara Tenenbaum states, the *agiotistas* "embraced centralism and national authority as well as the Lerdo law, a strong affirmation of the right of private property, and a dedication to law and order. The empresarios found a home with the liberals of the Reform and [in] the Porfiriato their true roots." In effect, they established an indigenous base upon which foreign enterprise could be grafted.[19]

As mentioned earlier, the period between 1855 and 1861 is known in Mexican history as La Reforma. It was an era of unrelenting liberalism in which the rising central government used all of its power to eradicate corporatism and revive liberty. The Reform was led by Benito Juárez, a Zapotec Indian from Oaxaca, and its essence was found in the federalist constitution of 1857. This document abolished ecclesiastical and military *fueros*, that is, the privilege of priests and army officers to be exempt from ordinary civil and criminal jurisdiction, and prohibited the corporate (church, communal, municipal) ownership of urban and rural real estate.[20]

Although ostensibly federalist, in actuality the national government created by the constitution of 1857 was strongly centralist, with powers to impeach state governors and invalidate state elections. And, more important, the constitution was silent on religion, an omission that meant Roman Catholicism was not recognized as the national religion of Mexico. Enforcement of the liberal ideology led to a three year civil war with the church and a major liberal-conservative struggle. By 1861, the liberal crusade was victorious, the church had lost its property without compensation, and separation of church and state had become a reality.[21]

The financial woes of the nation caused the victorious Juárez to issue a two-year moratorium on all government payments to foreign creditors. This was the pretext Napoleon III used to satisfy his imperialist urge. In 1864, he established a monarchy over Mexico with the French army supporting the imperial regime of Archduke Maximilian of Austria as Napoleon's nominee for the Mexican throne. Juárez eventually defeated the French with American financial and military assistance, abetted in part by the good works of his diplomat in Washington, D.C., Matías Romero, and by a covert army of Mexican secret agents who recruited American soldiers of fortune. By 1867, with the execution of Maximilian and the expulsion of French troops from Mexican soil, Juárez was finally free to champion the liberal bourgeois cause.[22]

Surprisingly, it was during the period of the French occupation between 1862 and 1867 that foreigners, including North Americans, first began to invest and speculate in Mexican properties in a serious fashion. With Juárez seeking U.S. public and private assistance against the French interventionists and pursuing investments to further Mexico's modernization, northern businessmen ventured into mining, agriculture, mail-steamship communications, and petroleum.[23]

Meanwhile, the regional *caudillo* of Nuevo León y Coahuila and the enemy of Juárez, Santiago Vidaurri, developed the cotton industry of the Mexican North and promoted a flourishing trade between the Confederates in Texas and the northern provinces of Nuevo León y Coahuila and Tamaulipas. Piedras Negras, Nuevo Laredo, and other Mexican towns grew as confederate cotton was shipped to Europe and arms and munitions were transshipped to Texas via the port city of Matamoros. It was this same commerce and industry that made successful capitalists out of Texans like Charles Stillman and the aforementioned King and Kenedy.[24]

Even Emperor Maximilian brought infusions of capital to Mexico. French assets gave new life to the textile industry of Puebla. British capital resumed the work of the Veracruz-Mexico City railroad, and a branch of the London Bank of Mexico, the Banco de Londres y México, was established. Generally speaking, the imperial government created policies and passed laws that encouraged European immigration, promoted foreign investments, and guaranteed individual property rights, including those of purchasers of church property. Thus, the environment of investment was well developed when Porfirio Díaz grabbed power in Mexico in 1876.[25]

Mexico's population grew from eight million in 1854 to fifteen million in 1910. The increase, while not as great as that of its northern neighbor during the same period (which went from twenty-three million in 1854 to ninety-two million in 1910), was significant. It signaled the end of an era of slow growth, and, unlike the United States, was not due to immigration but to an increase of the native population. (Most immigrants, repelled by the low salaries of Mexican industry, were attracted to the better living conditions that could be found in the United States.) The northern frontier states of Sonora, Coahuila, Nuevo León, and Tamaulipas increased in population because of internal migration.

Economic progress was most noticeable in the export-oriented sectors of the economy, especially mining, petroleum, and agriculture. The developing railway system made possible the growth of these industries. Before the railroads, mule transportation was too expensive for anything but precious metal mining, mainly silver and gold. With the railroads, production of copper, zinc, and lead soared. Copper production alone increased from 6,483 tons in 1891–92 to over 52,000 tons in 1910–11.[26] As for oil, by 1911 Mexico ranked third among the world's petroleum-producing nations, thanks to the railroads and the activities of American-owned concerns like Doheny's Mexican Petroleum Company, the Standard Oil Company, and the Texas Company (Texaco). As already indicated, the British trust of Weetman Pearson was also an important producer of the black gold.

In order to foster railway growth, the Díaz regime alloted grants of land to foreign and domestic developers. By 1884, land concentration (caused by purchase of public lands, concessions, outright gifts, and usurpation) stimulated the new commercialization of ranching (cattle and hides) and agriculture and fostered an export trade in cotton, garbanzos (chickpeas), fine woods, henequén, rubber, guayule, coffee, cochineal, *ixtle*, cacao, and chicle.[27] In the process, many peasants lost their land.[28] In his study of the *porfiriato*, social historian William Beezley cites an 1881 account in which a Judas effigy, attached to the headlights of a locomotive by the local *campesinos,* was exploded. The Judas image, representing the people, was destroyed by the engine. This rite symbolized the rapacious technology of the railroad, a technology that consumed both the peasant and his corn.[29]

During the 1880s and 1890s, the growth of the railroads was phenomenal. By 1884, the National linked Corpus Christi, Texas, to Mexico City by way of Laredo. That same year, the Mexican Central completed its 1,970 kilometers of track from El Paso to Mexico City. Other lines connected Nogales to Mexico City and Eagle Pass to Durango. A trunk line ran from the copper mining center at Cananea, Sonora, to Bisbee, Arizona. Tropical goods were moved by the Tehuántepec Railroad from the Pacific port of Salina Cruz overland to Coatzalcoacos on the Gulf of Mexico. By the time of the revolution in 1911, the railroad system totaled over 24,000 kilometers (14,904 miles), almost twenty-four times the 1880 amount but only a fraction of the 250,000 miles of track that existed in the United States.[30]

Unlike the grid system of American railroads, the Mexican pattern was radially arranged. Although the Díaz government had hoped that the Mexican railway network would connect the west and east coasts of Mexico to markets in the interior, in reality the main lines ran north and south, linking the United States with Mexico City. The result was that the lines served as a pipeline through which the raw materials of Mexico flowed to the United States (see figure 9). The raylike pattern meant that goods intended for the Mexican interior often had to go hundreds of miles over an indirect route to reach their market. For example, a shipment of goods from Mazatlán on the west coast intended for the Durango market a hundred miles away would have to travel north to Nogales, east to El Paso, and south to Torreón before reaching Durango—a trip of over a thousand miles. Mining camps in Coahuila and Sonora were more intimately connected to the American Southwest than to Mexico City as a result of the mining legislation of the *porfiriato.*[31]

The railroads that facilitated export production and the import of manufactures also allowed for the introduction of agricultural produce from the United States, especially during times of crop failure and

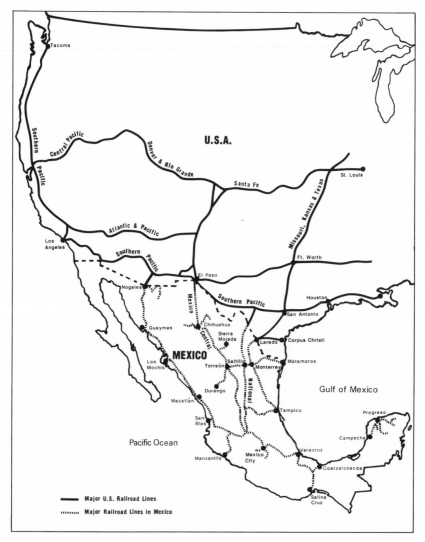

Fig. 9. Major Mexican and American Rail Lines, Early 1900s

drought in central Mexico. Thus, maize was imported to Mexico from the United States in large numbers during the arduous years of 1892, 1896, and 1910, with imports rising to over 10 percent of national consumption.[32]

In 1884, when the American-controlled Mexican Central railroad completed its line to Mexico City, the Mexican government created a new mining code that made no mention of the colonial tradition of state ownership of subsoil resources. The omission gave surface proprietors ownership of bituminous and nonmetallic materials. In addition, the tax law was revised in 1887 to exempt coal, iron, sulphur, and mercury from all mine taxes. It also provided for lowering of freight rates on mineral products destined for export and encouraged concessions to foster new mining enterprises. The Code of 1884 and the Tax Law of 1887 meant that Mexico was moving toward a laissez-faire mining policy.[33]

The first result of the new legislation was the development of rail lines to the mining fields. The Mexican Central linked the mining camps of Chihuahua to El Paso and made it possible to process Mexican ores in Colorado, Missouri, Oklahoma, Kansas, and Texas. In the 1890s Robert S. Towne opened the Mexican Northern Railway, which connected the silver-lead ore of Sierra Mojada, Coahuila, with the smelters of El Paso. After 1900 the Río Grande, Sierra Madre, and Pacific Railroad of American entrepreneur William C. Greene linked the timber and copper resources of Sonora with Arizona and the American West coast. Greene's Cananea Consolidated Copper Company was the most productive copper mine of *porfirian* Mexico.[34]

The McKinley Tariff of 1890 and the Sherman Silver Purchase Act aroused American interest in high-grade silver ores and stimulated the building of smelters in Mexico to avoid the new duties in the United States. In the early 1890s, Daniel Guggenheim built several smelters in the state of Nuevo León and by 1910 Guggenheim's American Smelting and Refining Company (ASARCO) was the largest privately owned business in Mexico; and another American owned mining corporation, the Anaconda complex, was its nearest competitor. By the end of the *porfiriato*, U.S. investors held 81 percent of the industry's total capital, while their British counterparts controlled nearly 15 percent.[35]

An increase in trade with the United States was the major result of railroads that were overwhelmingly owned and controlled by a consortium of U.S. capitalists. Exports from the mines, forests, ranches, and farms of Mexico went to the United States. From the United States came finished goods such as chemicals, steel rods and sheets, copper wiring, machine belts and tools, electrical machinery, motors, railway rolling stock, and equipment for mining, agriculture, and local factories.[36] To be fair, not all finished goods were produced on foreign soil. The textile industries of Orizaba and Puebla, although French owned, did supply the domestic economy, as did a host of many other Mexican-owned light industries that produced paper, glass, shoes, beer, and food. Both U.S.- and Mexican-owned ore smelters in Monterrey provided steel for the Mexican economy. Yet, with the exception of the steel and related Mexican industries of Nuevo León, heavy industry in Mexico always lagged far behind light industry.[37]

Industrialization that occurred during the *porfiriato* established the pattern for the later revolutionary and post-revolutionary era. Unlike the situation in the United States or Great Britain when they were beginning their industrial development, the Mexicans did not have a home market that could absorb the vast quantities of a modern manufacturing plant. With sophisticated and capital-intensive technology acquired from the developed nations, the industries of Mexico were always producing under capacity. Overproduction and high costs eventually led to concentration of ownership and monopoly. The home industries that produced steel, glass, cotton, paper, soap, beer, cigarettes, dynamite, and the like, had to rely on constant government protection and subsidies to compete in a market that was restricted to the underdeveloped economy of Mexico.[38]

The boards of these industrial oligopolies usually consisted of merchant bankers, often of European descent, who manipulated the market and the state to maintain their position of dominance in the economy. Some of these entrepreneurs included German-born Hugo Scherer; Austrian Adolfo Prieto y Alvarez; Basque financier Antonio

Basagoiti; French industrialist León Signoret; Americans Eugene Kelly and Thomas Braniff; and Mexicans Julio Limantour (brother of the finance minister), Pablo Macedo, Juan Terrazas, and Enrique Creel.[39] The Mexicans in the group were included for their political influence. These entrepreneurs used the *porfirian* state for their own private, economic purposes, acquiring subsidies, tax breaks, and protective tariffs and in turn providing the state with loans and revenues. By so doing they assured that Mexican industry would never become self-sufficient, nor the state ever independent of the industrial class.

The growth of the railroads soon brought the isolated Mexican countryside into contact with urban centers, port cities, and the global economy. Legislation was designed to support elite interests and the expansion of commercial agriculture. The anticorporate tradition of the Ley Lerdo, coupled with new *porfirian* land laws that enabled private companies to survey public lands and retain one-third of what they found for themselves, led to the expropriation, foreclosure, and seizure of many rural lands. These laws not only expanded new markets and fed the speculative motives of capitalists, but also transformed peasants into laborers and sent the surplus labor of the countryside into mining camps, industrial towns, or commercial estates. According to Friedrich Katz, communal villages of central and southern Mexico, which controlled approximately 40 percent of all agricultural lands in 1810, held only 5 percent when Díaz left office in 1911. In other words, over 90 percent of Mexico's peasants were landless due to the modernization and land laws of the *porfiriato*. For the period after 1910, this translated into a loss of village autonomy, decreased mobility, new fears and insecurities, and violence.[40]

The *porfirian* enclosure process was a necessary development in the country's transformation to capitalism, and American investors were in the vanguard. John Hart observes that "over 100 million acres, more than 22 percent of Mexico's land surface, came into the possession of American owners." After 1900, many of these corporate owners subdivided their tracts and sold them to thousands of American colonists who occupied properties in all parts of the country. Americans invested in, worked on, and held more than a hundred properties of between 100,000 and 500,000 acres. The U.S. publishing magnate William Randolph Hearst alone owned landholdings in Chihuahua, Oaxaca, Tabasco, Chiapas, and Campeche that amounted to over seven million acres.[41] The Mexican countryside that greeted these new owners was a patchwork quilt. The southern coastal states of Veracruz, Tabasco, Yucatán, and Chiapas, as well as the northern borderlands, were areas of sparse population that soon developed export-oriented agriculture. The north-central plateau of the Bajío, San Luis Potosí, and Zacatecas were populated by large, private estates, while the central and southern highlands remained a stronghold of peasant villages with communal traditions.[42]

Important discrepancies appeared in the agricultural sector in terms of the stage of technical modernization employed in each area. Generally, lands that produced cash crops like sugar and henequén underwent a technological revolution, while food staples production, although increasing throughout the *porfiriato*, still utilized antiquated and traditional methods. Though a scarcity of labor may have led to technological advances in the northern borderlands and the southern coasts, Mexico's abundance of cheap labor in the central zones did not induce much modernization when it came to producing wheat and corn. In fact, one study cited by Katz indicates that in 1911 the costs for producing a similar amount of wheat were the same for the modern American farmer as they were for the Mexican *hacendado* using cheap labor and primitive technology.[43]

The impact of the railroads was uneven. Railroads meant new markets for the country's peripheries. The southern coastal states began producing export commodities like Yucatecan henequén or Chiapas coffee, while livestock raising expanded in the northern borderlands, and cotton farms sprouted up in the Laguna (where Durango and Coahuila come together). In the central state of Morelos, linked to Mexico City and Veracruz by the railroad, production of sugar cane increased. While slave and debt labor were common in the tropics, higher wages and increased mobility were the rule in the Mexican North.

Contrary to conditions elsewhere, the impact of the railroads in central Mexico often meant that *hacendados* now had new competition from outsiders, and labor was often further restricted with peasants becoming tenants, tenants becoming sharecroppers, and sharecroppers becoming laborers. By the time of the revolution, these differing conditions elicited a variety of responses from the inhabitants. In the Bajío, estate workers and peasants remained passive, while in Morelos and the northern borderlands, peasants and *rancheros* (middle class farmers) were rebellious.[44]

A tremendous change took place in the Gran Chichimeca, especially the northern Mexican states of Sonora, Chihuahua, and Coahuila during the *porfiriato*. This area underwent transformation from a frontier to a border, a place in which U.S. capital greeted Mexican labor under rules created by politicians and their foreign allies in Mexico City.[45] The removal of the Apache threat and the arrival of the railroad set the stage for immigration into the Mexican North. More than 15,000 Americans came to the area as wealthy investors, landowners, railway workers, managers, and technicians. In addition, 300,000 more migrants from central and southern Mexico arrived to work in the mines, smelters, foundries, breweries, textile factories, ranches and cotton farms of the North. By the turn of the century, the northern borderlands was the most modern section of Mexico.[46]

The North was characterized by high wages, labor mobility, and high technology. Owners of the mining camps of Cananea and Batopilas paid some of the higher wages in Mexico. The Laguna cotton district and the garbanzo fields of the Yaqui valley were equipped with newly designed irrigation systems. Alexander Sheperd's reduction plant at Batopilas was as modern as any existing at that time in either the United States or Mexico. Modernization spread throughout the North, affecting Yaqui peasants, Tarahumara miners, Baja fishermen, Chihuahua cowboys, and Coahuila railway workers alike.[47]

Another dimension of the northern borderlands was urbanization. Overnight isolated pueblos like Torreón were changed into major cities, and steel towns like Monterrey began to swell in population. Monterrey's development came when the rails linked it to the United States via Laredo, to the seaport of Tampico, to the coal and iron ore deposits west of the city, and to Mexico City. With tremendous hydroelectrical potential, and capital from the United States, Monterrey became the leading industrial town of Mexico by the end of the *porfiriato*. Monterrey's two major industries were the Cervecería Cuauhtémoc, a brewery that produced Carta Blanca beer, and the steel factory Fundidora de Fierro y Acero, with its smelters, ironworks, and foundries. These industries spawned related enterprises producing glassware, cement, textiles, pottery, and foodstuffs.[48]

The *porfiriato* also witnessed the development of an indigenous capitalist class in the North. Elites like the Sonoran Triumvirate of Luis Torres, Rafael Izábal, and Ramón Corral; the Luis Terrazas-Enrique Creel clan of Chihuahua; the patriarchal Evaristo Madero household of Coahuila; the Monterrey mill owner families; and the Nuevo León *hacendados* promoted capitalism in northern Mexico. In some ways they constituted a Mexican equivalent to the Guggenheims, Vanderbilts, and Rockefellers in the United States.[49]

Modernization was not only an economic but a political phenomenon. An important dimension of the *porfiriato* was the partial emergence of the apparatus of a modern state, with its expanded police and judicial and administrative powers spread throughout the provinces, hamlets, and municipalities of the Gran Chichimeca. Not only American capital transformed the Mexican North, the political and military arm of Mexico City changed a frontier into a border. When Díaz became president in 1876 he immediately began consolidating his power.[50]

Making use of the classic tactics of effective rule, Díaz practiced the politics of divide and conquer with the military, church, and even foreign powers like the United States and Britain. In addition, he added to the security of his regime by influencing the appointment of state governors, approving candidates for the national congress, dispensing patronage to his friends, developing shifting commands for the military, controlling the courts, subsidizing and suppressing the press, and cultivating the support of the church.[51]

Taking for his political and economic creed the positivist slogan "Order and Progress," Díaz was determined to curb Mexico's tradition of anarchy so that economic development and modernization could occur. Aided by the genius of his financial minister, José I. Limantour, Díaz was able to restructure the monetary system, establish a fixed ratio between silver and gold (a consequence of America's return to the gold standard in 1900), balance the budget, abolish the *alcabalas* (interstate tariffs), acquire new revenues (mainly from import duties and taxes on rare metals), and secure new international loans. The laws of Mexico were reformed so as to meet the needs of the creditor nations.[52]

A Mexico City clique of politicians, lawyers, bankers, financiers, and industrialists (known as *los científicos*) advised Díaz on the niceties of scientific management and rationalized the excesses of technocracy and capitalism that characterized his rule. This group acted as intermediaries for foreign companies that wished to penetrate the Mexican economy. Overall they reasoned that foreign wealth (especially European capital since it would act as a counterbalance to American investments) combined with indigenous capital would lead to economic progress for Mexico. However, to assure this development, the state would have to protect and promote the interests of the investor.[53]

The Pax Porfiriato was maintained, in part, by a liberal use of the police powers of the state. Díaz augmented the military budget, established a modern military academy, and bought arms and advice from Saint Chamond and other French suppliers. Aided by the development of the electromagnetic telegraph and the railways, communication and transportation advances facilitated the mobilization and deployment of the army and police. Federal troops moved quickly to pacify the frontier. They were also used to protect the National Palace, guard the federal prisons, and when needed, to break strikes. Díaz also employed the services of the national guard, the Rurales (Rural Police Force), and specially commissioned gendarmes, like those led by Colonel Emilio Kosterlitzky in Sonora. These paramilitary forces not only repressed the enemies of the state, but were an important counterweight to the influence of the army. Political rivals were either shot on the spot (under the provisions of the infamous Ley Fuga, law of flight), sent to the federal prison at San Juan de Ulúa, or absorbed into an expanding bureaucracy.[54]

Díaz also developed an elaborate spy system that he hoped would make his regime secure. The Ministry of Gobernación soon acquired a *policía secreta*, while the War Department developed its own military and police forces that could be used covertly to acquire information on Don Porfirio's enemies. More important, a bicultural and binational spy and police system was directed by Enrique Creel, who, between 1906 and 1911, had been governor of Chihuahua, the Mexican ambassador to the United States, and the minister of foreign relations. As informal chief of Díaz's espionage service, Creel secured the cooperation of U.S. authorities, gathered information from thirty-one Mexican consulates in the United States, and employed several American detective agencies (for example, Furlong Secret Service Company of St. Louis) to assist in the arrest and prosecution of revolutionary exiles. He coordinated the activities of these detectives with those of governmental authorities, forwarding intelligence reports to the Mexican vice president, the U.S. Department of State, and the various consulates in the United States.[55]

Creel was aided in his attack on the revolutionists by members of America's developing espionage system. Information from private detectives was funnelled by Creel to members of the U.S. State Department, which in turn handed it over to Justice Department marshals and Bureau of Investigation agents (who would eventually become FBI G-men), individuals in Treasury's Secret Service, and employees of the Bureau of Immigration and Naturalization. In addition, U.S. military personnel, customs officials, and immigration officers worked hand in hand with private detectives. Most important of all were the consuls. Representing the twenty-five U.S. consulates that were in Mexico in 1911, the consul was America's major source of political and military intelligence at the time. Thus, the late *porfiriato* saw the beginnings of an institutionalized spy system in both Mexico and the United States.[56]

It was on the provincial or state level that Don Porfirio's modernization had its greatest impact, especially when the national *caudillo* set out to destroy the almost autonomous kingdoms that regional *caudillos* such as Ignacio Pesqueira in Sonora and Luis Terrazas in Chihuahua had established. The office selected for this assault on local autonomy was the prefect, or *jefe político*, traditionally a district administrator with limited authority who was either appointed by a state governor or elected directly by the *municipios*. Under Díaz the office was upgraded, and most prefects now took their orders from Mexico City and exercised increased powers that involved commanding district police forces; naming municipal officers (including mayors); appointing local judges, constables, and, on the hacienda, lords of the domain; and promoting the interests of foreign investors. In addition, Díaz and the governors were successful in reducing the number of *municipios* in the country and diminishing the authority of the *ayuntamientos* (town councils), especially in Sonora and Chihuahua.[57]

All of this came to a head in the 1890s in Chihuahua when villagers rose in arms to rebel against the expropriation of lands and the loss of political autonomy. Peasants, peons, cowboys, and Yaqui Indians participated in violence against the authorities. The most famous instance took place in 1891 at Tomochi in western Chihuahua. There the inhabitants rebelled against the arbitrary actions of the local *jefe's* nephew and the mayor's threat to subject them to the *leva* (military draft). The rebel leaders were adherents of the Teresita cult of the Saint of Cabora and, knowing God was on their side, defeated the first armies that were sent after them. Eventually, the rebellion resulted in the destruction of Tomochi, yet the government suffered nearly five hundred casualties.[58]

Again, between 1903 and 1907, as one solution to the "Indian problem," several Yaquis, peaceful (*mansos*) as well as rebellious (*broncos*), men, women, and children, were either killed or taken from their homeland and shipped to the Yucatán or the Valle Nacional in Oaxaca and sold as slaves to henequén and coffee planters. More than fifteen thousand Native Americans were eventually exiled. Deportation was to be expected from "civilized" whites who for years had been deporting Yaquis (along with Opatas, Pimas, and Mayos) from their native homes to the seaports, farms, mining camps, presidios, and towns of Sonora. They were cheap labor that could sail boats, dive for pearls, push plows, dig for ore, march in armies, and work as masons and carpenters in the *municipios*.[59]

While the advent of the apparatus of a partially modernized state was changing the landscape of Mexico, it also meant that the Mexican state was emerging as a force (a secondary force to be sure) in international and hemispheric relations for the first time since the wars of independence. Of course, the genius of Limantour and the importance of Mexico for the global economy gave Díaz and the Mexican state a new status and position in the world community of nations. Mexico could then perform the international politics of a middle power when it came to great power conflict with the lesser states of Central America. Most of these actions, such as sending Mexican gunboats to the coasts of Guatemala in 1909, were designed to maintain political stability in Central America so as to diminish U.S. influence in the region (especially the Roosevelt Corollary), or at the least, to prevent a great power intervention that would eventually undermine Mexican influence.[60]

Thus, the Mexico of Porfirio Díaz witnessed "peace, order and progress." Certainly the political system was orderly. Only a few years earlier a military opportunist by the name of Antonio López de Santa Anna had occupied the office of the presidency no fewer than eleven times and had waged war against Spain, France, and the United States. Then Mexico witnessed the efficient and peaceful rule of one man, Don Porfirio (excluding Díaz's colleague and friend Manuel González, who was president from 1880 to 1884). In contrast, between 1876 and 1911 the United States experienced eight presidents, eleven administrations, and assassinations of two presidents, James A. Garfield and William McKinley. There can be no questioning the orderliness of Don Porfirio's Mexico.

Economic progress and modernization also characterized the Mexico of Don Porfirio. Mexico's middle classes expanded, and foreign capital found a welcome home in Mexico. The railroads boomed, mines were revived, commercial agriculture developed, oil wells sunk, harbor and dock facilities were constructed, roads were built, and commerce grew. Electric tramway hearses replaced the horse and carriage in Mexico City. Limantour's reforms had changed Mexico's image abroad. The regime started to receive lavish praise by foreign heads of state. Many held with Judge Peyton Edwards of Texas that "Porfirio Díaz is the greatest statesman in the world today." For the first time Mexico began to participate in international conferences; yet there were also costs to progress.[61]

After the depression of 1907, many Mexican investors and regional elites found it more difficult to compete with foreign capitalists. At the same time, their political role was diminishing on the municipal and state levels of government as the *porfirian* state continued to expand. Many rural peasants found themselves intimidated by local *hacendados, jefes políticos,* and Rurales. The peasants were exploited by foreign entrepreneurs and Mexican loan sharks. Peons on the haciendas were worse off financially than their ancestors had been a century before, with corn and beans costing much more in 1910 than in 1810.

The plight of urban labor had changed little throughout the last half of the nineteenth century. Workers in the factories and mines were without political rights and suffered from long workdays, industrial hazards, meager pensions, and no compensation. The education, diet, and public health of the lower classes were inadequate. Life expectancy was about thirty years of age (it had been twenty-two for Indians during the colonial era), and infant mortality remained undesirably high.[62]

Perhaps Porfirio Díaz had paid too high a price to modernize his country. The material benefits of the age of modernization did not filter down to the people. The trickle down theory was as inadequate then as it is today. Very quickly the Mexican masses would demand a different reality. *Serrano* (cowboys, miners, and other mountaineers from the North) and agrarian revolutionaries, allied with ambitious northern *hacendados,* merchants, and local elites, would call for the overthrow of the regime.

The internal struggle would be reflected externally as the United States competed with the British and other European nations to shape the flow of events in Mexico. The "long nineteenth century" had ended, and the United States was now a major economic power that was threatening British hegemony in Latin America. As for Mexico, its nascent modernization did not change its peripheral status in the global community, but its economy was on the periphery of the new core in the United States. The dependency of Mexico and the modernized Mexican borderlands on the United States was greater than ever. As the residue of progress led to social change, conflict, and violence in Mexico, the United States found itself strategically important as a source of recruits, munitions, and monies for the *revoltosos*. The Mexican Revolution in the United States was about to begin.

6 The Mexican Revolution in the United States

> After some months, Pershing returns to the United States. He brings back a long caravan of soldiers fed up with breathing dust, with the people throwing stones, with the lies in each little village in that gravelly desert. From the crest of a hill, Pancho Villa looks down and comments: *"They came like eagles and they leave like wet hens."*
>
> From Eduardo Galeano, *Memory of Fire*

Between 1907 and 1908 the world marketplace was in trouble. The banking crisis was started when American speculators tried to corner the market in copper, resulting in the destabilization of banks in London, Amsterdam, and Hamburg. Panic swept Wall Street. Banks closed; 20 percent of them were in Texas. New investment money for Mexico dried up. New York banker and financier J. Pierpont Morgan had to import $100 million in gold from Europe to momentarily halt the hysteria.

Mexico's dependency on the United States meant that it would not be spared a crisis of its own. The economic growth that had characterized the *porfirian* years before 1900 was at an end. Government income declined, foreign debt increased, prices soared (especially for corn, beans, and wheat), consumption decreased, labor was cutback, and wages declined. All of this happened in the midst of the social and political unrest of 1906–1907, from strikes at Cananea and Río Blanco to factory closings in Mexico City. The only happy note in all of this was the visit of baseball's world champion Chicago White Sox to Mexico City for spring training in March of 1907.

As in the United States, the origins of baseball in Mexico are hazy. The mythmakers who claim baseball is indigenous to the United States and that Abner Doubleday from Cooperstown, New York, was its inventor also tell us that Doubleday, a West Point graduate who served in the U.S. Army during the Mexican War, promoted the game of baseball among the militia units stationed in the Halls of Moctezuma. Supposedly, one Illinois volunteer who captured Santa Anna's cork leg as a war trophy used it as a bat in one of these contests. Whatever, there is no doubting that American baseball became popular in Mexico in the 1890s at the same time British cricket began to decline in Mexico City circles. This change in recreational preferences paralleled the declining influence of the British business community and the rise of U.S. interests. By 1911, the Mexicans had initiated a coup d'etat that brought down the old regime, and New York entrepreneurs, although unhappy over the World Series loss of New York to Philadelphia in six games, were ready to renew business in Mexico with the new administration of Francisco I. Madero.[1]

Madero had come to power in May of the year of the New York World Series loss. Just a year earlier, on 18 May 1910, Halley's Comet had brushed the earth with its tail. According to the village shamans, this was a sign that the powerful Old Ones were to come and sweep the wicked away and prepare for the arrival of an Apostle of Democracy called Madero. Although democracy would have to wait, an apostle named Madero did arrive to sweep Díaz away. By 1913, after the assassination of Madero, a major civil war developed in which various revolutionaries emerged, fought, and died. First there were Emiliano Zapata and Francisco Villa, then later Venustiano Carranza, and finally Álvaro Obregón. Through it all, the constitution of 1917 was born, a document containing the aspirations of millions of Mexicans for social justice.

Meanwhile, the United States had emerged from World War I a creditor nation for the first time in its history. New York City, not London, was the financial center of the global economy, and the United States had its own empire in the Caribbean. By 1923, the military and violent phase of the Mexican Revolution was over, and the United States's influence in Mexico was greater than ever. Once again, however, in 1923 the National League's New York team would lose the world series in six games, perhaps in its own way an omen testifying to the difficulty of obtaining ultimate greatness.

The events of World War I would be pivotal for the United States. Applied science and engineering were advanced, of course, through German and Allied developments. On the German side, trench warfare was eventually overcome with the introduction of the flamethrower, submachine gun, and light artillery. The Germans also used the submarine and torpedo to threaten surface ships. The Allies dealt with the challenges of trench warfare by inventing the tank. Both sides made use of balloons, dirigibles, and aircraft to move supplies, engage in reconnaissance, and combat the enemy. Aircraft posed a serious threat to surface shipping and thus were a complement to the submarine.[2] As for the United States, by 1914 its navy was the third largest in the world, and its regular army had tripled in size since 1900.

But it was in the economic arena in which World War I was important for American history. The power of a nation-state not only consists in its armed forces but in its economic and technological resources as well. On the eve of World War I, for example, while Russia was a "military" power with a front-line army ten times that of the United States, the latter was an "industrial" society that produced six times as much steel as Russia and consumed ten times as much energy. In 1913, the per capita level of industrialization in the United States was the highest among the Great Powers—greater than Great Britain and over six times that of Russia.[3]

Between 1914 and 1919, the center of world finance moved across the Atlantic as Europe's international debts increased and the United States became a creditor nation. American aid to France in the form of exported coal, coke, steel, machine tools, foodstuffs, and loans made it possible for French factories to concentrate on armament output. In 1917, with Germany possessing the military advantage after the Russian collapse, the entry of the United States into the conflict facilitated Allied manufacturing production to become more than twice that of Germany and Austria-Hungary—the economic balance was tilted heavily in favor of the Allies. More important, the sheer size of Europe's trade deficit with the United States (which was supplying Europe with billions of dollars' worth of foodstuffs and munitions, but requiring few goods in return) forced Europe to not only transfer gold to the United States but to borrow on the New York and Chicago money markets to pay their American suppliers. Overall, this meant that the Allies were becoming more and more dependent on American financial aid to sustain their war effort. In effect, the global conflict of 1914–17 distorted the natural patterns of world production and trade and accelerated the United States to a position of greatness and postwar global power relative to Europe.[4]

Meanwhile, the U.S. neighbor to the south was undergoing a complex civil struggle often referred to as the Mexican Revolution. The geographical proximity of the United States (with its Caribbean empire) to Mexico, in addition to the developing U.S. role in the Latin American economy, meant that the Americans and their government would be almost obliged to intervene and shape that not-only-Mexican event. The cardinal rule for the United States in hemispheric affairs was that the United States was creating a sphere of influence in Central America, the Caribbean, and Mexico, and in that sphere indigenous revolutionary nationalists who threatened the American market would have to be curtailed, and the influence of competing empires—Germany, Japan, or Great Britain—would have to be contained. Although Great Britain was a U.S. ally on the European front, in America's backyard the British were competitors worthy of being vanquished.

The United States contributed to the conditions that fostered revolution in Mexico. The growth characterizing Díaz's Mexico had been ultimately, as John Coatsworth reminds us, a "modernization from without, not from above." U.S. capital and markets had created the commercialization of agriculture, the proletarianization of the peasantry, and the expansion of an export-oriented economy. To sustain this situation, Díaz was forced to maintain a balanced budget and low levels of taxation. When financial trouble occurred after 1906–1907, he lacked both the mind-set and the tools necessary to stimulate the economy or calm the political waters. When Madero and his *hacendado*, peasant, and labor supporters challenged the *porfirian* government in 1910–11, they were questioning the role of U.S. imperialism in Mexico and the regime's relationship to the United States.[5]

The cessation of American silver purchases in 1902, the devaluation of the peso in 1905, and the recession of 1907 combined to weaken Mexican capitalists in relation to foreign investors. Deunionization made labor more powerless, while land grabs by thousands of American colonists uprooted the peasantry. In Chihuahua, lands were reorganized to favor American and state elites. In Sonora, American and Mexico City intruders displaced Yaqui and Mayo Indians and developed the newly vacated lands. And in Coahuila and Nuevo León, Madero family interests were losing out to mining, ranching, agricultural, and banking elites from outside.[6]

Worse off than the Madero family (who were wealthy and at least had access to the Mexico City elite through their contacts with José Limantour) were the hundreds of provincial elites and middle-class groups that were losing economic power to Americans and political autonomy to the Mexican state. While alienation among the northern provincial elites was central to the revolution, it was also true that the "offended" were quickly joined by the "oppressed." The revolutionary crisis of 1910 was the result—a multiclass movement that involved *hacendados*, bankers, merchants, schoolteachers, lawyers, journalists, *rancheros*, workers, and peasants against the old regime—and Francisco I. Madero was its nominal leader.[7]

From San Antonio, Texas, in November of 1910, Madero published his political program, the Plan de San Luis Potosí. Denouncing the recent presidential election as fraudulent, he called for a national insurrection on 20 November and promised democratic elections for a new government. While angry landlords, farmers, and merchants rallied to his cause, dispossessed peasants in Morelos were attracted by a minor clause in the Plan that promised a review of any land confiscations. By May, before Díaz was forced from office, peasant land seizures had taken place in Chihuahua, Coahuila, Sonora, Durango, and throughout the central region of the country. This rising tide of rural unrest was finally halted by an elite arrangement that sent Díaz to Paris and resulted in the election of Madero to the presidency on 1 October 1911.[8]

Madero's pro-Texas and pro-American policies were crucial to his revolution. Although relations were becoming strained between the United States and Mexico after 1908, there is no evidence that the U.S. government abandoned Díaz until after the victory of Pascual Orozco's *maderista* troops at Ciudad Juárez on 10 May 1911. Since 1908 Díaz and Limantour had been pursuing a pro-European policy that seemed to favor Europeans and the Japanese over American interests, from foreign loans and leases to oil and railway concessions. But until the *orozquista* victory at Ciudad Juárez, Madero's followers in the United States were just another anti-Díaz *revoltoso* group, often being confused by Justice Department officials with *magonistas* (disciples of anarcho-communist Ricardo Flores Magón). By May, the ambivalence of Taft's policy was redefined to favor Madero. Neutrality laws and embargo acts were soon used to curtail the activity of Madero's enemies in the United States, from the anarchistic *magonistas* and reformist *orozquistas* to the more conservative *reyistas* (followers of Díaz's ex-minister of war, Bernardo Reyes).[9] During Madero's brief presidency, from October 1911 to February 1913, the Mexican economy was growing. Smelting profits grew, oil production boomed, and agriculture yielded large harvests. Yet economic progress did not beget political order, and it was the lack of such order that eventually led to Madero's downfall.[10]

Madero's enemies appeared on all sides. In November of 1911, disappointed *zapatistas* issued their own revolutionary Plan de Ayala and declared war on the traitor Madero for his failures at land reform. From the North, the adherents of first Bernardo Reyes and then later of Pascual Orozco led rebellions in December 1911 and March 1912 that soon merged with the violence of the countryside. By October, the *científicos* had organized a revolt around General Félix Díaz, Porfirio Díaz's nephew. The rebellions and nationwide *campesino* violence (much of the latter was directed against Americans) ruined the U.S. government's confidence in Madero. By February of 1913, the American ambassador, Henry Lane Wilson, in conjunction with several *científicos* and ex-*porfirista* generals, especially Victoriano Huerta, had overthrown Madero. On the night of 22 February, Madero and his vice-president, José María Pino Suárez, were murdered. Now the *maderistas* had a martyr and a cause. A few days later, on 4 March 1913, Woodrow Wilson replaced Taft in the White House.

Wilson, much to the surprise of Huerta, the American business community in Mexico, and the British ambassador, was not anxious to recognize the new Mexican government. Morality and ideology were one and the same for Wilson. The Puritan ethic, for Wilson, sanctioned capitalism and free enterprise, and natural law required free trade, a "natural" international division of labor, and republican institutions. Dollar diplomacy meant the U.S. government would promote industry, commerce, and investments abroad, and that these expanding markets would be protected by the police powers of the United States. Wilson's reforms included the development of a strong merchant marine, a downward revision of the tariff (the Underwood Tariff, what the critics called free trade imperialism), and laws permitting foreign branch banking (the Federal Reserve Act). These all reflected Wilson's moralism and commercialism.[11]

Unfortunately, Huerta's military dictatorship was a form of government that, for Wilson, was a throwback to feudal times—a landed oligarchy willing to use America's competitors in Mexico to maintain the status quo. Madero's overthrow was, in Wilson's view, a heavy blow to the solutions of Mexico's problems. Free enterprise and parliamentary democracy were those solutions, and underdeveloped countries like Mexico would have to be brought into the western world of commerce and industry and in the process taught the arts of self-help, self-control, and self-government. In addition, Washington held that Huerta's coup was a *científico* counterrevolution designed to favor British oil interests, especially Sir Weetman Pearson's El Aguila, over those of the United States. Huerta would have to go.[12]

In Mexico, the resurgence of the *científicos* revived hostilities. A chickpea farmer and politician from Sonora, Alvaro Obregón, organized several state militias into an eight-thousand-strong regular state army. In Chihuahua, Durango, and Zacatecas, several rebels and militia units rallied to Francisco Villa's cause. In Coahuila, Governor Venustiano Carranza led the resistance and established the Constitutionalist Army. Elsewhere, Emiliano Zapata from Morelos directed an independent guerrilla war to regain for the villages their lost lands.

Huerta's government met the challenge of its adversaries by increasing the regular army's share of the national budget to 30 percent and its size to eighty-five thousand, promoting its officers, enlarging the arsenals, and expanding the Rurales. In general, Huerta looked to Great Britain, Germany, and Japan for support, while Wilson's United States tended to support the opposition, especially Villa and Carranza.[13]

As Huerta's power grew, the United States became increasingly hostile. American businessmen in Mexico, especially the oil interests who had originally supported Huerta, now moved closer to his rivals. Edward L. Doheny, in 1913, began to advance money to Carranza even before his troops occupied the oil fields of Tampico. Standard Oil's Henry Clay Pierce had his own negotiations with Carranza. Meanwhile, Wilson was active. He first recalled Henry Lane Wilson and opened the border to arms shipments to the rebels. After unsuccessfully seeking Huerta's resignation (with the bribe of a loan), Wilson then threatened to support the Constitutionalists if Huerta did not go. By April of the next year, twelve hundred marines and bluejackets occupied the port of Veracruz, posed to move by rail into Mexico City if Huerta refused to resign. Under pressure from Villa and the Constitutionalists in the north and Zapata in the south, cut off from European credit by an Anglo-U.S. agreement, and with the military threat of the United States, Huerta on 15 July 1914 resigned and set sail on a German ship into exile.[14]

Without a common enemy, the anti-*huertistas* began to divide into factions. Obregón's Army of the Northwest joined with the Northeast Corps, a sixty-thousand-armed force under the authority of First Chief Carranza. Obregón eventually brought the anarchist Casa del Obrero into the Constitutionalist alliance with five thousand workers fighting as Red Battalions. Opposing Carranza was Pancho Villa's Division of the North. Headquartered in Chihuahua and Durango, it consisted of thirty thousand regularly paid soldiers and was the strongest military body in Mexico. Unlike the Constitutionalists, Villa's army consisted of many peasants, miners, cowboys, and bandits and was generally a more heterogenous group than that of the Constitutionalists. Other revolutionary troops clustered around Zapata and the village chieftains of Morelos and Guerrero. They were not professionals, received no pay, and consisted of around fifteen thousand regulars and ten thousand guerrillas. After the October 1914 convention of war chiefs in Aguascalientes (from which Carranza was absent), a combined force of *zapatistas* and *villistas* occupied Mexico City while Carranza retreated to Veracruz.[15]

In July of 1914 when Huerta finally went into exile, the United States found itself with a greater concern on its hands—hostilities were openly declared in Europe. With Europeans combating each other across the Atlantic, the Americans practically received a mandate from European leaders to maintain hegemony in the Western Hemisphere. The world's shipping was in disarray, and Mexico's oil exports declined. In addition, the chaos of civil war had left Mexico's economy in disorder, especially the mining, industrial, and financial sectors. Mexico appeared to Washington to be in need of U.S. economic direction. What the U.S. government and its business allies wanted was a restored, constitutional government that would seek American loans to reform the foreign debt, fund the claims of foreigners for damages, and develop an economic policy favorable to the major corporations doing business in Mexico. Until Villa's defeat at Celaya in April of 1915, it was he who won Wilson's favor as the man who could best meet Washington's objectives in Mexico.[16]

Villa received Wilson's initial blessing for a number of reasons. The large American companies in Mexico demanded protection of their interests. This meant no confiscations of property, reasonable taxes, and protection from bandits. In the beginning, Villa was able to finance his revolution by confiscating only Mexican estates; he did not expropriate American property. In exchange for Chihuahua cattle and Laguna cotton, he was able to get arms and ammunition from the United States. The taxes he levied on Americans were lower than those of other revolutionary leaders, especially Carranza who preferred to tax foreigners rather than seize the wealth of the domestic oligarchy. Villa expelled organizers of the Industrial Workers of the World (IWW) from Mexico, prevented rival bandits from attacking Americans, curbed strikers, and did not allow his supporters to engage in anti-American rhetoric. Finally, he had the assistance of two intermediaries who sent friendly messages to Washington on his behalf—the U.S. consul in Torreón, George Carothers, and the head of the Southern Command of the U.S. Army, General Hugh Scott.[17]

The Villa–U.S. relationship quickly turned sour. By the end of 1914, Villa's cattle and cotton resources were exhausted, and unlike Carranza he did not control any oil fields. Villa reversed his earlier policy by taxing American *hacendados* and putting new pressure on American mine owners to increase production. Conditions worsened as Villa found himself competing with Russia, France, and Great Britain to obtain American arms at increasing prices. Villa became very unhappy with Uncle Sam when the United States, in November 1914, turned over the port of Veracruz with its many warehouses to the Constitutionalists. Not only did this allow Carranza to collect customs revenues and export freely but the armaments (machine guns, rifles, carbines, shotguns, bullets, barbed wire, radio sets, pistols, grenades, poison gas, and so on) shifted the balance of power from Villa's army to Carranza's forces.[18]

Because of Villa's military defeat at Celaya by Obregón, and the American fear of German intrigues in Mexico to foment disorder along the border, U.S. policy took a decided turn. In October of 1915, de facto recognition was extended to the Carranza government and, in effect, closed the border to Villa's trade in arms. In addition, Wilson allowed Carranza to transport his troops from El Paso to Douglas, Arizona, via the railroad to reinforce the Constitutionalists in Sonora. Finally Villa, in desperation, led his army of 485 across the border at Palomas, Chihuahua, and assaulted the bleak, sun-baked adobe town of Columbus, New Mexico, in March 1916. Although the costs to Villa were heavy, the town was burned and eighteen Americans lost their lives.

The motives for Villa's actions were many, but most likely he sought retaliation against the Americans for their betrayal of his movement and desired to forestall what he believed to be an alliance between the

United States and Carranza that would make Mexico a U.S. protectorate. Following the raid, the clamor for a U.S. intervention was loud
and immediate and led to the dispatching of a small punitive expedition (originally six thousand men, later expanded to ten thousand)
under the command of General John J. Pershing, a hero of past wars
against the Apache.[19]

Carranza's efforts at consolidating a new Mexican state were interrupted by the U.S. invasion. Before that event, American recognition
had legalized the imports of arms and ammunition to his government,
and this was followed by recognition from Germany and Britain. On
the strength of the U.S. war boom, the Mexican economy started to
recuperate; mining and manufacturing growth provided new revenue for Carranza's government. To curb the influence of labor, he
mustered out the Casa's Red Battalions from his army and outlawed
independent unions. Estates were returned to their landlords, and
businessmen formed alliances with him. Then the *villistas* struck, and
Carranza had to deal with the embarrassment of a U.S. invasion. To
bind the Mexican army to his new government, Carranza made Obregón minister of war (an office Obregón quickly vacated so as to go
into early "retirement" on his Sonoran farm).[20]

The punitive expedition lasted from March 1916 to February 1917.
Mexican officials believed that the expedition was more than a bandit-
hunting force and that an army of pacification could easily be given
the new mission of cleaning up Mexico, taking on Carranza's troops,
and shaping the Mexican civil war in a direction that Wilson approved. In other words, the Americans might use force to bring an end
to Carranza's brand of economic nationalism. The American occupation led to several serious incidents, especially at Carrizal and Hidalgo
del Parral, any one of which could have escalated into a war (see
figure 10). Ultimately, Wilson had to choose his priorities; European
war and the deteriorating state of U.S.-German relations took prece-
dence over Mexico's assertion of independence. When the last of
Pershing's saddlesore "wet hens" retreated across the Río Bravo, the
United States broke off relations with Germany. Meanwhile, the Mexi-

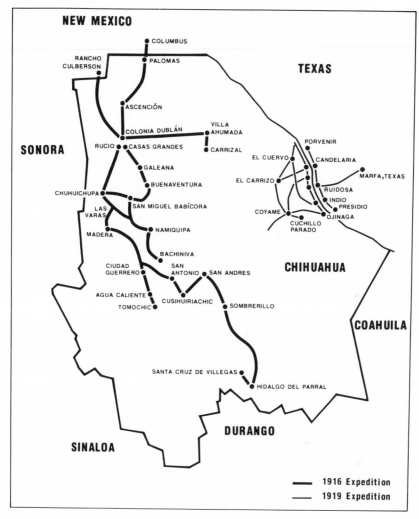

Fig. 10. U.S. Punitive Expeditions into Mexico

can constitution was being promulgated and along with it came new difficulties in the U.S.-Mexican relationship.[21]

The constitutional convention that met in Querétaro between November 1916 and February 1917 was composed of individuals (220 delegates and alternates) known to social scientists as petty bourgeois and bourgeois. They were young and middle class. Apart from the twenty-two senior military officers, the delegates were professionals (lawyers, teachers, engineers, physicians, accountants, pharmacists), artisans, merchants, labor leaders, railway workers, and employees. They had very little governmental experience but were politically ambitious. Generally, they either supported the conservative Carranza or the Jacobin Obregón. The 220 individuals did not represent Villa and Zapata or any enemies of the state. But they did share the anti-American nationalism that the punitive expedition had evoked from Mexicans of all classes and factions.[22]

In creating the constitutional charter, the *obregonistas* succeeded in writing the social and economic sections, especially Articles 27, 33, 123, and 130 (although Carranza won on some issues such as a stronger presidency and authorization for a central bank). Article 27 evoked the spirit of Zapata by calling for the breakup of large landed estates. It placed conditions on the right of foreigners to acquire real estate and mineral resources, affirmed the principle of nationalization, and asserted the right to expropriate private property. Under this provision, the Mexican state had the right to deprive foreign oil companies of the ownership of subsoil reserves. (It should be noted that in 1917 foreigners owned 90 percent of Mexico's petroleum resources and that Mexico was the third largest producer of oil after the United States and Russia—most oil went to the United States, which enabled it in turn to export fuel to the Allies, especially England.) Article 33 provided for extraditing foreigners without a trial, while Article 123 was literally a worker's bill of rights, from a guaranteed eight-hour day to the right to unionize and strike. Article 130 guaranteed freedom of worship and prohibited priests from criticizing the constitution or the government. In all, it was a federalist, anticlerical, nationalistic document that subordinated individual property rights to the Mexican nation and, if put into effect, would repudiate the established rule of international intercourse and Wilson's ideal of free enterprise.[23]

While Wilson, with his attention on European affairs, could not do much to prevent the birth of the constitution of 1917, he could try to prevent implementation of its more odorous provisions. Article 27 was the most troubling. If it were interpreted retroactively, it would become a major threat to U.S. oil interests in Mexico. During the course of the war, Wilson attempted to prevent Carranza from concentrating too much power that would threaten American property interests. He would have to wait to deal effectively with Carranza until after the war and then from a position of strength.

Meanwhile, Germany wanted to deny Mexican oil to the Allies and, if possible, foment war between Mexico and the United States, forcing the United States to divert troops to Mexico. In February 1917, the German Secretary of Foreign Affairs, Arthur Zimmermann, sought a German alliance with Mexico in which, after the inevitable German victory, the southwestern United States (Mexico's lost provinces) would belong to Mexico as spoils of war. While Carranza refused the offer, it did not reduce Wilson's suspicions that Germany would continue to make mischief in Mexico, from generating anti-American propaganda to sabotaging the oil fields. Although after April 1917, when the United States entered the war on the Allied side, Carranza professed neutrality, he still sought German loans and allowed German spies and agents to operate with impunity on Mexican soil. He did not want an alliance that would anger the United States, but he did seek to use Germany as a countervailing influence to limit U.S. power in Mexico. This was not unlike the nationalistic policies of the last few years of the Díaz era.

On 11 November 1918, World War I ended, allowing the United States to deal with Mexico without interference from any other foreign state. The United States threatened to withdraw diplomatic recognition if Carranza refused to negotiate on Article 27. Recognizing the realities of power, Carranza suspended earlier wartime decrees that required the oil companies to exchange their titles for state concessions and wisely waited for the Mexican Congress to implement any retroactive interpretations of Article 27.[24]

Meanwhile, Obregón started organizing his presidential campaign for the 1920 election, receiving much assistance from his supporters in the states of California, Washington, Arizona, and Texas. He was the candidate of the Gran Chichimeca country and was inadvertently aided in his quest of power by Carranza, who successfully plotted to kill their old adversary Zapata. On 10 April 1919, Zapata was shot by *carrancistas* at the Hacienda de Chinameca in his own home territory. In 1920, when Carranza attempted to name his successor to the presidency, Obregón, allied with his fellow Sonorans, declared himself in revolt. In May, Carranza was forced to flee office and was assassinated by a loyal *obregonista* on his way to Veracruz and exile. Obregón became president.

In the United States there was also a new executive, President Warren G. Harding, a Republican who, even more than Wilson, knew that his major concern would be that of safeguarding American property rights against Mexican confiscation. Harding listened to his Republican advisers, especially the anti-*carrancista* Secretary of Interior Albert Bacon Fall. Through Fall, oilmen like Edward Doheny and the Oil Producer's Association successfully lobbied the president into becoming more active in defending their interests. Secretary of State Charles Evans Hughes refused diplomatic recognition to the Obregón government until Obregón would agree to a Treaty of Amity and Commerce, which would prevent Mexico from treating Article 27 retroactively. Obregón refused to agree to the terms dictated by the United States. To have done so would have been tantamount to political suicide. From 1920 to 1923, Obregón was not recognized by the United States.

Before the impasse was settled, Francisco Villa was assassinated in Hidalgo del Parral, Chihuahua. Although evidence is lacking, it is supposed that the assassination was committed with the approval of Obregón and his Sonoran ally Secretary of Gobernación Plutarco Elías

Calles. From confidential sources, U.S. military intelligence agents (G-2) concluded that Villa's death was probably linked to his ties with Adolfo de la Huerta, provisional president in 1920 and a critic of the Obregón regime. It was assumed that Villa had intended to lend his considerable presence to the de la Huerta cause. When Obregón and Calles learned of this, they sent secret agents to Chihuahua to recruit an assassination squad. Thus, one more potential enemy was reduced from Obregón's list of rivals.[25]

Finally, during the summer of 1923, the dispute between the United States and Mexico was resolved with the assistance of the Mexican Supreme Court. That court handed down a decision on the retroactive application of Article 27 in which it pronounced the doctrine of "positive acts." Article 27 would not apply retroactively provided that the owners of oil fields had undertaken, before 1917, some "positive act" (such as erecting drilling equipment) intended to look for and remove oil from the soil. The Bucareli agreements allowed the United States to limit revolutionary nationalist legislation, and Obregón received recognition without subscribing to the original treaty. When Adolfo de la Huerta rebelled against the Obregón government in December 1923, he was defeated easily. Diplomatic recognition brought U.S. assistance to Obregón in the form of arms, munitions, shared intelligence, and a strict application of the neutrality laws against de la Huerta.[26]

By 1923 the civil war was over. Obregón and U.S. business and governmental interests had reached a rapprochement. The Bucareli Accords had momentarily resolved the oil question but at some limited cost to Mexican sovereignty. Several American companies in Sonora and Texas endorsed his rule. Obregón repaid a personal debt to W. R. Grace, the American entrepreneur who had financed many of his earlier military victories. Obregón successfully refinanced the Mexican debt with U.S. banking houses, consolidated his family holdings in Sonora, and outflanked his regional enemies.[27] Opponents like Villa and most of the leading *revoltosos* were dead, victims of the violence of revolution, class struggle, and power politics. Two *magonistas*, Librado

Rivera and Enrique Flores Magón, were released from U.S. federal prisons and returned to Mexico, their radical cause exhausted. The Sonoran dynasty of Obregón and Calles was intact.[28]

Obregón's seizure of power and consolidation of rule coincided with the victory of the Mexican middle class and its indigenous and American corporate backers. A population of around fourteen million, reduced by war and disease, now, more than before the World War, had to do business with the omnipotent neighbor to the north and its corporate interests. For example, American oil companies had outflanked the Europeans and were now more powerful than ever in Mexico. In fact, since the turn of the century, Mexican economic history has been largely a function of United States economic history (see figure 11).

On the domestic front, the new Mexican revolutionary army was absorbing over 60 percent of the budget. Although society was less castelike in structure than it had been under Díaz, lower class ambitions could only be satisfied from above—labor was not independent, and the peasants were still without land; the hacienda emerged from the revolution intact.[29] Moreover, the Mexico of 1923 was still characterized by an industrial structure that enabled powerful barons to monopolize manufacturing and seek protection from government. In many ways the revolution, rather than tearing down the industrial arrangement of the *porfiriato*, reinforced it.[30]

The new state acted as the nation's bourgeois party, reforming from above to diminish any threats to capitalism and national sovereignty. As John Womack, Jr., notes, for all of the violence, the main historic meaning of the Mexican Revolution was a "capitalist tenacity in the economy and bourgeois reform of the state," a tendency that helps to explain the stability of the 1930s and Mexico's discordant growth after 1940.[31]

In taking a violent path toward modernization, Mexico differed from the rest of Latin America. During the late nineteenth century, most of these countries were, in varying degrees, being integrated into world capitalism. As noted, these economic changes brought about

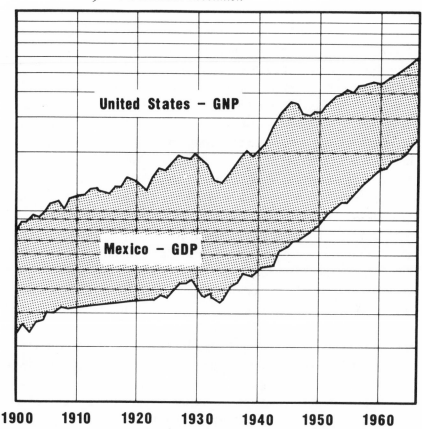

Fig. 11. Comparative Growth of Mexican and U.S. Economies, 1900–1965. Source: Adapted from John Womack, Jr., "The Mexican Economy during the Revolution, 1910–1920: Historiography and Analysis," *Marxist Perspectives* 1 (Winter 1978): 100.

the growth of centralized states not only in Mexico, but Argentina, Brazil, and Chile. Modernization meant the rise of state bureaucracies, an expansion of the armies, an extension of the tax powers, and more mass participation in politics. In Argentina, for example, traditions of parliamentarianism made it easy for the middle class to seek more economic and political power with a minimum of violence. There, in 1912, the Saénz Peña law created universal male suffrage, and by 1916 the Radicals (a middle class party) came to power under Hipólito Yrigoyen. Yet Mexico underwent major violence to achieve a similar effect. Why this difference in the history of the two countries?

Although the causes were many, three of the more important factors can be isolated. First, while anarchists and syndicalists were repressed in both Argentina and Mexico after 1917, the working class of Buenos Aires consisted of unnaturalized immigrants who, insecure in their new surroundings and in transit between Italy and the pampas, avoided political action movements and union activity. They were, in general, more apolitical and less able to participate in politics than their Mexican counterparts.[32] Second, the countryside of Argentina was filled with colonists, foreign-born tenant farmers, and displaced laborers, but no classic peasantry. Land reform would never become the vital issue that it was in Mexico. The absence of a peasantry meant no power bases and coalitions for rural farmers in the political history of Argentina. Mexico had the only peasant revolution in Latin America before 1920, and it was due to the existence of an indigenous, rural population that was angry over the state's policy of expropriating free-village lands and subordinating their inhabitants.[33] Finally, the proximity of the United States to Mexico meant that Mexico could launch its many rebellions from American soil and had easier access to sanctuary, arms, munitions, recruits, and finances than Argentine (or, for that matter, Latin American) revolutionaries. The dominance of border Mexicans in shaping the destiny of the nation throughout the 1920s was one result of this special geographical situation.[34]

In this last respect, the Mexican Revolution was not simply a Mexican event, but an episode in the history of the United States as well. The impact of the United States on the Mexican Revolution is well known (for example, the U.S. alliance with anti-*huertista* revolutionaries that brought about the end of the *porfirian* state, or the U.S. campaign to prevent Carranza from reconstituting a powerful new state), but the influence of Mexico on the United States is less well known.[35] Texas, Arizona, and New Mexico (the last two acquiring statehood during the revolutionary era) were, as border provinces, especially affected by events in Mexico. This was where hundreds of Mexicans (and some Chinese) sought refuge from the fighting. One estimate suggests that as many as a million and a half people migrated into the Southwest from Mexico between 1910 and 1920.[36]

Racial incidents and labor unrest in Texas and Arizona were exacerbated because of troubles in Mexico. Between July 1915 and July 1916, thirty raids from Mexico into Texas (the Plan of San Diego) produced several American deaths that led to reprisals against hundreds of Mexicans and Mexican Americans by Texas Rangers and vigilantes. From Sonora, laborers came into the Arizona copper fields to escape the violence and unstable economy of Mexico, and, on several occasions, including the infamous Bisbee strike of 1917 (in which twelve hundred miners, many of whom were Mexican, were rounded up, loaded in cattle cars, and shipped to a remote part of New Mexico where they were stranded), class conflict turned into racial war.[37]

As for private enterprise, Texans and Arizonans engaged in a profitable business in the arms trade (legal and illegal) with Mexico. Sonora and Chihuahua sent hundreds of cattle to Nogales and El Paso where the meatpacking industry thrived. Obregón's skill in organizing the garbanzo growers of Sonora and his work as an export-import agent impressed many Arizona businessmen. Revolution created big profits as Texas oilmen financed Sonoran strongmen, Tampico bandits, and *carrancista* forces along the Gulf. In return, they received protection for, and lucrative earnings from, their operations in Mexico.[38]

Politically, events in Mexico affected the United States. *Revoltosos*, that is, Mexico's rebels in revolt, were active in the United States between the Immigration Act of 1903 and the end of the Red Scare era in the early 1920s. These groups, ranging from the radical socialists and anarchists who followed Ricardo Flores Magón (*magonistas*) to the reactionary followers of Félix Díaz (*felicistas*), desired to use the United States as a revolutionary (and counterrevolutionary) base. Generally speaking, the radical rebels, as revolutionary nationalists, were the object of suppression by the Department of Justice and the Bureau of Immigration. *Magonistas, orozquistas, huertistas*, and *reyistas* were consistently pursued and harassed by federal, state, and private detectives and police.

On some occasions, a *revoltoso* group would be privately supported by the U.S. government in order to affect affairs in Mexico, such as allowing the *felicistas* to operate so as to complicate matters for the Carranza government. Domestic politics would be muddled by the constant charge (by Senator Albert Bacon Fall, among others) that revolution in Mexico was spreading sedition in the United States. Most often, Mexico's rebels in the United States were suppressed. The general reaction of the U.S. government (for example, arrests, surveillance, imprisonment, unofficial kidnappings, forced deportations, illegal seizures and searches), coming in an era of nativism, antiradicalism, and wartime hysteria, was extreme and seriously threatened the nineteenth-century traditions of humanitarianism and civil liberties.[39]

The civil war in Mexico allowed the United States several opportunities to develop its own military establishment. Mobilization of troops along the border during the Taft era, the intervention by the navy and marines at Veracruz in 1914, and the Pershing expedition of 1916 led to developments that would later aid the U.S. cause in World War I, from training exercises and organization schemes to intelligence operations and improvement of hardware.[40]

In particular, Pershing's activities served as a prelude to the larger undertaking of the American Expeditionary Force in World War I. New technological advances came from his mission in Mexico, not the least being aerial surveillance and signals intelligence. The former soon led to the development of an Army Air Service Armed Patrol that secured the border with DH4s (De Haviland two seater, light bombing, and observation planes). Some of these planes reached France in early 1918 and saw some combat service. As for the latter, signals intelligence involved the use of codes and codebreaking, with mobile radio-intercept stations being deployed along the border to monitor Villa's radio nets. By 1918, a new Military Intelligence Division (MID) had been created that had a technical capacity unknown to earlier agencies, and a new era in the history of American espionage had started.[41]

Of all of the American economic interests in Mexico, only oil underwent a boom between 1911 and 1921. For example, although wartime demand increased prosperity for the copper companies, after the war mining and its related enterprises declined in production. However, after 1911 and continuing into the postwar era, the market for petroleum was wide open due to several factors, including the beginnings of assembly-line production in the automobile industry, the conversion of the world's navies from coal to oil, and the advent of World War I.[42]

Americans sought to meet this demand by exploring for new oil fields and seeking increased reserves, first in California, Texas, and Oklahoma, and then along the Gulf Coast of Mexico. In spite of the revolution, businessmen, engineers, geologists, and laborers left the American Southwest for Mexico and participated in bringing Mexican oil yields up to 25 percent of total world production by 1921 (when the initial Texas boom had begun to dwindle). In 1911, American investments in Mexican oil only amounted to 38.5 percent of a total of $51.9 million (U.S.) invested in Mexico, while British participation totaled 61.5 percent. However, by 1921 the situation had reversed itself when American investments amounted to 61 percent of a total of $819.6 million. By the end of the decade, the oil companies had financed the Mexican Revolution in the form of taxes, forced loans, and theft, and in return, North American companies had gained preeminence in the industry by having outmaneuvered their British competitors in Mexico. Finally, several individuals made small fortunes.[43]

One Southwesterner who epitomized the assault of American oilmen on Mexico was William F. Buckley (father of the well-known conservative writer and editor of the same name). A native of Washington, Texas, and resident of Eagle Pass, he obtained his law degree from the University of Texas in 1905 and in 1911 went to Tampico, Mexico, to open a law office with his two brothers. Buckley not only advised American oilmen on contract matters, but also got involved in a direct way by becoming founder and co-owner of the Pantepec Petroleum Company of Tampico.[44]

An enemy of the Mexican Revolution, Buckley established a network of agents and informants to spy on alleged revolutionaries in

Mexico and the United States. After 1919, he aided the unfriendly senate inquiry of Mexican affairs by Albert Bacon Fall. Buckley forwarded to Fall data on Carranza's ties to bolshevism and radical labor in Mexico and the United States. The assumption was that revolution in Mexico was spreading sedition in the United States, a popular idea during the era of the postwar Red Scare. In the 1920s, he was a bitter opponent of Obregón and sympathetic to President Harding's hard-line Mexican policy. Buckley was expelled from Mexico in 1922, and, like his better known compatriots, Edward Doheny and John D. Rockefeller, he profited well from his pursuit of the black gold.[45]

In spite of the violence of revolution, the Mexican economy continued to react to business cycles in the North American economy. Between 1910 and 1920, with the exception of 1915, the bulk of commerce between Mexico and the United States continued to expand. Imports into the United States from Mexico and exports to Mexico from the United States increased more than three-fold during this period. Commerce boomed during the wartime era when the U.S. market expanded and declined after 1918 in some sectors, like copper, when the North American market contracted.[46]

Legal trade involved imports into the United States like copper, oil, cotton, ixtle, cattle, and garbanzo beans, and exports from the United States of oil and mining machinery, banknotes, horses, clothing, firearms, ammunition, and explosives. Many arms and munitions were smuggled into Mexico, while the illegal trade from Mexico involved beef and cattle on the hoof, mescal and other liquors, and even Chinese and Mexican aliens. New York City remained the leader in exports and imports, but New Orleans and El Paso were also important ports.[47]

North American merchants, creditors, munitions dealers, and import-export agents proved to be Obregón's major supporters in the United States between 1920 and 1923 when U.S. diplomatic recognition of Obregón's government was in question.[48] In this respect they differed greatly from their counterparts in the oil industry. While Mexican commerce was only a small part of the total trade of the United

States in the global economy, it had an important impact on the politics and pocketbooks of those involved.

By 1923, the radical, heroic, epic phase of revolution was over. It was a time of rapprochement with the United States. Uncle Sam now had an economic hegemony in Mexico unseen even in the days of Díaz. Standard Oil had outmaneuvered its rivals and was ready to combat the Mexican government over any attempts to expropriate its properties. A new bourgeoisie was in power in Mexico and more than willing to practice the politics of populism with workers and *campesinos*.

The Mexican regime had an army of almost 100,000 men claiming over 60 percent of the national budget and of uncertain loyalty. The church, both individuals in the hierarchy and laymen in the National Republican Party, were ready to resist any attempts by the state to enforce the anticlericalism of the constitution of 1917. And the large landowners and industrialists were still in evidence. Until 1940 these groups—army officers, priests, landlords, and oil and industrial barons—would attempt to shape Mexico's destinies. The United States would be more than an interested bystander.

7 Soldiers, Priests, and Lords of Land and Industry

> Once't there was a Bolshevik, who wouldn't say his prayers, So Kellogg sent him off to bed, away upstairs; An Kellogg heerd him holler, and Coolidge heerd him bawl, But when they turn't the kivers down he wasn't there at all. They seeked him down in Mexico, they cussed him in the press. They seeked him round the Capitol, and ever'where I guess.
>
> Parody of a Popular Poem, 1927

World War I intensified the penetration of underdeveloped societies by the colonial powers. The world-economy brought these countries into an expanding global network of commerce, trade, and western ideas. Yet, in many instances, this contact provoked indigenous reactions that were highly nationalistic and anticolonial. Mohandas Gandhi's passive resistance movement to British rule in India was only one of many worldwide rebellions that were known collectively as the "revolt against the West." Others occurred or were brewing in Africa, Egypt, China, Indonesia, Tunisia, Turkey, and Mexico. In Mexico the counterpart to Turkey's Kemal Ataturk was Plutarco Elías Calles. In the early and mid-1920s, he was a revolutionary nationalist who, like Carranza in 1918 and Lázaro Cárdenas in 1938, asserted that Mexico was equal in sovereignty to the United States and that Mexico had a right to control its own internal resources.[1]

The United States confronted a revolutionary Mexico as its relative power in the interwar years vis-á-vis Europe and the USSR was declining. From a relative strong position in the early 1920s, the United States went into a depression in the 1930s that did not end until the resurgence of the wartime market of World War II. As noted, after World War I, the United States was the world's greatest financial and creditor nation, holding huge stocks of gold and having a domestic market that allowed massive economies of scale by giant firms. It was

126

the largest producer of manufactures and foodstuffs. Yet the financial collapse of 1929 and the subsequent depression injured it much more than any other advanced economy. By 1933, the nation's GNP had fallen to half that of 1929, the value of manufactured goods was one-quarter of the 1929 figure, exports had decreased by over 69 percent since 1929, and fifteen million workers were out of jobs. After the panic of 1937, the U.S. share of world manufacturing output was lower than any time since 1910. Although the American economy had tremendous potential, by the late 1930s it was greatly underutilized. Only the giant rearmament programs initiated by the army and navy in 1940 and afterwards improved the economic situation.[2]

Mexico experienced the effects of a world depression three years before the Wall Street crisis of 1929. The crash came early, hit hard, but was over by 1932. Between 1926 and 1932 demand declined, output fell, profits disappeared, and investments evaporated. Political and social unrest paralleled the economic situation with unemployment, labor strikes, peasant revolts, increased emigration, and army rebellions occurring between 1927 and 1929. Along with the economic problems, the political costs of law and order placed heavy demands on the federal budget, especially for military expenses. Mexico possessed a fragile economy that relied on exports to the United States and a mining and hydrocarbon industry to drive it forward. Traditionally, exports had fueled imports, the consumer market, and had brought revenues to the government. In 1920 exports peaked. Then in 1926 they began to decline, and after that date they fell drastically, causing a similar drop in government income.[3]

Oil was the first product to cause problems. Political unrest and rising production costs in Mexico, plus the discovery of easily tapped oil deposits in Venezuela, led to a contraction in output. By 1927, Venezuela's oil production was surpassing that of Mexico. As of 1932, Mexico was only producing 18 percent of what it had generated in 1922. Duties on petroleum, which represented one-third of all government income in 1921, had fallen to one-eighth of national earnings by 1927.[4]

The contraction in the export sector was not confined to the oil industry. In 1926, the world market price of silver dropped, and Mexican silver exports collapsed. Lead, zinc, and copper followed in 1929, with output in the mining sector losing half its value between that year and 1932. Agriculture also declined after 1928. All of this led to a diminishing in the manufacturing of consumer goods and, as stated above, a decline in the consumption of consumer products.[5]

Mexico recovered much faster from the Great Depression than either the United States or Europe. The recovery began in 1933 and was aided by the unorthodox monetary and fiscal policies of the Cárdenas government from 1934 to 1940. After 1940, the wartime demands of World War II assured Mexico's economic growth. There are at least three explanations for this rejuvenation of the economy: first, the buffering effect of an agrarian sector in the relationship of Mexico to the world capitalist economy; second, a rise in commodity prices after 1932, especially for oil and silver; and finally, the change in government policies after 1933.

In spite of the recent modernization, Mexico in the 1930s was predominantly rural. Almost three-fourths of the economically active population was in agriculture, with many of these people functioning as a peasantry outside of the national economy and, therefore, unaffected by the stresses of capitalist production and exchange. In the nation's rural states, these individuals spoke indigenous languages, went barefoot, lived in small villages, and engaged in subsistence agriculture. Cárdenas's agrarian reforms generally encouraged an even greater reliance on subsistence agriculture. The overall effect was one in which the nation, fortunately in this instance, had a built-in buffer against the impact of world capitalism and the Great Depression.[6]

Mexico also benefited from a relatively diversified group of export items, including fruit, coffee, staple crops, silver, and oil. The volume of these exports were, by 1936, once again on the upswing. In the case of silver, the upswing was due in part to the 1934 silver purchase program, which enabled the United States to acquire large volumes of Mexican silver.[7]

Finally, the Mexican government also played a role in the recovery by changing its practices from fiscal and monetary conservatism to expansionism. In 1936, the government began to run deficits as an explicit antidepression tactic, and moved away from administrative payments (such as military spending) toward economic and social expenditures (railroads, irrigation facilities, schools, and so on). The engine of growth of this recovery was the industrial sector, with steel and cement works leading the way, while other industries attracted new groups of entrepreneurs from Eastern Europe and the Middle East. The result was the end of depression and the beginnings of the "economic miracle" that lasted into the 1970s.[8]

Meanwhile, the U.S. State Department was pursuing a policy designed to end the depression in North America. Franklin Roosevelt's Good Neighbor Policy was an extension of New Deal thinking into foreign affairs. Following the practices of his predecessor, Roosevelt wanted an end to "gunboat diplomacy" and military intervention and the creation of an inter-American alliance that would isolate the hemisphere from European and Asiatic troubles. By withdrawing marines from the Caribbean and Central America, he hoped to substitute trust and confidence for Latin jealousies and fears of the United States. (In 1933, he did not intervene militarily in the Cuban Revolution, and in Nicaragua the marines were replaced by a home-grown Guardia; in that same year the marines left Haiti.)

Roosevelt wanted to fight the depression by stimulating trade and investments in Latin America. To do so, he blocked regional alliances, prevented barter arrangements with extrahemispheric powers, extended credits to Latin nations, and established an inter-American banking system. America's underutilized economy needed customers to purchase its industrial goods and absorb its capital surpluses. Mexico needed a restored market to buy its raw goods and precious metals. This was the inter-American ideal; abandoning force for a cooperation that would be mutually beneficial to both parties—a kind of good neighborliness between Mexicans and Americans.

Inter-American security was not to be abandoned, however, even if the marines were called home. The War Department continued to revise and update a series of contingency plans that called for the unilateral invasion of several Latin American countries. The United States proceeded to issue threats of military intervention, as it did during the Cuban Revolution of 1933. And, as noted, in Nicaragua a Guardia Nacional was created to replace the departing marines, while loans from the President's Emergency Fund were sent to the Nicaraguan dictator.

In 1935, the FBI received new authority to establish secret service organizations in Latin America. J. Edgar Hoover quickly sent a police mission to Colombia, and by 1940 the FBI's Special Intelligence Service was instituted in Mexico. In addition, ITT (International Telephone and Telegraph) and Pan American Airways were subsidized by the American government and directed to erect a communications and air transportation monopoly in Latin America. So, under the Good Neighbor Policy, mercenaries and covert police operations supplanted the traditional reliance on military intervention for maintaining internal security and protecting American investments.

The Good Neighbor Policy almost drowned in Mexican oil after the 1938 expropriation. Eventually, however, U.S. military intervention was avoided as agreements were worked out with the Mexicans over the oil question and prevented any further barter arrangements between Mexico and Germany. The Export-Import Bank was also initiated to provide public loans to Latin countries so they could purchase American exports and improve their own trade structures. By 1946, U.S. policy had succeeded when Mexico's president Miguel Alemán pledged his support for the Good Neighbor Policy in return for a hundred million dollar loan from the U.S. government.[9]

The interest of the United States in Mexico during the interwar years was not only governmental. The cessation of the violence of civil war in 1917, normalization of relations with the United States in 1929, and the construction of new roads linking Mexico with the United States led to a new type of contact. Many Americans were attracted to Mexico, either as intellectuals enthralled by the fever of the first twentieth-century revolution in the Americas or as tourists seduced by the Mexican countryside. Accounts written by these visitors about pre-Columbian sites, art, and folklore appealed to others. By the 1930s, large scale tourism had developed, which was reflected by the decision of the Ministry of National Economy to institute a Tourism Office.[10]

During the early revolutionary period, many American journalists and essayists had been interested in the Mexican struggle, including John Kenneth Turner, author of *Barbarous Mexico* (what some have called the *Uncle Tom's Cabin* of the Mexican Revolution), who attracted to his retreat in Carmel, California, other literary luminaries, such as Sinclair Lewis, Upton Sinclair, and Jack London. All these men penned works about Mexico. The *villista* movement enticed writers John Reed and Ambrose Bierce to its cause. After Bierce's peculiar death in Mexico, his writings and life story attracted a following on both sides of the border. In the United States in 1929 alone, four biographies of Bierce appeared, and his works later attracted the attention of several Mexican intellectuals, not the least being Carlos Fuentes.[11]

Throughout the Roaring Twenties and the Dismaying Thirties, the two countries exchanged their creative artists, with journalist Carleton Beals, folklorist Frances Toor, historian Frank Tannenbaum, and photographer Edmund Weston visiting and living in Mexico City. Meanwhile, muralist Diego Rivera toured and painted in San Francisco, Detroit, and New York City, and José Clemente Orozco and David Alfaro Siqueiros frescoed other walls in the United States.

Rivera's tour of the United States involved painting murals on several public walls, including the now famous "Making of a Fresco" at the San Francisco Art Institute in 1931. Orozco worked at New York's New School for Social Research. Their American works, plus the Mexican muralist tradition of the early 1920s in which education, art, cultural nationalism, and public policy were merged, inspired a similar program in the United States. Roosevelt supported the arts as an antidepression program designed to propagandize the values of New Deal America. Like the murals of Rivera, Siqueiros, and Orozco, the American artists expressed powerful scenes that criticized the excesses of capitalism and the plight of the exploited, a style of art known as social realism. This fashion can be seen today in the several murals of Coit Tower in San Francisco that portray California industry and social conditions in the 1930s. This and other art around the country received funds from the Civil Works Administration, which established the Public Works of Art Project (PWAP), an undertaking designed to employ over twenty-five hundred artists and five hundred workers in an American artistic renaissance.[12]

Meanwhile, the most significant trends of the interwar years in Mexico were the taming of the army, the struggling against organized religion, and the curtailing of haciendas and foreign oil enclaves by the new revolutionary state. It was a partial process. Soldiers and priests still have a voice in political affairs; haciendas continue to exist. The American oil companies no longer dominate the Mexican petroleum industry, but dependence on the U.S. economy is greater than ever.

However, the heritage of Calles and Cárdenas was one of overthrowing the military and semifeudal oligarchy that clung to the fringes of modern Mexico and, through a populist program and the assistance of a corporativist state, paved the way toward the agribusiness and commercial capitalism of today. In this struggle, the U.S. government, with its strategic concerns and economic interests, was an interested observer and participant.[13]

The importance of Mexico to U.S. strategic interests continued during the interwar years. The original 1911 Contingency War Plan for Mexico was upgraded and revised, incorporating both a cooperative and interventionist approach to Mexico. In 1919, a revitalized Military Intelligence Division (MID) developed a contingency scheme that, when needed, would have U.S. forces seizing oil and coal fields in Mexico, blockading Mexican seaports and sealing the U.S. border, cutting the railway lines from Guatemala, advancing into Mexico City, and eventually replacing U.S. troops with a Mexican constabulary under U.S. direction and control. These goals were constantly updated in a series of Special Green Plans and were not considered obsolete until 1946.[14]

From 1919 to World War II the MID, through its G-2 "negative" branch, conducted counterpropaganda and counterintelligence in Mexico, maintaining surveillance on labor groups, political radicals, and others. In addition, during and immediately after the World War I era, agents of the Office of Navy Intelligence (ONI) were sent into

Mexico to locate transmitters and offer aid to any pro-American groups that would overthrow provincial governments unfriendly to the United States. After 1935, Nazi leaders were compromised and converted into informers. With the assistance of the FBI, MID agents penetrated the Communist party of Mexico and used their influence to affect party policy.[15]

While "negative" intelligence was preoccupying one branch of the MID, G-2's "positive" wing, which included intelligence, information-gathering, translations, maps, photographs, codes, and ciphers, was active in gathering information about Mexico. American military attachés reported on a wide range of topics relating to military affairs (for example, Mexican troop movements, training, command structures), economic matters (foreign capital in Mexico, debts, monetary and banking matters, the petroleum industry, agriculture and so on), and domestic politics (such as revolutionary activities, Mexico's foreign affairs, communist influences in the government). MID's activity, always in conjunction with the ONI, was comprehensive and indicated the importance of Mexico for U.S. policymakers.[16]

On several occasions the U.S. government provided Mexico with military assistance to deal with internal threats. In 1923, Washington sold Obregón's government eleven De Haviland airplanes (and hired U.S. pilots to fly them), thirty-three machine guns, fifteen thousand Enfield rifles, five million rounds of ammunition, and other military goods in order to suppress the de la Huerta rebellion. The U.S. government also shared MID intelligence with Obregón and used gunboats stationed at Veracruz and Tampico to thwart the *de la huertistas*. The price for this aid was the deradicalizing of the revolution.[17]

Later, in 1929, the U.S. government assisted Calles when General Gonzalo Escobar and half of the Mexican army engaged in insurrection against his rule. The United States sent weapons to Calles directly from its army arsenals and stringently enforced its neutrality laws against the *escobaristas*. Mexico paid out over 1.5 million dollars for planes, arms, and munitions. The privilege of purchasing war materials in the United States aided in the modernization of the Mexican army and made Mexico more stable, and more dependent on the United States.[18]

Throughout the 1920s and 1930s the Mexican government, in an attempt to professionalize the army, sent promising junior officers to the United States and Europe for training. During the mid-1940s, U.S. influence increased, with the Ávila Camacho administration restructuring the Mexican military using the U.S. armed forces as its model. U.S. army field manuals were incorporated into the military training program, and major acquisitions of military hardware were made.[19]

Obregón was the first Mexican president to deal with the problem of the military, a conglomeration of over one hundred thousand men in the federal army (consuming over 60 percent of the total budget), plus thousands of militiamen, hundreds of private warriors, and assorted vigilantes. The revolution had created a corps of independent military chieftains dedicated to the obtainment of self-enrichment. Many were of questionable loyalty and were as willing to follow the lead of a state governor, a local *jefe*, or a self-appointed savior as they were willing to abide by the rules of the Sonora clique in Mexico City.

Being a realist, Obregón was willing to purchase their loyalty as evidenced in his famous saying that "there is no general able to resist a *cañonazo* (cannonball) of fifty thousand pesos." As the partially crippled president was fond of noting, the crooked generals allowed him to become president because with only one arm (lost in the Battle of Celaya) he would be able to steal less. Allowing the generals to exchange their political independence for material gain, he eventually merged all generals into the regular army.[20]

In building a national army, Obregón incorporated several generals, colonels, and junior officers into the Reserve and discharged all the enlisted men under their command. In three years, from 1920 to 1923, he had reduced the army by forty thousand and cut military expenditures in half. He also increased the number of military districts, overhauled the instruction program of the Colegio Militar in Chapultepec, and sent promising young officers to Spain, France, Germany, and the United States to study modern fighting techniques.[21]

During the Calles years (1923–29), the modernization and professionalization of the armed forces continued. To initiate these reforms, Calles selected General Joaquín Amaro, a poor Tarascan Indian boy during the 1910 fighting, as his war minister. Amaro reorganized the whole army structure, reducing the officer corps, their troops, and the military's share of the federal budget from 36 percent to 25 percent in just three years. He reopened the Colegio Militar and overhauled its curriculum, and the newly commissioned cadets from the academy were assigned to regiments of doubtful loyalty. More important, he developed a civilian counterpoise to the army by mobilizing the agrarian irregulars (volunteer peasant forces variously known as *defensas sociales, guardias blancas,* or *cuerpos de voluntarios*) during the rebellions of 1923 and 1929. After the rebellions, the army was ordered to confiscate their weapons, and regional chiefs were placed under the command of the national army. Yet, although their allegiance was to the national government, the *defensas sociales* retained significant autonomy.[22]

What Amaro started, Cárdenas completed, first as war minister from 1932 to 1934, and then as president from 1935 to 1940. Under his leadership, the Superior War College was established, a school of intensive training for the most promising officers. New educational programs that focused on technical training were started for the rank and file. Enlisted men also received a 10 percent raise, life insurance, and improved living conditions in the barracks. Military expenditures were kept down by reducing the size of the officer corps, initiating retirement programs, and by increasing the army's public works activities. The military's share of the federal budget declined to 19 percent in 1938, a downward trend that would continue after Cárdenas left office.[23]

As a counterpoise to the army, Cárdenas organized militia brigades as proletarian defenders of his regime. In 1938, the uniformed workers' militia numbered 100,000 strong, twice the size of the regular army. However, it should be noted that many of these militiamen had little or no access to arms and arsenals and often drilled with wooden rifles. Finally, the institutionalization of the political system in 1938 created the Party of the Mexican Revolution (PRM) with four sectors—military, peasant, labor, and popular. In effect, the political influence of the army was divided into four interest groups, since individual military men belonged to all of the party sectors. The creation of a *sector militar* made it difficult for the army to assume an anti-PRM posture during the Cárdenas presidency.[24]

Reorganization of the party threatened the interests of many regional military *caudillos*. Two months after the PRM reforms, General Saturnino Cedillo rebelled. A follower of Obregón and Calles, he had been active in opposing the de la Huerta and Escobar rebellions. A radical *agrarista* with a popular following in San Luis Potosí, Cedillo had a large private army. Unbeknownst to the Mexican public was the fact that Cedillo was also the leading figure behind the operations of an opium ring in the United States and Mexico. From the United States came capital that was sent to plantations in Mexico where the poppies were grown, and then the opium would be returned to Chinese tongs in the United States. Others involved in the ring included the chief of the federal district secret police, the secret police chief of Gobernación, and several deputies and senators from the federal district, Veracruz, and San Luis Potosí. In spite of his resources, Cedillo was no match for Cárdenas, and he was soon defeated. A similar misfortune happened to General Juan Andreu Almazán in 1940, the last revolutionary general to threaten the state. The knockout blow had been delivered—the military would now assume the role of guardian of the state.[25]

Simultaneous with the struggle against the army was the state's battle with the Catholic church. This was a church-state rivalry with roots in the colonial past, as well as the liberal-clerical struggles of the nineteenth century. The opening salvo in the Cristero rebellion was fired on 21 February 1925 when the government supported the establishment of an Orthodox Catholic Apostolic Mexican Church. This attempt to set up a schismatic church headed by a dissident priest—a submissive state-controlled religious corporation—was met with denunciations and riots by angry Catholics.

The earlier anticlerical provisions of the constitution of 1917, especially those secularizing education, limiting the number of clergy, and restricting Catholic political activity, were condemned in a pastoral letter issued by Mexican bishops. Calles reacted by closing Catholic schools and deporting all foreign-born clergy. As matters reached a crisis, the church authorities suspended public worship and Catholics in various parts of the country rose in arms.[26]

Lay direction of the revolt took place under the auspices of the National League for the Defense of Religious Liberty (LNDLR), with passive support from the Mexican hierarchy and the Vatican. Initially, open rebellion spread across western Mexico throughout the states of Colima, Jalisco, Durango, Guanajuato, and Michoacán. After the army crushed the initial rebellions in late 1926 and in January 1927, there followed almost two and a half years of indecisive guerrilla warfare characterized by brutal excesses on both sides, from looting and rape to the massacre of civilians and execution of prisoners. While the Cristeros often made the *agraristas* (those who participated in the state's agrarian reform programs) and rural schoolteachers pay, with blood, for their connection with the state, the *federales* would retaliate by decapitating village priests and burning the property of their followers.[27]

The Cristeros, who numbered over twenty thousand in July 1927, were down to 14,000 when they laid down their arms after the 21 June 1929 settlement between the church and the state. According to Mexican War Department figures, the number of Cristeros killed in Jalisco alone between 1 January 1928 and 31 July 1928 was 3,235. Most of the guerrillas were *rancheros,* small farmers, and cattlemen, while the League's membership was largely middle class. It was mostly a rural revolt that lacked support from *hacendados* and urban businessmen. Although the 1929 agreement, arranged through the intercession of U.S. Ambassador Dwight Morrow, allowed the church to perform its own spiritual affairs under its own direction, the spirit of the settlement soon evaporated and religious strife continued for another decade before President Cárdenas finally arranged a permanent settlement.[28]

The reaction of the U.S. government and the American Catholic church to affairs in Mexico took place in the context of the postwar Red Scare concerns of the 1920s. By far the most important political event shaping popular politics was the threat of bolshevism. The

new communist leadership in Moscow was atheistic and was advocating an international class war against imperialistic capitalists, including those who were profiting in Mexico. In 1926–1927, when U.S.
marines were sent into Nicaragua and two Italian anarchists, Nicola
Sacco and Bartolomeo Vanzetti, falsely accused of communism, were
convicted of murder and executed in the electric chair, the Coolidge
administration was concerned with the "bolshevist" government of
Calles in Mexico—a government that was unfriendly to American oil
interests and was sending arms to the anti-American, anti-imperialist,
liberal forces of Juan B. Sacasa in Nicaragua.[29] In the popular press,
Mexico was portrayed as a chaotic country led by bloodthirsty and
dishonest enemies of private property and the church; men who had
no respect for religious toleration and no fear of God. Apprehensive
over the "bolshevising" of Mexico, Catholic leaders and newspapers
raised the red specter in an attempt to arouse public opinion against
the persecution of the Mexican church.[30]

At the same time, the resurgence of nativism in the United States
and the Ku Klux Klan in the mid-1920s, plus the negative reaction to
the bid of Alfred Smith for the presidency in 1928, indicated that anti-
Catholicism was again on the rise. In 1926, the Protestant Presbyterian
Synod adopted a resolution of sympathy for Calles and his church
policy, while Methodist leader George Miller declared, referring to the
persecution of the church in Mexico, that "it is delicious to hear our
tormenters pleading for religious liberty and conscience."[31]

When the Cristero campaign began, the LNDLR coveted the financial backing of U.S. Catholics, but in the final analysis it got only
expressions of sympathy. Before the educated classes of San José de
Gracia in Michoacán would join the rebellion, they had to be assured,
according to historian Luis González, that "the *agraristas* of the neighboring towns in Jalisco would come with their rifles . . . and that the
Catholics of the United States would help with money and military
supplies."[32] American bishops deplored the persecution in Mexico
and rendered assistance to Mexican bishops, priests, and nuns who
came to the United States during the crisis. The Catholic Church Extension Society appropriated $25,000 for a Mexican aid fund, while the

Knights of Columbus propagandized against the Calles government and raised funds for a Catholic relief charity. But the bishops refused to bankroll a rebellion, and the Knights of Columbus assessed their membership to meet the costs of relief work, not arms shipments. Eventually, a conciliatory viewpoint prevailed from within the church, as Father John J. Burke aided the American ambassador in negotiating the settlement of 21 June 1929.[33]

As for the U.S. government, before 1927 it generally agreed with the viewpoint of the Catholic review *America* that the religious question was merely "a smoke screen, raised by Calles to conceal from Mexicans his difficulties with us and to make it hard for our State Department to take action on civil matters [oil, mining, and land law issues] without being accused of doing the bidding of the Catholic Church."[34] Coolidge and his secretary of state, Frank Kellogg, were less than pleased with Mexico's power play in Central America. Yet, the Bucareli agreements of 1923 had indicated that diplomacy could defend U.S. interests. In addition, Protestant arguments in favor of Calles and the general antipathy to intervention by a majority of Americans (as voiced by senators William Borah and Robert M. La Follette, Jr.) led the U.S. government to back Calles and seek an honorable end to the conflict. As Coolidge, and later Franklin D. Roosevelt, knew, only a strong central authority in Mexico could prevent trouble between the two countries.[35]

As indicated, Ambassador Morrow initiated the original settlement. Yet the first years after the 1929 truce did witness even harsher anticlerical laws and more conflict. In 1933, Article 3 of the constitution of 1917 was amended to read "education imparted by the State shall be socialistic." Anticlerics and Communists became entrenched in the departments of education and communication of the Cárdenas government. Throughout the 1930s, state authorities continued their persecution of the church—in Veracruz the bishop was arrested; the state of Durango issued a decree limiting the number of priests; in Tabasco the churches were closed, religious images forbidden, and priests required to marry.[36]

Under Roosevelt, however, Ambassador Josephus Daniels quietly persuaded the Mexican authorities to call off the campaign against the church and succeeded in countering the negative stereotype of the government that was publicized by American Catholics during the 1930s. By 1938, Cárdenas was respectful of Catholicism, and relations with the church improved. When the government expropriated foreign oil properties in 1938, it had the support of the church hierarchy. The war against the church was now over. The constitution and ultimate power of the state had been upheld, and the government was now an active force in the educational life of the nation.[37]

Another heritage of the Calles-Cárdenas era was the attack by the state against the lords of land and industry. Agrarian reform and cries of "land and liberty" had shaped the revolution. Article 27 of the constitution advanced several ideas, including that lands could be expropriated "for reasons of public utility" without compensation and that the state would "take necessary action to break up large estates" and develop small holdings and new centers with sufficient land and water.

Throughout the 1920s and early 1930s, in spite of the violence in the countryside, land distributions were minimal. Several peasant leagues were formed, and angry peasants in Veracruz, Morelos, and the Yucatán seized land, while Tarascan Indian communities led by Primo Tapia rioted in Michoacán. Yet, in spite of the occasional concessions to the peasantry, after 1928 most state assistance went to large, commercial *hacendados* in the form of liberal credit arrangements and irrigation concessions. In the context of the depression and the improved relations with the United States, Calles agreed with Ambassador Morrow that land distributions should cease and the agrarian debt reduced. This was the case until the Agrarian Code of 1934.

The Agrarian Code divided the nation's agrarian producers into *ejidatarios*—individuals and families who lived in communities and worked on state-owned lands in which the *ejido*, or community, enjoyed the right of usufruct—and so-called small landowners (*propiedades pequeñas*), a group that included many *hacendados* and foreign owners who were anything but small landowners in spite of how they appeared on paper. After the Agrarian Code, years of sweeping reform came to the countryside, with land grants totalling nearly 17.9 million hectares between 1934 and 1940. This was more than two and a half times the amount of land that had been distributed by all previous post-1917 regimes.[38] In addition, consistent with his philosophy of corporativism, Cárdenas incorporated several regional peasant leagues into the National Peasant Confederation (CNC), and made the CNC an integral part of the aforementioned Party of the Mexican Revolution (PRM).

Cárdenas's redistribution program lasted from 1934 until 1937, when labor difficulties, military riots, and bureaucratic corruption put the government in a difficult political position. *Ejidos* were created in the Yaqui valley of Sonora, the sugar growing areas of Sinaloa, the Laguna cotton district (some eight million acres on the Coahuila-Durango border), and the henequén fields of Yucatán. Some lands changed hands in the older Mexico of the central and south central highlands. Yet, less than 10 percent of all *ejido* farmers worked on a collective basis (most farmed small parcels within an *ejido*), and the *ejidatarios* who did acquire lands often fought with the peasants, *peones*, sharecroppers, and migrant workers who had received nothing.[39]

By 1940, over 60 percent of the cultivable land was in parcels of over 1,000 hectares, with over 40 percent being large haciendas of 10,000 or more hectares. Small private landholdings also increased in number between 1930 and 1940.[40] As earlier, many *hacendados* benefited by state actions that provided them with access to capital, technology, and markets, and a legal code that allowed them to exempt 150 hectares of irrigated land from expropriation. Although about fifty U.S. settlers were adversely affected when *ejidos* were created in the Yaqui valley of Sonora, and Cárdenas's reforms distressed American property owners in Chihuahua and Baja California, most principal producers in Sinaloa (such as the United Sugar Company), the Laguna district (twelve corporations, 70 percent of which were foreign owned), and the Yucatán either evaded the law outright or were purposely excluded from its effects.[41]

Ultimately, the agrarian reforms only destroyed those landlords who refused to modernize and, while allotting some parcels of land to *ejidatarios* and hacienda peons, opened the way to monopoly agriculture and a new class of entrepreneurial farmers, mostly northerners, who could control credit and markets and knew the benefits of technology, fertilizers, tractors, and a degree for their sons from Texas A&M College. In 1940, scarcely an *ejido* could be found in Sonora, but there were highways and irrigation programs that represented over one quarter of the public investment that had been expended during the previous decade and a half. Obregón's dream had come true—Sonora and the North had become a Mexican variation of U.S. agriculture.[42]

Meanwhile, the lords of the petroleum industry were making threats from behind their barricades on the oilfields. The struggle between Cárdenas and the oil companies, like the Cristero rebellion, had its origin in the constitution of 1917, especially those aspects of Article 27 that enunciated that "the nation shall have at all times the right to impose upon private property such restrictions as the public interest may require," including the prerogative to confine concessions to own and exploit natural resources to Mexican citizens. In effect, the revolution had returned Mexico to pre-*porfirian* days when subsurface rights were the property of the nation and not individual entrepreneurs or corporations.

In 1918, President Carranza, who initially and privately did not seek to make an issue out of oil, nonetheless declared that Article 27 would be interpreted retroactively. Companies that had developed during the *porfiriato,* such as the U.S. owned Standard Oil and the British Royal Dutch-Shell, would be adversely affected by this decision. After 1920, the U.S. government refused to recognize Obregón's government until he agreed to the terms of the Bucareli agreement of 1923. In 1925, Calles initially took a tough stance with the companies, requiring them to exchange perpetual ownership rights for those limited to fifty years. By 1927, however, after a long process of bargaining, Calles and the Mexican Supreme Court held that those properties on which "positive acts" had been performed before 1917 could be developed to perpetuity. Thus the matter stood until Cárdenas came to power.[43]

Until 1938, various Mexican administrations had been unable to effectively apply Article 27 of the constitution and carry out the nationalization of the subsoil. In the end, foreign corporations, backed up by the U.S. government, had held their ground. Yet, by 1938, conditions were favorable for Cárdenas to act against the companies. As Cárdenas himself stated:

> Various administrations since the Revolution have attempted to do something about the subsoil concessions being enjoyed by foreign firms, but up until now domestic problems and international pressure have mitigated against this effort. Today, however, the circumstances are different: there are no internal struggles going on, and a new world war is about to begin. It is a good time to see if England and the United States, which talk so much about democracy and respect for the sovereignty of other countries, will in fact stand up to their spoken convictions when Mexico exercises its rights.[44]

And on 18 March 1938, conditions were right. Cárdenas issued a decree nationalizing the surface possessions of sixteen oil companies, including the properties of Standard Oil.[45]

As in the struggle against the army and the church, corporations, or labor syndicates and unions, were used as allies of the state. Encouraged by the sympathy of the chief executive for the working class, the *petroleros*, on 15 August 1935, organized the National Petroleum Workers' Union (STPRM), which merged the next year into the Mexican Confederation of Workers (CTM). In 1938, of the 600,000 affiliated workers of the CTM, 15,000 worked for the oil companies. Late in 1936, the petroleum workers demanded a new contract with higher wages and benefits. When negotiations between management and workers broke down, the union called a strike in May 1937. In August, the Board of Conciliation and Arbitration issued a report in favor of the workers and critical of the companies. Following a company appeal, the Mexican Supreme Court, in March of 1938, denied the appeal and backed the decision of the Board of Conciliation and Arbitration. When the companies still balked at the decision, the order of expropriation was delivered on 18 March 1938.[46]

Acting under the authority of the Mexican expropriation law of November 1936 (which had been used in 1937 to expropriate the Mexican National Railways), Cárdenas nationalized the almost wholly foreign-owned oil industry. On the evening of 18 March President Cárdenas read an address over the radio announcing his actions:

> It is evident that the problem which the oil companies have placed before the executive power of the nation by their refusal to obey the decree of the highest judicial tribunal is not a simple case of the execution of a sentence, but a definitive situation which must be solved urgently. The social interests of the laboring classes of all the industries demand it. . . . It is the sovereignty of the nation which is thwarted through the maneuvers of foreign capitalists who, forgetting that they have formed themselves into Mexican companies, now attempt to elude the mandates and obligations imposed by the authorities of this country.[47]

Cárdenas then established a public corporation composed of labor and government to operate the new national industry. Founded earlier in December 1933, for social rather than economic ends, Petróleos Mexicanos (PEMEX) would be used in the post–WWII era for developmental purposes—subsidizing energy, assisting the petrochemical industry, and, in general, providing technology for the overall growth of the economy.[48]

As to be expected, the companies responded aggressively to the expropriation. Trained engineers and geologists were called home, and a boycott was established preventing Mexico from acquiring machinery, chemicals, and transport for its industry. A vicious propaganda campaign was carried out in the United States through company subsidized magazines like Standard Oil of New Jersey's *Lamp* and also in such periodicals as the *Atlantic Monthly*. Mexicans were accused of being thieves, debased thugs, fascists, and bolshevists.[49]

It was alleged that Cárdenas was a captive of the Communist party who supported socialistic labor movements against foreign capitalists (some congressional critics went further to suggest that the Roosevelt administration had encouraged the establishment of communism in Mexico).[50] This was in spite of the fact that the Mexican Communist party (PCM) had been officially suppressed after the Escobar revolt of 1929, and, by 1930, diplomatic relations had been terminated with the USSR. Although Cárdenas ended the persecution of the PCM in 1934, he did not restore relations with the USSR.[51] When, in 1938, he allowed Leon Trotsky asylum in Mexico, many of his opponents in the United States and in the Military Intelligence Division of the U.S. Army interpreted this as an act friendly to the communist camp.[52] *Cardenismo* was a statist doctrine, a philosophy of corporativism in which Cárdenas controlled the party—the party did not control him.

For several reasons the campaign against Cárdenas failed. The oil workers and the Mexican people in general, including the church, supported the expropriation and had a united will to resist foreign pressure. The eighteenth of March 1938 became a national holiday. In the United States, many investors, mining proprietors, and manufacturers opposed a policy of intervention that would seemingly aid big oil producers at their own expense. Roosevelt, and his ambassador to Mexico, Josephus Daniels, did not want to see the Good Neighbor Policy "drown in Mexican oil." Although the U.S. government could have joined the boycott and refused to purchase silver from Mexico as a form of economic pressure, to have done so would have caused a bankrupt Mexico to cease purchasing American goods and services altogether. Finally, the threat of Germany and a European war meant that Roosevelt wished to curry favor with the strategically situated southern neighbor.[53]

Consequently, by late 1941 a general agreement was signed between Mexico and the United States that compensated American firms.[54] The oil barons, chiefs of a once domineering foreign enclave, were finally slain. They would join the corpses of ambitious army officers, rash priests, and feudal landlords. Mexico was to become a modern state.

In spite of the reformism and nationalism, Calles, as a member of the Sonoran dynasty, and Cárdenas, a radical from Michoacán, pursued policies of capitalist development and state aided private enterprise. They created a heritage of economic corporativism, government intervention, labor reform, civilian rule, state supremacy (especially over the church), and agrarian reform. In addition, Cárdenas initiated deficit spending in his fight against the depression. He also attempted reconciliation with all groups—the church, the oil interests, and hacienda owners—who had lost lands to peasants. He banned some, but not all, foreign capitalists from power. The communists were never incorporated into the government party and were excluded from positions of political authority. Cárdenas eventually espoused the Grand Alliance and supported the war against fascism. He was the great modernizer who led Mexico toward corporate capitalism and the economic recovery of the next era—an economic "miracle" that would last from World War II to the 1970s.

To speak of a Calles-Cárdenas heritage and of the continuity of capitalist development is not to deny the differences that existed between the decades of the 1920s and 1930s. Certainly the problems created by the Great Depression and the rise of Nazi Germany caused the PRM of 1938 to face unusual circumstances not present when the Party of the National Revolution (PNR) was first formed in 1929. Corporativism in the 1920s was a system that appealed to democratic socialists in Germany and England, and even Hoover Republicans in the United States. However, after 1934, corporativism became increasingly associated with fascism and Nazism—ideologies opposed to either the traditions of Mexican revolutionary nationalism or the egalitarianism of the New Deal in the United States. The distinguishing features of the 1930s—a depressed economy, industrial unionism, Communist party activity, and so on—resulted in the creation of a powerful minority voice critical of and resistant to capitalism. Cárdenas, as national *caudillo* and patriarch of all Mexicans, gave a sympathetic ear to the cries of the underclass. This call of anguished radicalism lives on in the current history of Mexico—a socialistic *grito* that the name of Cárdenas, father or son, still evokes today.[55]

In the final analysis, when the career of Cárdenas is viewed through the wartime era of the early 1940s, Cárdenas was not so different from FDR, the New Dealer, who also wanted to save capitalism and make the hemisphere secure from the inroads of fascist dictatorship. Thus, the diplomatic agreement of 1941 signaled a new era of cooperation in the history of the United States and Mexico, a cooperation that would be tested by the realities of a global war.[56]

8 Preening and Ruffling the Serpent's Plumage

> As long ago as 1986, Treasury Secretary James Baker was privately predicting that "the day is not far off when an American president is going to devote more attention to Mexico than the Soviet Union."
>
> *Newsweek*, 8 January 1990

Immanuel Wallerstein, famed sociologist and architect of the world-system theory, argues that 1967–68 was a pivotal time in the history of the world-economy. Until then, the United States dominated the military arena and the political economy. After 1967, a steady process of erosion of the hegemonic position of the United States in the world-economy occurred. Wallerstein notes the tremendous psychological shock to U.S. political and business leaders in response to events of 1967–68: the currency and gold crisis (in which the price of gold fell below the official price of $35 an ounce by 1970), signaling the tumble of the U.S. dollar from its pedestal; the Tet offensive against South Vietnam in which a small Third World people appeared to be thwarting the military will of the United States; the student-worker rebellions at Columbia University, Paris, Tokyo, Prague, and Mexico City.[1]

During the early 1970s, the United States entered a period of decelerated growth in which relative decline could be measured in terms of productivity figures, exports to and shares in the world market, research expenditures, currency strength, rates of inflation, and unemployment. By the 1980s, the uncompetitiveness of U.S. industrial goods and the declining sales of agricultural exports produced immense deficits in the "visible" trade. The trade deficit, in turn, was affected by the national debt ($2.8 trillion in 1990; over $4 trillion by 1992) and a $150 billion federal deficit (as of 1990). To finance this debt, the United States was not able to rely on earnings from "invisibles" (as

Great Britain's banks and insurance houses did before 1914). Instead, the United States was forced to import ever-larger sums of capital and in the process was transformed in a few years from the world's largest creditor to the world's largest debtor nation. New York, London, and Toronto now shared their monetary power with Tokyo/Yokohama—as of 1990 a megacity of over 17.2 million people that was fast becoming the world's leading financial center.[2]

The late sixties and early seventies was a critical season for Mexico as well. Politically, there was the 2 October 1968 incident at Tlatelolco square in Mexico City in which soldiers and secret police were responsible for the deaths of hundreds, the wounding of hundreds more, and the arrest of at least fifteen hundred student-worker demonstrators. This was followed by the Corpus Christi massacre of 10 June 1971 when at least fifty student demonstrators were killed by *porristas* (paid provocateurs posing as students) and *halcones* ("falcons," paramilitary troops sponsored by Monterrey capitalists and trained by Federal District police). These political events marked the end of the Mexican "miracle" of postwar economic growth and the beginning of social justice and political democracy movements in Mexico.[3]

In simple terms, Mexico's contemporary economic history can be divided into three periods. In the Mexican "miracle" phase from World War II to 1970 the government sought, through "import-substituting industrialization" (ISI), to create new wealth and promote economic growth. In the "shared development" pattern of the Luis Echeverría-José López Portillo administrations (1970–82) social spending and rural development programs were instituted along with a shift away from ISI toward export oriented growth (with the corresponding rise of the *maquila* industry in the North). And in the period since 1982 first Miguel de la Madrid (1982–88) and then Carlos Salinas de Gortari (1988–94) moved to "belt tightening," as Mexico abandoned ISI to enforce an IMF austerity program in which export revenues have been used to repay the interest on Mexico's national debt.[4]

Between 1940 and 1970, while the U.S. population was growing from 131.6 to 203.2 million, Mexico grew from 19.6 to 50.4 million. During the same period, Mexico became an urban area with the proportion of people living in regions of over ten thousand increasing from 22 percent in 1940 to 42 percent in 1970 (and in 1990 over 55 percent). By 1950, Mexico City had only 3 million inhabitants, but in 1970 it had swelled to 9.2 million, a growing process that has continued so that by 1990 the capital had 21.3 million and was the world's leading megacity. Similarly, northern Mexico had become a major urban zone. Most of these population shifts and growths started during World War II and continued throughout the Mexican "miracle" phase, when the economy grew at over 6 percent per annum.[5]

Wartime cooperation between Mexico and the United States signaled the beginning of a new era in diplomatic relations. Not since the age of Benito Juárez and the U.S. Civil War—a time when the liberal and nationalist aspirations of Juárez were supported by the United States—had the two countries seen their interests become so reciprocal. After June of 1941, it became clear to Mexico that there would be no final German victory in Europe. By the end of May 1942, after German submarines had sunk Mexican tankers, the United States and Mexico became formal allies.[6]

The United States considered Mexico to be geographically strategic, as well as an important source of raw materials and cheap labor for its war effort. Mexico, moving away from its revolutionary past to the economic orthodoxy of its new president, General Manuel Ávila Camacho, desired foreign capital to finance its industrial revolution, either in the form of public and private loans or direct foreign investment (DFI). This was an open invitation to North American bankers and investors. Thus, a "neo-*porfirian* era of good feelings" was initiated.[7]

In early 1942, after Mexico had broken diplomatic relations with Germany but prior to its alliance with the United States, the Mexican-American Joint Defense Commission was formed. Ávila Camacho also created a Pacific Military Region consisting of all the states from Baja California to Chiapas. This placed the West Coast, then seemingly threatened by the Japanese, under a coordinated defense plan commanded by ex-president Lázaro Cárdenas, an antifascist who also had a reputation as a staunch defender of Mexican sovereignty. The

Commission eventually oversaw the installation of a series of radar stations in Baja California and, under the Lend-Lease Act, funneled millions of dollars of military assistance to Mexico, resulting in new aircraft for the air force and a mechanized ground division for the army. U.S. aid meant that the Mexican military could develop without taxing the resources of the state and the national budget. A modernized air force squadron of three hundred men was eventually sent to the United States for training and, by 1944, was transferred to the Pacific. Mexico's 201st Squadron saw service in the Philippines.[8]

To counter the operations of a Nazi Fifth Column in Mexico, the United States appointed Gus Jones, a veteran FBI agent who, since 1921, had been the Special Agent in Charge (SAC) of the San Antonio office, to the office of U.S. counterspy chief in Mexico. A member of J. Edgar Hoover's Special Intelligence Service (SIS, created in mid-1940) for Latin America, Jones acquired diplomatic cover in the U.S. embassy in Mexico City as a civil attaché. He worked in conjunction with Secretary of Interior Miguel Alemán; Colonel Alvaro Basail of the Secret Service (attached to the ministry of the interior); General Maximino Ávila Camacho (the president's brother and minister of communications); and the postmaster general, General Fernando Ramírez. Together these individuals succeeded in eliminating subversive activity in Mexico.[9]

In the United States, the Federal Communications Commission (FCC) and the cryptographic section of the FBI aided the process by intercepting and decoding Nazi messages. In fact, Mexico was the first Latin American country to allow Radio Intelligence Division agents of the FCC to employ mobile radio detectors on its soil. Eventually, the NSDAP (Nazi Party) in Mexico was broken up, and the Abwehr's V-men (German military intelligence agents) were unable to operate. Gestapo officers Werner Georg Nicolaus and Karl Hellerman were arrested. Clandestine radio stations relaying messages to German submarines in the Atlantic were uncovered, including the ham operation of Carlos Retelsdorf in Coatepec, Veracruz. The legacy of wartime cooperation of Jones and SIS-Mexico was continued afterwards, with today's Mexican secret police operations (for example, the campaign of the U.S. Drug Enforcement Agency in Mexico) being dependent on the United States for technology, training, and equipment.[10]

Equally important were the strategic war materials Mexico provided for the Allied war effort. In 1941, the United States agreed to buy all Mexican production of copper, lead, zinc, graphite, mercury, and cadmium, as well as hard fibers. Formal trade agreements were signed that reopened the U.S. market to Mexican oil following the 1938 nationalization. The treaty also encouraged the export of cattle and agricultural products, and enabled the United States to acquire at fixed prices Mexican surpluses of rubber, henequén, and other items, including opium, a narcotic that contains morphine, from which heroin is derived. Morphine, of course, was used chiefly in medicine as a painkiller and sedative.[11]

Franklin D. Roosevelt and Ávila Camacho also agreed to allow Mexican workers (*braceros*) to serve as agricultural laborers in the American West, in part to replace the American farm workers who had been drafted into the armed forces. Eventually, *braceros* were also used in the railroad industry. By July 1945, there were some fifty-eight thousand *braceros* in agriculture, and another sixty-two thousand working on the railroads—not to mention the thousands of illegals called "wetbacks" or *mojados*. This wartime contract-labor program was continued into the postwar era until 1964, when, curiously enough, the *maquila* industry began a new phase in the history of cheap labor production.[12]

By 1943, 90 percent of Mexico's foreign trade was with the United States, the European market being lost because of the war. In order to cope with the demand from the United States, Mexico had to improve its internal transportation system and open lines of credit with its northern neighbor. By the end of Ávila Camacho's administration, Mexico had obtained $90 million in credit. The international loan market, closed to Mexico between 1913 and 1941, was now reopened.[13]

Credits from the Export-Import Bank in the United States were followed by private investments from both Europe and the United States. While the Mexican government promoted its own "statist" interests in the communications, transportation, fishing, and entertainment industries, private foreign capital flowed into the manufacturing and trade sectors of the economy (even though after 1944 foreign owner-ship was legally limited to 49 percent control of any enterprise, with 51 percent of the enterprise to be Mexican—a rule that was breached more often than enforced). Because of the wartime demand, new Mexican industries were initiated while older concerns expanded and increased in number. The range of industries included textiles, chemicals, food processing, beer, and cement. Electrical capacity rose and steel production grew. Industrialization created new wealth, with the national income almost tripling during the war years from 1940 to 1945.[14]

Throughout the 1940s and 1950s, Mexico embarked on the road toward "import-substituting industrialization" (ISI), a strategy that attempted to substitute domestically manufactured goods for commodities traditionally imported from abroad. The goal was to not only meet the needs of the domestic market, but produce a surplus of manufactured goods that could be exported to Latin America. To initiate ISI, Ávila Camacho replaced Marxist labor leader Vicente Lombardo Toledano with the much more conservative Fidel Velásquez. The administration was able to shift resources from labor to capital. As predicted, labor became the first victim of ISI thinking, as wages did not keep pace with cost of living increases. In addition, during the war, Velásquez curtailed the use of strikes as a corrective for social wrongs. Along with a tamed labor movement, ISI initiatives involved incentives to business such as subsidies, tax exemptions, and tariff protection. The Nacional Financiera, a government-owned bank, was created to provide loans to industry and supervise the industrial process.

Under Miguel Alemán (1946–52) and Adolfo Ruiz Cortines (1952–58) the Mexican program of industrialization became an irreversible fact. Like Ávila Camacho before him, Alemán (the first civilian president since the revolution) reduced land distribution to a trickle and restricted it to small families and private owners. He also reorganized the official party, renaming it the Party of the Institutionalized Revolution (PRI), made up of three sectors: peasant, worker, and popular (the military being merged into the other sectors). The party now became the dominant political force that gave direction to the state's ISI program, and under PRI guidance public works projects boomed. In addition to modernizing the railways, Alemán's administration oversaw the construction of dams and highways, promoted tourism, constructed the new University City, and expanded the activities of PEMEX (now receiving private loans from the United States), from building new pipelines and refineries to developing the new indus- tries of petrochemicals and fertilizers.[15]

In 1954, the Mexican government initiated a monetary and economic strategy generally known as stabilization development, a hard-money, low-inflation strategy to set an exchange rate and then manage the economy in a conservative manner to maintain that exchange rate. The overvalued peso was devalued from 8.65 pesos to the dollar to 12.5 pesos to the dollar. As a result, prices were stabilized, inflation decreased, exports were stimulated, tourism increased, and Mexico became attractive to foreign investors.[16]

U.S. capital flowed into the country. The signs of corporate North America were everywhere: General Electric (of Mexico), Ford, Gen- eral Motors, Dow Chemical, Pepsi-Cola, Coca-Cola, Colgate, John Deere, Goodyear, Sears and Roebuck, Proctor and Gamble, to name a few. Direct foreign investment, most from the United States, in- creased 60 percent between 1952 and 1958, and almost half of it ($497 million) went into industry. Direct U.S. investments increased from $922 million in 1959, to over $1,300 million at the end of the Adolfo López Mateos administration in 1964. In addition, funds from the Interamerican Development Bank, plus earnings on exports (78 per- cent of Mexico's total foreign trade was with the United States in 1955) and remittances from Mexican workers in the United States produced additional capital that aided the industrialization effort.[17]

The Mexican "miracle" was not unique to Mexico, as so-called Third World countries in general experienced expanding growth rates, in- creasing their share of total world manufacturing production from 8.5 percent in 1963 to 9.9 percent in 1973 (and 12 percent in 1980). In the postwar period, Germany, Japan, and other industrialized nations were booming, and their demand for primary products led to faster growth rates and increasing industrialization for the less-developed countries (LDCs, or as the State Department calls them, NICs— newly industrializing countries). Mexico was now a relatively wealthy "peripheral" country, under Argentina and Venezuela in terms of GDP per capita, but akin to Brazil in the Third World and Poland in the Second World. The productivity gap between Mexico and the United States had, in fact, narrowed slightly between 1950 and 1980, as the U.S. GDP per capita, 4.31 times that of Mexico in 1950, was only 3.10 times greater in 1980.[18]

Yet, in terms of quality of life (literacy rates, infant mortality, life expectancy, and so on) for the early 1970s, Mexico ranked well below the rich core countries of Europe and North America (as well as Japan). In this category, Mexico was similar to the Third World nations of Asia, such as the Philippines and Thailand (countries with lower GDP per capita figures than Mexico). In fact, even in economic terms, while the average core economy grew by 231 percent between 1950 and 1980, the average Third World economy had grown by only 92 percent. On a global scale, the gap in wealth that existed in 1950 was even bigger by 1980.[19]

Even more disturbing was the distribution of wealth. As previously noted, Mexico's population by the early 1970s was over fifty million, growing at an average annual rate of 3.3 percent. In spite of economic growth, in real terms there were more impoverished people in Mexico in 1970 than before the Mexican "miracle" began. Between 1950 and 1970, the income share going to the poorest tenth of the Mexican population dropped from 2.43 percent to 1.42 percent (0.35 percent in 1975). Meanwhile, the richest tenth increased their share of national income from 49 percent to over 51 percent. With twelve million Indians suffering from malnutrition, it looked as if Mexico's miraculous growth had only increased the maldistribution of income. Once again it would appear that the mystery of Guadalupe was the only miracle most Mexicans would experience.[20]

The political shortcomings of the promise of the Mexican Revolution during the Gustavo Díaz Ordaz administration (1964–70) and the lack of social justice reflected in the Mexican "miracle" led to the collision between a PRI-modern state and its citizens at Tlatelolco in 1968 and Corpus Christi in 1971. The government's reaction to these problems was the "shared development" strategy of the Echeverría-López Portillo years (1970–82), in which Echeverría attempted to share the wealth by establishing rural development programs to assist the *campesino* while curtailing the quick profits of the industrialists. This program was slightly amended by López Portillo who, with the benefit of newly discovered oil reserves, attempted to both create wealth for the few and share the wealth with the many.

Echeverría's agrarian development program guaranteed price supports, improved marketing and credit facilities, attempted to insure subsistence crops against failure, and provided social services to the rural poor. The National Staple Products Company (CONASUPO), a decentralized state agency, purchased basic foodstuffs at guaranteed prices from the farmer and distributed them at low prices to the urban poor. This agency forced down retail prices and undercut the profits of the middlemen. Many private businessmen were unhappy with this competition from the state. Costs for the new bureaucracy to implement these initiatives were borne by the government.[21]

Echeverría's industrial policy moved Mexico away from ISI and protectionism. Import duties originally intended to protect domestic industry were to be reduced to force Mexican producers to improve the quality of their goods. Subsidies and tax waivers were to be phased out. Only those industries producing goods for the popular market would receive government assistance. The 1973 Law to Regulate Foreign Investment required foreign investors to put their factories in underindustrialized areas and place their capital into job-creating areas. The restrictions led to a decline of direct foreign investment from the United States between 1970 and 1977. A more attractive alternative proved to be indirect foreign investments (for example, bank loans) as commercial institutions replaced individuals as the major source of Mexico's investment capital by 1981.[22]

The Echeverría administration implemented a foreign policy similar to that of the earlier government of López Mateos (1958–64). This was derived from the tenets of economic nationalism. The president attempted to broaden the political and economic horizons of Mexico by traveling to thirty-six countries and concluding 160 international agreements. He sought to break the dependency of Mexico on the United States by forging new trade agreements with Canada, Japan, China, the Soviet Union, and Western and Eastern Europe. He also attempted to expand Mexico's trade in manufactured articles with the LDCs of Central and South America.[23]

The realities of a multipolar world changed the Mexican-U.S. relationship. The Vietnam War had not only been a military defeat for the United States, because of the involvement of the mass media it had been a personal and psychological tragedy for Americans. Above all, it demonstrated the limits of military power, nuclear or conventional. The CIA's economic indicators revealed a decline of the U.S. share of world GNP between 1960 and 1980, dropping from 31.5 percent in 1960 to 25.9 in 1980. While the Soviet Union's economy was also in relative decline, other powers were rising, especially Japan (and the four tigers—South Korea, Taiwan, Singapore, and Malaysia), China, and the European Community. While the passing of the European Age apparently occurred in 1950, by the 1980s it appeared that some of the promises of the Thousand-Year Reich and the Greater East Asia Co-prosperity Sphere were being realized, not through warfare, but through the peaceful acts of trading states.[24]

One reaction to the brave new multipolar world was the attempt by Mexico to broaden its commercial landscape. This involved presidential trips, new trade arrangements, and international agreements outlined above. The 1973 Law to Regulate Foreign Investment was another example. In the diplomatic arena, the growing warmth of Mexico's relationship with Cuba signaled a new era, one in which the Mexican president visited that country for the first time. After the United States engaged in its destabilization program for Chile, an action that eventually led to a CIA-backed coup and the overthrow and death of Salvador Allende, Mexico broke off diplomatic relations with the military *junta* that assumed power, denounced the dictatorial nature of the new regime, and gave asylum to many of Allende's followers. All of this was an assertion by Mexico of its longstanding principles of nonintervention in the hemisphere, self-determination of peoples, and solidarity with Latin America. The Mexican proclamation was hostile to the United States and an affirmation of Mexico's intent to strengthen its hemispheric and world economic position. For Mexico, it signaled the end of Cold War politics, that is, bipolar politics, in the hemisphere.[25]

Since World War II, the United States had been accustomed to pursuing its anti-communist and anti-Soviet actions throughout Latin America, in spite of Latin reservations. At the close of the war, with the division of Germany and the loss of Japan's colonies, the United States and the Soviet Union were the only military powers of the first magnitude. While the U.S. GNP had surged by more than 50 percent in real terms during the war, Europe (minus the Soviet Union) had slipped by 25 percent. In Latin America, the United States retained wartime institutions and connections in order to funnel and foster its Cold War (bipolar) concerns—spreading anticommunist propaganda throughout the hemisphere and attempting to get the countries of Latin America to expel communists and break diplomatic relations with the Soviet Union.[26]

Mexico was always in the vanguard in resisting the interests of the United States and in maintaining the traditions of revolutionary nationalism and economic sovereignty. This was one heritage of Mexico's revolutionary past. Although willing to support the United States in the United Nations in key confrontations with the Soviet Union, there were limits to Mexican support. After the war it did not break diplomatic relations with the Soviet Union (reestablished during World War II) or send troops to Korea. In 1952, it was the only country of Latin America not to sign the Inter-American Reciprocal Aid Treaty, a U.S. military assistance pact. In 1954, its O.A.S. (Organization of American States) delegation, meeting at Caracas, defended the principle of non-intervention when the United States sponsored a CIA overthrow of the Guatemalan reformer, Jacobo Arbenz. The 1959 Cuban Revolution led by Fidel Castro once again increased tensions between the two countries, with Mexico maintaining diplomatic relations with Cuba and openly condemning the U.S.-backed invasion by exile forces at the Bay of Pigs (Playa Girón) in 1961. Although Lyndon Johnson sent troops into the Dominican Republic in 1965, the relationship normalized in the late sixties as Mexico disappeared into the background while the United States was preoccupied with Asian affairs and the Vietnam War.

It must be admitted that Mexico's independent policy in the Americas, while a source of unease for many Washington bureaucrats, did not seriously impair bilateral relations. It is true that during the early Castro years direct U.S. financial and economic aid to Mexico was minimal, perhaps one effect of Mexico's autonomous practices. Yet the Mexicans benefited when the United States closed its market to Cuban sugar and increased its trade with Mexico. Although travel back and forth between Havana and Mexico City was permited, travelers were placed on a blacklist and had their goods confiscated. It was obvious that the Mexican and American secret police establishments were cooperating in anti-revolutionary actions. In addition, the Mexican military continued to send individuals to the United States for training in counterinsurgency warfare. And, finally, with rumors of a military coup circulating in 1973, Echeverría gave the army a 15 percent pay hike, promoted mid-level officers, and became an official booster of these "professional patriots" with their Brazilian and American ties.[27]

By 1976, at the end of the Echeverría years, Mexico was in the midst of a political and fiscal crisis. Under attack by the conservatives who constantly reminded Echeverría of Allende's fate, as well as leftist rural and urban guerrillas, the president made concessions right and left. His rhetoric was louder than his reforms, and the result was unfulfilled expectations for the poor. Echeverría's attack on ISI and his attempt to diversify markets had only changed the dependency from U.S. investors to transnational corporations (TNCs) operating in an international market. They did not reduce the national debt or increase the domestic demand for manufactured articles. Mexico was still dependent on foreign imports for capital goods and high technology industry.[28]

This situation was not unique to Mexico, for Brazil, Argentina, and other Latin American countries faced a similar situation, exacerbated in the mid-1970s by worldwide inflation and recession. Yet, ultimately the president's unorthodox economics had led to bankrupt steel works, increased unemployment, a balance-of-trade deficit, and a decline in the output of basic foodstuffs. When the 1976 statistics were in, inflation stood at over 30 percent, and the accumulated public debt was near the $20 billion mark. The last act of surrender was the devaluation of the peso by 60 percent, changing it from 12.5 pesos to the dollar to over 22 pesos to the dollar. A depreciation process had been started that would continue throughout the 1980s.[29]

José López Portillo, the unorthodox minister of treasury in the previous administration, assumed the presidential office in 1976 and immediately announced an alliance for profits between the public and private sectors. The discovery of new oil fields in the Gulf of Campeche, verified in 1981 to amount to 72 billion barrels (placing Mexico second only to Saudi Arabia in reserves), opened Mexico's doors to international credit without the restrictions of the International Monetary Fund (IMF) agreement that had been first negotiated by the Echeverría government. Petrodollars created by oil exports enabled Mexico to forgo the austerity program of tight credit, wage freezes, and low public spending so dear to the hearts of industrialists, bankers, and managers of transnational corporations.[30]

As director of PEMEX, Jorge Díaz Serrano oversaw a massive undertaking to develop the oil fields. Thousands of rigs were built, platforms constructed, deep water ports dredged, tankers leased, and Texas "roughnecks" brought in to assist the project. Private banks overloaded with OPEC deposits eagerly loaned capital to Mexico. At least one-third of them were from the United States, such as the Bank of America, Citibank, Manufacturers Hanover, Chemical Banking Corp. of New York, and Chase Manhattan.

In its haste, the Mexican government made some miscalculations, such as the ambitious project to build a 1,350 kilometer gas pipeline from Cactus, Chiapas, to the northern border at Reynosa, Tamaulipas, to feed six U.S. companies with gas at a price eight times higher than that of the Mexican domestic market. When the Jimmy Carter administration opposed the plan, the project came to a sudden halt.

The only problem was that the Mexican government had not waited for final approval from the U.S. government before starting construction of the pipeline. Not learning from its history of bilateral relations with the United States, the Mexicans assumed that the American oil companies were allied with the U.S. government, a situation that was not true on at least two prior occasions—the 1927 oil dispute of the Calles years and the 1938 oil expropriation incident.[31]

During the López Portillo years, Mexico's role as a leading oil producer allowed it more independence in its foreign policy. In 1978, while refusing to allow the Shah of Iran to reenter Mexico, the Mexican government broke off relations with the Anastasio Somoza regime of Nicaragua. That next year it recognized the revolutionary Sandinist government and offered it technical and economic assistance, including oil. In 1980, PEMEX entered into a protocol with Cuba in which the former agreed to use Mexican technicians to explore Cuba's sea platform in search of oil. The San José Pact of 1980 allowed the countries of the Caribbean and Central America to purchase Mexican and Venezuelan oil at below market prices with long-term, low-interest loans. Finally, in August 1981, the Mexican and French governments circulated a joint statement recognizing the insurgents in El Salvador as "a representative political force."[32]

Needless to say, these acts of oil diplomacy by Mexico ran counter to the United States, an energy hungry country that feared the results of black gold blackmail, and its interests in the hemisphere. While private groups spoke of the creation of a North American Common Market that would allow Mexican hydrocarbons free access to the U.S. economy, the government of Ronald Reagan (1981–89) talked of free enterprise and discussions within the framework of existing international organizations (in which the U.S. had a dominant voice). For his part, President López Portillo, in his annual report of September 1981, reiterated his government's support for Cuba, Nicaragua, and the leftist forces in El Salvador by saying that by "tightening the links of friendship and cooperation that bind us with the revolutions of Cuba and Nicaragua, we have underscored Mexico's attachment to the political principle of the free determination of peoples."[33]

The promise to Mexico of moving from an underdeveloped to a developed country, and a major leader of the Third World bloc, vanished in June of 1981 when the price of oil took a drastic drop. A surplus world supply of fuel changed what had been a seller's market into a buyer's market. The origins of the price drop go back to 1978–79 when the Iranian revolution supposedly resulted in a world-wide oil shortage. More likely, the U.S. and British concerns manipulated the situation to increase the price of oil and thereby make their operations in the North Slope (Alaska) and North Sea profitable. In 1979, U.S. companies began drawing down inventories, cutting back their domestic production, and exporting oil overseas, all while the U.S. administration was deploring the oil scarcity. By 1981, the new oil wells of the United States and the United Kingdom were flowing, and this oil, along with petroleum from the USSR and Mexico (as well as the OPEC countries) created the surplus and the downward trend in prices. Mexico's hopes were shattered.[34]

In February 1982, the government devalued the peso nearly 100 percent. Mexico's financial community panicked as Mexicans began to convert pesos to dollars, and capital took flight. By July 1982, Mexico's officials told the U.S. Treasury that it could not meet the payments on its $83 billion debt due in August. Mexico was near bankruptcy. Alarm spread throughout the offices of the international banks, including those in the United States that had financed most of Mexico's debt. The Federal Reserve, working with international institutions (mainly the IMF), restructured the loan with billions of dollars of credit. Mexico received $1.8 billion from the United States and an additional $3.85 billion from the IMF.[35]

The price of the bailout was high, as Mexico agreed to deliver the bulk of its prospective gas and oil to the United States at a favorable price and to multiple exchange rates in the future (a process of mini-devaluations interspersed with periods when the peso exchange rate is frozen). The government also agreed to an IMF-instituted austerity program that meant wage controls and a cut in government expenditures; price increases for goods and services provided by government agencies like CONASUPO; a move toward opening the market to international competition and eventually seeking membership in the General Agreement on Tariffs and Trade (GATT); promotion of exports via the *maquiladora* industry along the border; a flexible interpretation of the 1973 Foreign Investment Law to encourage foreign investment; and an agreement to reduce by more than 40 percent the number of public sector firms. On 1 September 1982, in his final State of the Nation address, López Portillo nationalized the private banks. A shrinking, if not zero-growth, economy faced the Harvard trained Miguel de la Madrid (1982–88) as he took the presidential office in December.[36]

The immediate result of austerity was Mexico's first favorable balance of trade in many years—$5.5 billion in 1983. Initially, the rate of inflation was reduced, as was the public sector deficit. Between 1983 and 1984, the country's international reserves increased by over $4 billion. Then a devastating earthquake hit Mexico City in September 1985. By 1986, the economy worsened as a drastic plunge in oil prices translated into a drop in oil revenues for the state.[37]

The decline of oil revenues and the continuing economic problems forced Mexico to retreat from its earlier assertive and direct oil diplomacy and cede its role as a power broker in Central America and the Caribbean. The concerns of supporting the Sandinist government, seeking a negotiated settlement in El Salvador, and establishing global initiatives to relieve tensions remained the same, but the methods were now multilateral and indirect—for example, the creation of the Contadora group (Mexico, Venezuela, Colombia, and Panama) in 1983 to promote a negotiated settlement that would bring peace, avoid an East-West conflict, and indirectly reduce U.S. hegemony in the region.[38]

These goals of Mexican foreign policy, although tempered with the niceties of diplomatic language, still placed Mexico at odds with the U.S. position in Central America and the Caribbean. In October 1983, U.S. troops invaded Grenada (only forty-eight hours after 241 U.S. marines and sailors were killed in Beirut), and, throughout the Reagan era, the United States continued to support counterrevolutionary troops operating in Honduras against the Nicaraguan govern-

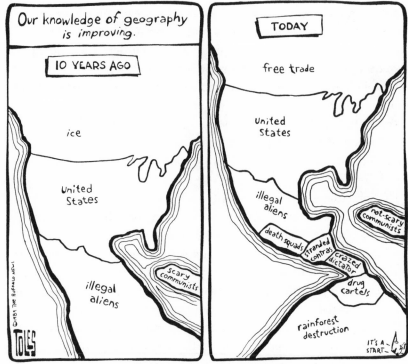

Fig. 12. Editorial cartoon by Tom Toles that appeared in the
19 December 1989 *Buffalo News*

ment. After peace talks broke down in the Mexican resort town of
Manzanillo in 1984, the Reagan administration initiated a destabilization program for Nicaragua that involved extralegal covert forces
(outside of and, perhaps, even unknown to the CIA), laundered drug
money, and violations of congressional rules concerning aid to the
Nicaraguan insurgency (eventually resulting in the Iran-Contra scan-
dal of 1985).

When the George Bush administration was sworn into power in
1989, the Contras had tired, Soviet expansionism had declined (a
portent of the 1991 disintegration of the USSR), and a conservative
government was on the verge of replacing the Sandinistas in Nicaragua. Yet, as the December 1989 military invasion of Panama demon-

strated (ostensibly to arrest Manuel Noriega), the United States was unwilling to relinquish peacefully its hegemony over Central America. Again, between January and March 1991, the United States went to war against Iraq, a relatively weak Third World nation (at least by First World standards). These actions increased again Mexico's suspicions of its northern neighbor.

Despite the economic and diplomatic setbacks between 1983 and 1988, the government of de la Madrid continued its program of reconstruction. Exemptions were made to the 1973 investment law in an attempt to attract foreign capital. In opposition to many of Mexico's businessmen, Mexico was admitted to GATT in July of 1986. And most surprising, the Mexican government sold, liquidated, or transferred over two hundred "low-priority" state enterprises to private concerns. On the target list were many well-known enterprises, including the Nacional Hotelera chain of five-star hotels, Vehiculos Automotores Mexicanos and Renault de Mexico (automobile concerns), Mexicana airlines, the Monterrey foundry, and in 1988, the state-owned copper mine at Cananea—expected to be sold to an industrial conglomerate for $910 million, it had been a symbol of revolutionary nationalism since the June strike of 1906.[39]

Since the fiscal crisis of 1982, the private and public members of the U.S. financial community have been hyperactive in their attempts to assist Mexico's economic recovery and maintain in the process their own solvency. In 1984, Mexico negotiated a second agreement in which the banks agreed to multi-year rescheduling. In 1985, their negotiating stance boosted by the Mexican earthquake and with support from the U.S. government, the Mexicans agreed to the Baker Plan (named for then Secretary of Treasury James Baker), a "gentler" (than IMF) austerity plan that combined loans and easier repayment terms with promises to privatize state-owned businesses. After the 1986 plunge in oil prices, the IMF and the World Bank recognized the need for compensatory finance with a $2 billion contingency fund that linked Mexico's growth rate to the amount of money they were willing to loan. Mexico also received lower interest rates than any hitherto charged to LDCs. Then, after the CIA in late 1986 alarmingly warned about destabilizing trends in Mexico, Washington made available a $3.5 billion bridge loan after the Mexican election of 1988. Finally in early 1990, the Brady Plan was announced (developed by U.S. Treasury Secretary Nicholas F. Brady) in which the United States renegotiated Mexico's public sector debt to some 450 commercial banks around the world.[40]

The social costs of de la Madrid's program have been very high. The burden of austerity has fallen on the working class and the poor—the majority of Mexicans. During the 1982–86 period, Mexico's real GDP per capita dropped 17 percent. This translated into a deterioration in real wages and purchasing power for the working poor. Steep increases in controlled food prices meant that the Mexican people were consuming fewer proteins and calories than ten years earlier; or that, in 1982 47 percent of a family's salary was spent on food, while in 1985, 64 percent was committed to food expenses. Mexico's employment problem was aggravated by the stabilization program as well. One estimate suggests that during 1985 about 11 percent of Mexico's 24 million workers were either underemployed or unemployed. It was not surprising that the rate of illegal immigration to the United States increased during the 1985–86 period.[41]

In the final analysis, then, the benefits of what is euphemistically labeled "austerity" went to the creditor nations in general (the United States, Japan, the European Community) and the United States in particular—member states of the IMF and World Bank. More specifically, private capital in Mexico and the United States profited from the financial crisis. Foreign capitalists were invited to ignore investment laws that forbid foreign control of more than 49 percent of a company, and have been the recipients, along with their Mexican counterparts, of over 200 state-owned companies that have been turned over to the private sector. Mexico has facilitated the expansion of foreign corporations such as Ford, Chrysler, General Motors, and Nissan. Mexico's membership in GATT was a capitulation to the free-trade forces in the United States seeking new access to Mexican markets and safeguards for its corporations. Finally, in early 1990, President Carlos

Salinas de Gortari agreed to entertain the idea of Mexico's entry into a North American Common Market, a notion considered ludicrous a decade ago.[42]

Unlike the early 1970s, Mexico's elites in 1982 could not respond to the financial disaster by attracting foreign loans, nor, as in the late 1970s, could they use oil exports as collateral for foreign indebtedness. As scholar Jeffrey Bortz notes, Mexico's elites turned to the policy they knew so well from past emergencies, "making the working class pay for the crisis."[43]

One justification for the attentiveness of the United States to the Mexican debt crisis was the stake the United States had in maintaining political stability in Mexico, since economic problems in Mexico carried over to the United States. A major reason the United States negotiated a $3.5 billion bridge loan with Mexico was to signal its satisfaction with the results of the 1988 election (in which Cuauhtémoc Cárdenas and the leftist National Democratic Front were defeated), and to assure the new Salinas administration of U.S. cooperation.

With Mexico attempting to promote "export substitution," that is, to diversify its exports away from oil and toward export manufactures, imports have been cut drastically. Also, the Mexicans have been attempting to achieve a favorable balance of trade (exports over imports). Economic interdependence translates into fewer U.S. exports to Mexico. For example, exports from Texas to Mexico were, in 1983, one-tenth of what they were in 1981. The failure of Mexico to purchase U.S. goods has resulted in the loss of jobs of hundreds of thousands of Americans—from feedstock farmers and Boeing employees to workers at Dow Chemical and the laborers at Caterpillar Corporation of Peoria. In turn, recession in the United States (as in the early 1980s) led to a decline in the ability of the United States to purchase Mexico's exports, as well as a decline in tourism in Mexico. Again, as noted before, the economic plight of Mexico's workers has led to an increase of illegal immigrants to the United States. Finally, it was not coincidental that cultivation of drug crops expanded greatly after the public debt crunched Latin America's traditional economies. The economic tragedies of the 1980s were expressed in the cocaine boom and the flow of cocaine (along with Mexican opium and marijuana) through Mexico to the United States.[44]

Opium production was legal during World War II, and by the late 1940s the Mexican heroin industry was well established. The opium trade became illegal after World War II. During the 1960s and 1970s, illegal harvesting of opium poppies was initially centered in the Golden Triangle area of the mountains of Sinaloa-Durango-Chihuahua. The import of opium and marijuana to the United States led the Nixon administration to create the Drug Enforcement Agency (DEA) in 1973. During the Echeverría years, money, supplies, fixed-wing aircraft, helicopters, and DEA agents and pilots flowed into Mexico to assist the drug eradication campaign known as Operation Condor.[45]

Initially, the heroin business was monopolized by Jaime Herrera Nevares, a Durango patriarch who controlled the "heroin trail" between El Paso and Chicago. Across the Sierra Madre in Sinaloa was Pedro Aviles Pérez, a gunslinger whose marijuana network extended from Culiacán to Mexicali and Tijuana. When federal authorities raided Sinaloa in the late 1970s and early 1980s, Aviles Pérez's apprentices moved the operation inland to Guadalajara. Under the Guadalajara mafia, the production of marijuana became big business, operating large plantations with modern equipment and fertilizers.[46]

When DEA officials successfully cut off the flow of cocaine through Miami in the early 1980s, the Colombian dealers sought new channels to the American market through Puerto Rico and northwestern Mexico. In Mexico, cocaine traffickers channeled their illegal goods through the established networks in which marijuana and heroin moved. The narcotics traffic made multimillionaires out of cartel members as narco-dollars and firearms in the United States were exchanged for brown heroin, marijuana, and cocaine (and a crystalline form of cocaine that can be smoked called "crack") from Mexico. Along with the narco-dollars and illegal trade came a growing problem of corruption of Mexico's public officials—politicians, high ranking policemen, and members of the military.[47]

Between 1982 and 1984, a combined force of DEA agents, the Mexican army, and members of the Mexican Federal Judicial Police (MFJP) carried out raids on marijuana fields in Zacatecas, San Luis Potosí, and Los Bufalos, Chihuahua. The success of these forays had two results: marijuana growers retreated from the exposed foothills to the inaccessible mountainous interior of the Tarahumara country of Chihuahua and Sinaloa; and to deter future raiders, the narco-cartel of Guadalajara planned a series of attacks on Americans, including one that led to the kidnapping, torture, and death of DEA agent Enrique Camarena outside of Guadalajara in February 1985.[48]

The death of Camarena and the torture of another DEA agent, along with the initial unwillingness of the Mexican authorities (abated by their CIA colleagues) to investigate the murder and harassment of agents, led to a public outcry in the U.S. Congress. In 1986, the congressional Mexico-bashing resulted in legislation that would enable the president to refuse financial aid (including favorable loans) to any country unwilling to actively pursue drug traders. Given Mexico's financial problems, this was a form of leverage that could not be dismissed.[49]

After the Camarena affair, Rafael Caro Quintero, a member of the Guadalajara drug cartel, was arrested and convicted for crimes related to drug trafficking. Consequently, nineteen people were charged with kidnapping, drug trafficking, and murder in connection with the Guadalajara slaying. Several hundred federal police officers were fired, and the major agencies were eventually dissolved.[50] But, the major dilemma remained: the problem was as much one of demand as supply. The street value of drugs in North American cities continued to decline, indicating that drugs were more available than ever to meet what was evidently an increasing demand (with the single exception of marijuana in which demand was declining while higher potency varieties were being grown in greenhouses, basements and attics, and national forests across the U.S.). Even when the cocaine supply was temporarily limited during the summer of 1990, the immediate result was not less drug use but more gun smuggling and gang fighting in inner cities in America.

By 1989, President Salinas de Gortari promised Mexican cooperation in the struggle against the drug lords, noting for the first time the national security concerns of Mexico in which narco-kings can field their own armies and threaten the integrity of the state, either through military actions or bribery of public officials. As the Manuel Buendía and Camarena incidents of 1984–85 revealed, Salinas's apprehensions about outlaw police and corruption in the highest level of government were all too real. In June 1989, José Antonio Zorrilla Pérez, ex-chief of the Federal Directorate of Security (DFS), was implicated in the 30 May 1984 murder of Mexico's leading journalist, Manuel Buendía. Buendía, whose daily column appeared on the front page of *Excelsior*, was shot and killed as he left his downtown office. He had been highly critical of the CIA and the DFS, an internal security political police force assigned to the Ministry of Interior and at that time under the direction of Zorrilla.[51]

Again, on 1 February 1990, Manual Ibarra-Herrera, the former head of the Mexican Federal Judicial Police (a secret police force under the Attorney General's office that specializes in espionage and arms and drug trafficking), was indicted by a federal grand jury in Los Angeles on charges of murder in the 1985 death of DEA agent Enrique "Kiki" Camarena. Whatever the constitutional issues and legal rights involved, the fact remained that the security forces were out of control and police corruption had penetrated the inner circle of the Mexican government. And corruption, among the police or other groups, was the major political issue of the 1980s, in the gubernatorial and senate elections of 1985 and 1986 and the presidential election of 1988.[52]

The state elections of 1986 in Chihuahua spread far beyond the boundaries of the state, becoming a kind of referendum on the legitimacy of the ruling party, PRI. The opposition National Action Party (PAN), a conservative group that had its origins in the late 1930s, was strong in Mexico's North, especially Chihuahua, and was split between a traditional, pro-clerical faction and the "neo-*panistas*" who favored free trade, private business, and political struggle. PAN's candidate for governor was Francisco Barrio, a *panista* victor in the earlier mayoral race in Ciudad Juárez. With the world's press in attendance, it was commonly believed that PRI would have to run a clean election and could not risk the bad publicity of a rigged contest. When the returns came in, PRI candidate Fernando Baeza had defeated the PAN candidate by 59.6 percent to 34.4 percent. PAN cried fraud and immediately sent its followers to the street to demonstrate against a contest allegedly characterized by pre-stuffed ballot boxes, police raids, and the expulsion of PAN poll watchers from their stations.[53]

This set the stage for the controversial presidential election of 1988. PRI's candidate was U.S.-educated Carlos Salinas de Gortari, a man who desired to continue the policies of the de la Madrid administration and represented the internationalist wing of the bourgeoisie, plus some of the newer technocrats in the party. The free market National Action Party, strong in the northern private sector and supported by the conservative Monterrey industrialist group, chose neo-*panista* Manuel Clouthier as its candidate. A coalition of leftist groups, including the Democratic Current that split from PRI, formed the National Democratic Front and its nominee was Cuauhtémoc Cárdenas, governor of Michoacán and son of the former president, Lázaro Cárdenas.[54]

Cárdenas represented the Echeverría wing of PRI, a faction that included traditional politicians, the PEMEX union leadership, the army, a part of the public sector bourgeoisie, and Mexico City's federal bureaucrats. The National Democratic Front opposed the IMF austerity plan, called for restoration of protectionism and state enterprise, and generally opposed the rule of Mexico by bankers. Cárdenas, the *priista* turned reformer, wanted a new and easier repayment schedule of Mexico's $100 billion foreign debt; and, with revenues spared from the debt, he urged government spending in the areas of social security, health, education, and housing, with additional credit for *campesino* farmers. His critics called his program socialistic and communistic, the intellectuals called it populism, but Cárdenas knew his father would call it revolutionary nationalism.[55]

The national results—50.4 percent for PRI, 31.2 percent for Cárdenas, and 17.1 percent for PAN—very likely understated the strength of the opposition. Although PRI won the election as expected, its strength was weak in the *panista* North, and almost nonexistent in the

Federal District. Mexico City, containing one-fourth of the nation's population and the traditional power center of the country, gave Cárdenas 49.22 percent of its vote, with another 21 percent going to PAN. *Chilangos* (people born in the Federal District), now allied with the reform wing of PRI, were opposing de la Madrid's program of federal decentralization: participants once again in the perennial urban-rural struggle that has characterized the history of Mexico City with its provinces.[56]

As Salinas, the young bureaucratic infighter who had previously been the minister of planning and budget, faced the future, he was confronted with a variety of dilemmas. How could he manage a society that was becoming more urbanized every year with a party that was losing its urban base? Could he further the democratization process and still expect PRI to maintain power? If, however, he continued the traditions of cooptation and repression, would not political instability and revolutionary nationalism be the result? And how could he implement the IMF austerity plan without either increasing social unrest or becoming a captive of the international bankers?

And what about the rightist challenge from PAN and the *panista* stronghold in northern Mexico? Was this not in microcosm a North-South rivalry that reflected the larger realities of the conflict between the United States and Mexico? Once again, the borderlands mirrored the differences between *ricos* and *pobres,* creditor and debtor, gringos and greasers. Much of Mexico's future depended on events in the Gran Chichimeca—that halfway house for a transit Mexico of poor workers, drug traffickers, *maquila* laborers, and other assorted Me*chicanos.*

9   Mexamerica

> The cities [such as El Paso and Ciudad Juárez or Calexico and Mexicali] couple like reluctant lovers in the night, embracing for fear that letting go could only be worse.
>
> Tom Miller, *On the Border*

That region of North America where the two societies of Mexico and the United States come together and overlap is known as Mexamerica. Historically, it has been a shifting cultural zone, known to the Aztecs as the "land of the uncivilized dogs," or what the Spaniards called the Gran Chichimeca. That area has been called the Spanish borderlands during the later colonial period, El Norte and La Frontera during Mexican days, and the American Southwest in recent history. Of course, what is southwest for Americans is northwest for Mexicans; thus the term the Greater Southwest from a U.S. perspective, or Greater Northwest from the Mexican view. The last term attempts at least to express the notion that this is a geographical region with some unity and reflects traits of both parent cultures. These traits are collectively known as "border culture," a reference to the twin societies that have developed along the 1,952 mile international boundary legally separating the United States from Mexico.[1]

As a geographical zone, Mexamerica defies precise definition. If one considers demography, then Mexamerica is much more than the series of twin cities that dot the border; much more than the populations that are found on both sides of the barbed-wire fence dividing Sonora from Arizona, or along the Río Grande (or *Río Bravo* as the Mexicans know it) boundary. If Mexico City is the civic center of the populated heart of southcentral Mexico, then Los Angeles (along with Tijuana-San Diego), having the second-largest collection of people of Mexican ancestry outside of Mexico City, is the urban nucleus of Mexamerica.

As historian Lester Langley notes, the northern limits of Mexamerica can be delineated with a "swathlike brushstroke" that meanders "across southern California, through central Arizona and New

173

Mexico," and then plunges "across the arid Texas west toward San Antonio on to the Gulf," with its southern boundary the populated regions of central Mexico. Again, and no more precisely, it is the borderlands of California, Arizona, New Mexico, and Texas in the United States, and the six Mexican states of Baja California, Sonora, Chihuahua, Coahuila, Nuevo León, and Tamaulipas. Indian Mexico presses from the south to remind Mexamerica of its cultural and historical roots; industrial America pushes from the north to shape its economic realities. The resulting conflicting forces have collided in the state of mind known as Mexamerica, a psychic reality reflected in the self-portrait by Mexican artist Frida Kahlo in her 1932 depiction of the borderlands (see figure 13).[2]

The popular culture of Mexamerica reflects this blending of Mexico and the United States. Mexican (Spanish) architecture is an important part of the heritage, mythology, and tourist industries of the southwestern United States. Anglo-Americans enjoy Taco Bells and other "Mexican" restaurants (such as the quick food eateries on the West Coast called Macheezmo Mouse Mexican cafes—trendy places that merge fitness madness with Disneyland atmospheres to serve up low-fat, low-cholesterol fajitas and burritos), while Mexamerica is a culinary region based on the cow culture of Mexico's northern plains, from wheat tortillas in Sonora and New Mexico to the chimichangas of Baja California and Tucson, Arizona. The cowboy as a popular image is in actuality a combination of the *ranchero* and *vaquero* of northern Mexico with the six shooter and Stetson hat of Texas fame. Together they have provided a *macho* tradition for both societies. Currently the *Texas Tornados*, a pop rock group of Texan and Mexican players, are putting Tex-Mex music on the map in the 1990s.[3]

Although the term Mexamerica suggests an area that has undergone an organic process of bilingualism, biculturalism, and binationalism, the interpenetration of American and Mexican social and economic influences within the border region has not been that complete. University of California professor Raúl A. Fernández has suggested that to call the borderlands area "Mexamerica" is to engage in hyperbole, and

Fig. 13. Frida Kahlo's *Self-Portrait on the Borderline Between Mexico and the United States*, 1932. Oil on sheet metal, 12 × 13. Collection of Mr. and Mrs. Manuel Reyero, New York. Photo courtesy of Christie's, New York.

he may be correct if by so doing a false impression of homogeneity is created. As Fernández notes, the region may be one in which the flow of tourists, goods, people, and information between the two countries has created a bicultural economy, but an economy characterized by dependency as well as interdependency and populated urban centers as well as isolated rural villages.

At least three distinct geographic and economic zones can be distinguished—northwest (Baja and Sonora), central (Chihuahua), and northeast (Tamaulipas). Each is tied to its U.S. counterpart but has few links to central Mexico and no integration to each other. These

enclaves do not suggest a uniform degree of acculturation throughout the borderlands, a condition as true for the pre-Columbian Gran
Chichimeca as it is today.[4]

Yet Mexamerica is a region of interboundary activity and intraborder
commotion—of hustle and tumult, legal and illegal. A description
of Mexamericana in the late 1980s would include a wide variety of
peoples. The proud Mixtec Indians—the Cloud People of Oaxaca—
speak no English or Spanish and work illegally in the fields of far-
away California so that their earnings can be sent to the village hall in
Tequixtepec to pay for the cost of a new town clock. An Iowa couple
living in a mobile home in the Harlingen Fig Tree retirement community are so-called Winter Texans who eat Burger Kings with jalapeños,
resent the Mexican influence of the area, employ a *chicana* maid, and
shop for French perfume in Reynosa. A Polish-American executive
from Buffalo, New York, who works for Trico Products Corporation
leaves his home in Brownsville every weekday morning to commute to
the company's assembly plant in Matamoros. A Mexican citizen living
in Ciudad Juárez commutes each workday to El Paso where he has a
full-time job in a department store and resident status in the United
States. A black bow hangs in the village hall in the central Mexican
farm town of Pabellon de Arteaga, home for seven of the eighteen
illegal aliens who suffocated in a boxcar in Sierra Blanca—victims of
the Texas sun. A Tarahumara Indian abandons his cave dwelling near
Yoquivo in the Chihuahua Sierra and travels several hundred miles
to Ojinaga to barter for axe heads made in the United States. A pilot
from Tucson delivers guns to his contacts in Sahuaripa, Sonora, fly-
ing on to the rugged Barranca de Cobre country of Chihuahua to
make a hemp pickup and returning with his load to a remote landing
strip near Hermanas, New Mexico. And cowboy capitalists in Phoenix
and Chihuahua City, an Anglo and a Mexican, form a partnership to
furnish northern Mexican cities with satellite dishes, made from components assembled in Tijuana, so that Casas Grandes entrepreneurs
can receive NFL football games on Sunday.[5]

These Mexamericana scenarios reflect the diversity and dependency of the region—the result of a several-hundred-year process in

which the Greater Southwest, as a peripheral area, has been incorporated into the world-economy. Incorporation began in pre-Columbian times when several trading centers developed in the Gran Chichimeca through which items were channeled, swapped, bartered, and exchanged between nomadic bands living on the basins, ranges, and plains of the Gran Chichimeca and the highly developed urban centers of Mesoamerica. When the Toltecs ruled Tula between A.D. 900 and 1250, their traders or *pochteca* furnished technology (for example, the making of copper bells or intensive agrarian techniques, including the raising of scarlet Macaws) to the trading towns (such as Snaketown, Chaco Canyon, Casas Grandes) in exchange for turquoise goods, salt, peyote, herbs, and slaves. Chaco Canyon and Casas Grandes not only transmitted to the core raw materials obtained from the nomads, they also manufactured weapons, ornaments, and tools that went to both the nomads and the Mesoamericans. After A.D. 1300, the trading centers declined, and Gran Chichimeca life became increasingly less complex. Before the Spaniards came in the sixteenth century, Athapaskan bison hunters appeared and made trade contacts with the surviving Pueblo villages around the Pecos basin. By the time of Spanish contact, there were over a hundred Pueblo villages, including today's Hopi, Zuni, and Acoma Pueblos.

Best known of the Athapaskans were the Navajo and Apache. The Navajos settled northwest of the Pueblo heartland and soon acquired Spanish traits from their Pueblo neighbors. They were particularly successful in making use of the livestock that the Spaniards had introduced into New Mexico. The Navajos developed a pastoral life, centered around sheep raising and agriculture—the women owned and cared for the sheep, while the men adopted the horse as a tool of transport and warfare. In the seventeenth century, the Plains Apaches also adopted the horse for hunting, raiding, fighting, and trading. The livestock herds of Spanish presidios and missions beckoned to the Apache. Slave raiding and buffalo hunting increased. More trade goods translated into an expanded need for Spanish wares by Pueblos to meet the increasing demands. The spiral of dependency had been started.

While the Apache was a raider, not all of the fighting was initiated by the Native Americans (in spite of what the Spanish sources
tell us). Slave raiding was done as much by the Spaniards as by the
Apache. Many of these Indian slaves, Apache and otherwise, were
forced to labor in mining camps, haciendas, and towns. Documents
clearly reveal that the relationship between the Athapaskans and the
Pueblos was essentially peaceful and commercial before the coming of
the Spaniards. The Plains Apaches provided many commercial items
for the Pueblos, including buffalo hides, antelope skins, and dried
meat. Most of the fighting that took place during the Pueblo revolt
of 1680–92 was done by the Pueblos, not the Navajos or Apaches.
Even after that date relations between Athapaskans, and Pueblos and
Pimas, remained good. It was the Spanish policy of divide and rule
that eventually destroyed these friendly relationships.[6]

The Comanches form an interesting contrast with the Apaches.
Throughout the eighteenth century, until the end of the French and
Indian Wars in 1763 (in which the French were expelled from North
America), the Comanches reigned as lords of the plains. Located on
the southern plains, with the French to the northeast and the Spaniards to the southwest, they were strategically situated between the
gun and horse frontiers. Armed with firearms and horses, they were
highly skilled fighters who soon dominated the raiding and trading of
the plains. Exchanging buffalo skins, captives, and guns for Spanish
horses, they established extensive trading connections in New Mexico.

While Comanche fortunes improved, some Pueblo villages were
abandoned. Meanwhile the Apaches were wedged between permanent Spanish settlements near Santa Fe to the north and Chihuahua
to the south. Suffering the results of a Spanish policy that encouraged Comanche wars on them, the Apaches were forced off the plains
and into the range and basin country of southern Arizona, Sonora,
and Nueva Vizcaya. Comanche intrusions made it difficult for the
Apache to either acquire guns from French traders or horses from
Spanish merchants. As conditions worsened, many Apaches were
used as forced labor in the mines, factories, and farms of northern
New Spain. Remaining Apaches engaged in counter-raiding against

Spaniards, Pueblos, Comanches, and other indigenous groups. An era of endemic warfare ensued.

At the end of the Spanish period, between 1780 and 1820, the region of the Gran Chichimeca changed from a marginal periphery to a dependent periphery, with trading relationships no longer based on kinship ties but unequal exchange—that is, one trading partner (the Spanish) taking advantage of disparate values for some product. Spain initiated what Eric Wolf calls an advanced tributary mode of production. Its most telling feature was the use of the army (soldiers and presidios) and the church (the policy of *congregación*) to coerce and control the indigenous population.

Spain's so-called Bourbon reforms lowered the costs of defense and administration on the frontier and brought peace to the region. This was the result of a variety of policies and practices, including the creation of "a fund for allies" that induced peaceful behavior from the nomads with bribes of gifts, rations, liquor, and low-quality weapons for hunting; an alliance with Comanches that led to the military reduction of the Apaches, and, in general, a "divide-and-rule" policy that created Spanish allies who suppressed other nomads and increased Spanish control over all Native Americans; and the "tribalization" of Indian groups, or, the creation of political centralization so that a variety of bands were forced to unite under a *cacique* who would deal with the Spanish.

The initiation of peace accelerated trade. From Chihuahua came tools, arms, fabrics, boots, clothing, shoes, chocolate, tobacco, sugar, and liquors; from New Mexico came sheep, raw wool, hides (antelope, buffalo, deer), salt, pine nuts, El Paso brandy, and captives. Many Native American bands were destroyed; some, such as the Comanche, were tribalized and subdued. New Mexico became increasingly dependent on old Mexico, a periphery of a periphery.

During the Mexican period, from 1820 to 1845, the Gran Chichimeca underwent a transition from a dependent fringe to a full-blown periphery. Initially, the influence of Mexico City was weak, which allowed the region to gradually become economically incorporated into the developing U.S. economy. The initiation of trade between

Independence, Missouri, and Santa Fe, New Mexico (the Santa Fe Trail), meant that manufactured articles (such as cotton clothing) from the United States would eventually displace productive goods from Chihuahua. Mules and specie poured out of Mexico to pay for the new wares coming in from Missouri.

With the conclusion of the Mexican-American War, the northern half of Mexico was transformed into the vital expanding economy of the United States. Indigenous trade came to an end, Indian bands were destroyed or concentrated into reservations, and the practice of raiding and endemic warfare ceased. The Comanche Indians were forced by 1867 to settle in a small part of the Indian Territory (Oklahoma); the Apaches were destroyed by 1886 when Geronimo was captured. Nomadism ended with the Native American coming under the jurisdiction of the state—first American, and later, Mexican (during the *porfiriato*). By 1900, the Mexican frontier had been transformed into a border, politically influenced by the Mexican state but economically dependent on the United States. The Gran Chichimeca was fully incorporated into the capitalist market of the United States, and Mexamerica became the meeting ground between American capital and Mexican labor.[7]

Mexamerica is the home of several ethnic groups. The majority population on the U.S. side is Anglo (so-called whites for census purposes). As of 1980, whites outnumbered nonwhites by 4:1 in Arizona, 3:1 in California, and 2:1 in Texas. However, in New Mexico the number of Anglos to non-Anglos (Hispanics, blacks, and Native Americans) in 1980 was 695,203 Anglos to 604,765 non-Anglos, or about a 1.2:1 ratio. When all of California is considered, there are about 28 million Anglos in the border states. Asians, especially Chinese, play an important role in the history of California and Sonora. California is also home to large numbers of people of Japanese and Filipino ancestry. In 1980, blacks were 7 percent of the population of California, and 12 percent of the inhabitants of Texas (about 1.7 million in each state).

By 1990, it was estimated that there were 22.4 million Americans of Hispanic background in the United States, with California and Texas ranking first and second respectively in the United States in the size of their Hispanic populations. Of the total Hispanic population in the United States, 33.9 percent reside in California and 21.3 percent live in Texas. These 22.4 million Hispanics are a significant increase over the 14.6 million persons who listed themselves as Hispanics in the 1980 census. The growth in the last decade is due to increased birth rates, lower death rates, and immigration.

As for Native Americans, 40 percent of the U.S. Native American population (1,361,869 in 1980; nearly 2 million by 1990) live in the four border states, with the Navajo nation being the largest group. On the other side of the international boundary, the Mexican borderlands has some of the smallest indigenous-speaking populations in the country, with Tamaulipas, Nuevo León, and Coahuila having less than 1 percent native speakers. The largest group of Native Americans in Mexamerica, second only to the Navajo, are the Tarahumara of Chihuahua (over 50,000).

Finally, of a total Mexican population of 66.8 million in 1980, the borderlands region of Mexico had a population of 10.7 million. When undocumented migrants are factored in, there are probably as many as 20 million (plus or minus) speakers of Spanish in Mexamerica and another 20 million non-Hispanic inhabitants (considering only southern California as part of Mexamerica). The recent past has witnessed unprecedented growth. Since 1970, the metropolitan areas on the U.S. side of the boundary have increased three times more rapidly than the United States as a whole, as workers fled the Great Lakes to ride the Sun Belt's golden elevator of opportunity. Meanwhile, the Mexican *municipios* along the border have grown faster than Mexico's total population for several decades.[8]

Of all the groups in Mexamerica, Indians find themselves on the bottom of the social ladder, whether in the American Southwest or the Mexican border area. When the Treaty of Guadalupe Hidalgo was signed in 1848, Native Americans inhabiting the border area were required by the new rules to refrain from crossing a political line that had little or no meaning to them. While most tribes were reduced, many were destroyed by the encroachments of white men pushing west and brown men pushing north. Two groups were able to use the

boundary to their advantage: many Yaquis fled from Mexican exploitation in Sonora to refuges in Arizona, while the Kickapoos were able
to find deliverance from their Texas persecutors by establishing themselves across the boundary in Coahuila at their Nacimiento colony. Yet
both peoples today live at the edge of society.[9]

As a people who successfully resisted assimilation into the majority
"white" culture, the Yaqui of Sonora exceeded all others. Yaqui resistance to the *yoris*, the white men, and to *yori* domination followed
three patterns—accommodation, rebellion, and incorporation into a
larger political movement. Accommodation has occurred twice in their
history: first, was the long period in the sixteenth and seventeenth
centuries when they were missionized and under Jesuit tutelage; the
second came after 1940 and continues to this day. When the Jesuits
"reduced" the eighty widely scattered hamlets of the Yaquis to eight
pueblos, they consolidated and redefined Yaqui cultural pride. The
Yaqui developed an allegiance to the missionaries, who in turn protected them from Spanish outsiders. During this period, the Yaquis became economically self-sufficient, working on communal lands, producing the new crops of wheat and cotton, and developing a new
ranching industry, and, at times, loaning their labor to the mining
camps. Even when the Jesuits were expelled in 1767, the Yaquis were
able to maintain their independence. By contrast, Yaqui acquiescence
to the Mexican state today—working and living on a reduced reserve
of land—has been the result of a forced submission.[10]

The second type of Yaqui response was rebellion. Their first autonomous rebellion was the 1740 uprising, aided in part by their southern
neighbors, the Mayos. In 1825, Juan Banderas cleared the Yaqui valley
as a protest against levies of troops and produce. Banderas's call for
a separate Indian republic came close to realization when José María
Leyva Cajeme organized and governed a Yaqui state-within-a-state
from 1875 until his death in 1886. During the *porfiriato* (1876–1911),
the Yaquis entered the final phase of rebellion by developing the tactics of guerrilla warfare. The state responded by sending many Yaquis
into virtual slavery on the henequén plantations of the Yucatán. Many
escaped the terrors of captivity by fleeing to Arizona.[11]

Finally, after 1910, the Yaquis were incorporated into the Mexican nation because of the Mexican Revolution. They became national revolutionaries, especially gaining fame as the fierce fighters of Alvaro Obregón and Adolfo de la Huerta. Unfortunately for the Yaqui, the goals of the Mexican Revolution were modernization and nationalism, not autonomy for traditional groups. Today they are no more indispensable than other peasant groups, even though they still maintain their identity.[12]

As for the Kickapoos, in the seventeenth century they were an Algonquian-speaking group that lived around lower Michigan, between Lake Michigan and Lake Erie. They had been driven there by the Iroquois and other eastern Native Americans. In the eighteenth century, they were at times allies, and on other occasions enemies, of the French, British, and Americans. During the French and Indian Wars, the Kickapoos defended the Ohio-Mississippi perimeter of New France and allied themselves with the Ottawa Indian leader Pontiac. They later switched their allegiance to the British, and after 1779, the Americans. However, during the War of 1812, they were arrayed with the British and the Shawnee chief Tecumseh against the Americans. Throughout this period, the Kickapoos followed fur trappers of various nationalities, and the result of forced movements, broken treaties, and continuous warfare was fragmentation and dispersal.[13]

Some of the bands moved to the Osage River in Missouri, others went to eastern Illinois, while still others went on to Arkansas and Texas-Coahuila. When the Texans gained their independence from Mexico, the Kickapoo were again dispersed because of the Texans's fear that they would side with the Mexicans to regain their lost territory. By 1864, a contingent of Kickapoos had arrived in Mexico from Oklahoma to occupy land abandoned by the Seminoles. This was the Hacienda El Nacimiento, their current home. Between 1865 and 1885, the Mexican Kickapoos raided Texas ranches for mules and horses.[14]

During the Mexican Revolution, the Kickapoo fought with Victoriano Huerta, thereby earning the enmity of Venustiano Carranza and his forces. Hiding out in the sierra at night, they were not able to return to their tranquil existence until 1920.[15] In the mid-1980s a small band of Kickapoos made their home beneath the International Bridge connecting Eagle Pass, Texas, and Piedras Negras, Coahuila.[16] What had originally been an eastern woodlands Native American was now a permanent member of the Club de Chichimeca.

A current trend is illustrated by the fifty thousand Tarahumaras who live today in the canyon valleys, foothills, and eastern plains of the Sierra Madre Occidental of Chihuahua, an important remnant of the semiagricultural people who inhabited this area in the sixteenth century. Originally, like the Navajos, their lands lacked utility for outsiders. The early intrusions by Spanish miners, farmers, ranchers, and missionaries were met by violence and passive resistance. Eventually, the Tamahumaras adapted the goat to their agriculture ("a gift of the gods, not the Spaniards") and withdrew to the mountain interior to find more fertile lands and to escape the Spaniard. The Jesuit reductions were not completely successful in the Sierra Tarahumar, and the Jesuits themselves were expelled from New Spain after 1767. During the late eighteenth and early nineteenth centuries, Spanish and Mexican resources were too limited for frontier activity in the Sierra, and therefore, the Tarahumara regained some lost autonomy over their lives.[17]

The modernization of the twentieth century has witnessed a new mining era, the development of the railroad, and a forestry industry that has pushed the Tarahumara into marginal lands insufficient for adequate maize production. Being forced to supplement their agricultural incomes, the Tarahumara have left the Sierra to work for non-Indians. Those who remain have been pushed further west and south with the best lands being occupied by *mestizos* and outsiders. Tarahumaras, who in 1900 were equal in numbers to outsiders, are now outnumbered by *mestizos* more than six to one. The Tarahumara currently suffer from a 60 percent infant mortality rate, and more than four-fifths of them have tuberculosis. They are indeed the new poor of the Gran Chichimeca.[18]

Borderland Mexican Americans (also known as Latinos in California, Hispanos in New Mexico, and Chicanos elsewhere) face the dilemma of living in a micro-society in which the political and economic forces are controlled by Anglos; but their cultural, religious, and spiritual life (not to mention the realities of their Native American past) bind them to Mexico. Their nineteenth-century heritage has been one of being foreigners in their native land, where Anglos and Mexican Americans have clashed over property rights, religious freedom, and personal liberty, with the Mexican American, more often than not, coming out on the short end. This conflict has led to eruptions of violence, with the Chicano suffering discrimination, harassment, land invasion, rape, theft, murder, and lynching (in spite of the promises of the Treaty of Guadalupe Hidalgo). On several occasions, Hispanics have fled the United States for the safety of Mexico, the most recent and best known movement being the expatriation of over a half-million Mexicans during the Great Depression. Not all Chicanos are what Octavio Paz calls *pachucos*—people without a culture— but many have identity problems, not knowing if they should identify with the majority Anglo culture or their "hermanos y hermanas" south of the border.[19]

The legacy of a militarily superior English-speaking society imposing an international boundary over what had been a part of Mexico continues today. Language is one barometer of the changing Mexican-American reality. Traditionally, many Chicanos were punished for speaking Spanish in the public schools, with officials inflicting sanctions on Spanish speakers. In the process many Mexican Americans became ashamed to identify with either Mexico today or their Spanish-speaking past. The advent of bilingual education in the 1970s, an event bespeaking a certain degree of enlightenment, was opposed by many members of the Anglo majority. Part of the opposition came in the form of English-only groups who moved to make English the official language in several states.[20]

One association clustered around former Senator S. I. Hayakawa from California who succeeded in 1986 in making English the official language of that state. Like Hayakawa, many of the English-only crowd believed a conspiracy was afoot to divide the country into a bilingual and bicultural society. Yet, as a recent Rand Corporation study indicates, 95 percent of the children of Mexican immigrants can speak

English, and by the second generation more than half can speak *only* English. And perhaps, as Carlos Fuentes notes, when you get a proposition to make the English language the official language, it means one thing—"that English is no longer the official language of the state of California."²¹

Chicano ambivalence is increased when borderland Mexican Americans visit Mexico unable to converse in Spanish or at best speaking "Spanglish," a mixture of Spanish and English. Many learn to their horror that most Mexicans consider them culturally corrupt—show-offs who act superior with their flashy clothes and cars, imitating the worst features of American materialistic society, while either not speaking the language of the mother country or speaking a mongrel-ized version.²²

For their part, Chicanos also have inconsistent attitudes about Mexico and its sons and daughters (Mexican immigrants). Many, especially in working-class ranks, although sympathetic to the Mexican poor, see Mexican migrants as unwanted rivals and support those Anglos who want to increase quotas and employer sanctions. Many Chicanos, while looking south of the border in search for cultural pride, share the Anglo contempt for the corruption of the Mexican government and its unwillingness or inability to solve its many economic and social ills. This ambivalence in the Chicano community is in part generational, with first generation Mexicans attached to Mexico, the second generation seeking acculturation and integration into the majority culture, and a third generation stressing ethnic revival. Likewise, the Mexican government has shown its own ambivalence in its attitudes and relations with the Chicano community by seeking and opposing the aid of Chicanos in its attempt to influence U.S. policy toward Mexico.²³

Whatever the result of this 160-year-history of Chicano-Mexicano-Anglo relations, the future would appear to be one of both apprehension and hope for Anglos and Mexican Americans. One estimate suggests that in twenty years, at the current rate of growth, people of color (yellow, black, and brown) will be in the majority in California. The same estimate suggests that minorities will be the majority in the United States within fifty years. Whether these projections are correct or not, it is obvious that a major issue for all Americans will be whether the future of America's minorities will be one of repression or accommodation.

A third major group living in Mexamerica are those Mexican border-landers who dwell south of the international boundary in the Mexican North, the *norteños* or *fronterizos*. Unlike the Mexican American population in the United States, Mexico's North has few American Mexicans apart from assorted wealthy entrepreneurs who have "californicated" the Baja and Sonora, and those few Mormons who have sought Jehovah in Chihuahua (in 1960 only sixty thousand persons of U.S. birth lived in Mexico's six border states). Yet, the cultural and economic influence of the United States on the Mexican North is far greater than that of Mexico on Anglos in the American Southwest (apart from New Mexico). The dominance of the North American economy has made the Mexican North a distinctive region of Mexico, so much so that Mexicans from the interior refer to the region as *pocholandia* or *gringolandia* (a cheap imitation of the United States). The *pocho*, or northerner, is, as Américo Paredes says, "a poor soul wedged between the pyramid and the skyscraper." [24]

Generally speaking, the *norteño* lives in a relatively autonomous region of Mexico. Traditionally, remoteness from the central government has fostered regionalism and independence. The degree of autonomy has waxed and waned over the years, with the power relationship of the provinces to the central government changing over time. The first northern resurgence began in the nineteenth century during the wars of independence (1810) and ended with the modernization of the state by Porfirio Díaz (after 1876). The chaos and violence of the Mexican Revolution (1910–23) witnessed a second era in the development of *norteño* particularism, with the rise of the North and the successful conquest of the Mexican state by *norteños*. Paradoxically, the Sonoran dynasty, which created a national party system and rebuilt the state bureaucracy, succeeded in returning power to Mexico City. Finally, the end of the Mexican "miracle" and the financial problems of the 1980s has led to another period of political and economic revival in the Mexican North today.[25]

The political awakening is evidenced in the activities of the conservative Partido Acción Nacional (PAN). In 1983, PRI's dominance was challenged when PAN won the mayorships in Ciudad Juárez, Chihuahua City, and Durango. The next years saw PAN victories in congressional races throughout Chihuahua. Only PRI's blatantly fraudulent practices prevented PAN from claiming governorships in Nuevo León, Sonora, and Chihuahua in the mid-1980s.[26]

The general economic upswing in the North is confirmed by a growing mining industry, a vibrant cattle sector, a booming drug industry (legal and illegal), increased tourism, a swelling auto parts business, and expanding trade in winter vegetables. Leading the way, of course, is the *maquiladora* program of border industries. All of this activity has led to an increased dependency on the United States, from the "culture of sin" of brothels, gambling houses, and bars that was exported to the Mexican border during a period of reform and prohibition in the United States, to the population growth of Tijuana and Ciudad Juárez, which has been fostered by the American desire for cheap labor. (Tijuana is the gate city for illegal aliens to enter the United States, while Ciudad Juárez is the leading *maquila* site.) In any case, northern particularism is a constant reality and a concern for PRI and the powers in Mexico City.[27]

The relative wealth of the people of Mexamerica is a subject of much controversy, with many U.S. governors of border states arguing that the borderlands constitute a drain on their overall economies, even though there is no direct evidence for this contention.[28] The area is unique in that nowhere in the community of nations is there a boundary separating two nations with a greater degree of economic disparity than that which exists between the United States and Mexico. As for the border towns, U.S. border cities are generally less prosperous economically than comparable non-border cities. The Texas regions (especially Starr county) and the New Mexico counties tied to El Paso have relatively low levels of per capita income. San Diego, on the other hand, a border city not symbiotically tied to Mexico, has a higher per capita income than the national average. As for the Mexican border cities, they tend to have higher per capita incomes and greater economic productivity than comparable interior cities. Yet the tremendous redistribution of wealth during the 1980s in the United States and Mexico, due to Reaganomics, supply-side economics, trickle-down theory, IMF austerity thinking, and monetary devaluations, has resulted in relatively less money for many and greater affluence for few, in and out of the border region. *Maquila* workers in particular have suffered a decline in real standards during the last few years, while the transnational corporations have increased their profits substantially.[29]

Until 1982, Mexico's North was undergoing accelerated growth as an industrial and agribusiness zone. A long period of overvaluation of the Mexican peso, added to the oil bonanza, led to a closer interaction of the two border economies. The overvalued peso allowed border residents to have increasing access to U.S. commodities, while U.S. border businesses sought to service more oil-rich Mexican consumers. Meanwhile, Mexican agriculture was transformed after World War II, so that garbanzos, winter vegetables (especially tomatoes), cotton, citrus crops, grapes, and strawberries were produced with the assistance of the federal irrigation program and grown mainly to serve U.S. markets for fresh produce and to provide inputs to the agribusiness sector.[30]

This kind of growth was dependent on markets and capital inputs from the United States. Granted some local capital was accumulated with Mexican businessmen owning a few *maquilas,* modern farms, and cattle ranches; *maquila* facilitators (what Leslie Sklair calls the "comprador bourgeoisie"—Mexican bankers, lawyers, accountants, politicians, and land developers) got wealthy; and there has been a general upgrading of personnel in *maquila* management ranks. Yet most *maquilas* were foreign owned and managed. And while they expanded the industrial employment base in border cities in Mexico, they usually had no connections with other Mexican firms. In addition, the large assembly plants employ a semi-skilled transitory pool of cheap, female laborers who, until the devaluation of 1982, spent a high proportion of their earnings on the U.S. side of the border.[31]

The various border subregions mentioned above had few backward linkages with the productive activities of central Mexico and no integration among themselves. The pattern of regional development in the United States between 1950 and 1990 was the most important force affecting the changes between the Mexican subregions: for example, the contrast between the manufacturing city of Tijuana, influenced by metropolitan Los Angeles, and the less developed cities of Mier and Reynosa across from South Texas and far from populated centers. (In Texas growth has been in the capital intensive oil fields in the north away from the border.) The result has been to increase the dependency of the Mexican border area on the United States, rather than to integrate it more closely with the Mexican economy.[32]

In the mid-1980s, there were about seven hundred *maquiladoras* that employed over seventy-seven thousand people scattered along the two thousand mile border with the United States, with about one-fourth of them in Ciudad Juárez, and large numbers located in Tijuana, Mexicali, and Matamoros. These are mostly foreign-owned factories that import materials and components duty free to Mexican assembly plants and, until recently, marketed their assembled parts outside of Mexico. Most are American-owned industries with labor-intensive assembly plants in Mexico. For example: Trico Products Corporation of Buffalo, New York, assembles windshield wipers in Matamoros; Louisiana-Pacific Co. takes redwoods from northern California and mills them in El Sauzal, between Tijuana and Ensenada; Fisher-Price assembles toys in Tijuana, Matamoros, and Acuña; Buffalo China casts tea pots and sugar bowls in Ciudad Juárez; Zenith erects television sets in Reynosa and Matamoros.[33]

Interestingly, not all foreign enterprises are American. For example, Hitachi, the electronics company, taking advantage of loopholes in the U.S. trade laws, is one of several dozen Japanese companies operating *maquiladoras* in Tijuana. There are also border assembly plants owned by Mexicans, as well as factories formed around Mexican labor cooperatives.[34]

Whether the *maquiladoras* have a positive or negative effect on the total Mexican economy is difficult to access. After a careful study of the industry, Leslie Sklair concludes that, while the *maquila* strategy of development has achieved a measure of success, it can really only be understood in a global context and from that point of view, "unless the Mexican government and the TNCs can work out ways of transforming it into a more potent instrument for the development of Mexico and the advancement of its people, Mexico is better off without it."[35] On the other hand, El Paso scholar Ellwyn R. Stoddard concludes that most of the negative images of the industry are due to popular stereotypes mostly inaccurate, noting that "multinational corporation maquiladoras provide more extra-wage benefits, a better workplace (safety and comfort), and better worker relationships than do Mexican-owned factories or those formed around labor cooperatives."[36]

In the larger context of Mexican economic development, the *maquiladoras* are only one dimension of the Mexican program. Like other parts of the economy and the Mexican North in general, they are dependent on the U.S. market for capital inputs and product distribution. As for some of the specific criticisms of the program, many of the newer plants are excellent examples of good working environments. For instance, Trico's assembly plant in Matamoros has excellent health, educational, and recreational facilities; air conditioning; bright-colored walls; a modern assembly plant; and an up-to-date water refinery works.[37]

Many of the *maquilas* in Tijuana, Mexicali, Nuevo Laredo and Ciudad Juárez, taking advantage of Mexico's cheap labor and lax enforcement of environmental laws, exploit female workers and inundate with hazardous chemicals and untreated sewage the Tijuana River, the New River (stretching 80 miles from Mexicali into the Imperial Valley of California), and the Río Grande. Most have replaced U.S. workers with cheap Mexican labor, with resulting unemployment and plant closings in the United States. Perhaps the *maquiladora* issue is not one of "calamity or catalyst?" as Stoddard frames it, but "calamity and catalyst."[38]

A catalog of social problems can be constructed for the border area, mostly the result of the tremendous population growth of the last thirty years. Not only have Mexican border cities been growing twice as fast as their U.S. twins, but 19 percent of the 1980 population of the six Mexican border states was in the ten border cities. Of the twin cities with the largest populations along the boundary, eight of them had a total population of 3.6 million in 1980, with the largest twin city being Tijuana-San Diego with 1.3 million persons (36 percent of the total), and Ciudad Juárez-El Paso in second place with about one million inhabitants (27 percent of the total). The adjacent cities form in many ways a binational metropolitan zone, especially in the larger urban zones of Texas and Chihuahua-Tamaulipas (Ciudad Juárez-El Paso or Matamoros-Brownsville).[39]

Unsettled economic conditions in the interior have pushed Mexicans to the border, attracted by employment opportunities in the north and job possibilities and higher salaries of the American Southwest. Migration to border communities (and high birth rates and low death rates) has resulted in urban crowding and its corollary: the social problems of crime, poverty, underemployment, congestion, air pollution, diminishing water resources in an arid zone, insufficient housing, meager health services, inadequate communications, a poor transportation network, and limited waste management facilities. As binational metropolitan zones, these problems, caused by an expanding population with limited resources, can only be solved by national and, at times, international authorities. However, national leaders more often than not look at these problems as matters to be solved by regional politicians and local governments.[40]

One problem somewhat peculiar to the border culture is the phenomenon of the border underworld. The laws of unequal exchange apply with a vengeance to an area intersected by an international boundary, which, in turn, dictates differences in price and currency structures between the United States and Mexico, generally dividing a rich nation from a poor one. These disparities of wealth and income create many opportunities for crime and illicit exchange in a network that includes legitimate as well as illegitimate businesses.[41]

Many of these exchanges are conducted by organized crime groups with kinship ties to old border trading families that possess power and legitimacy in their communities. Examples of such organized crime syndicates would be the Syrian-Lebanese gang in El Paso, or the Herrera family of Durango.[42]

Other underworld characters include narcotics traffickers, cargo transporters (pilots and truck drivers), contractors (middlemen who link the underworld with the legitimate world), and salaried employees who carry the contraband across borders. The upperworld players include financiers (bankers, businessmen, etc.) who launder money and provide capital to the underworld elites, and attorneys, judges, politicians, and law enforcement officials whose support is rewarded by the border underworld. A cross-border service economy of contraband smuggling has evolved in which as much as one-fifth of all border trade may be in contraband goods.[43]

From the United States to Mexico comes firearms, stolen cars and trucks, pornography, VCRs, color TVs, electronics equipment, laundered money, and a host of unregulated manufactures. From Mexico *coyotes* move their human contraband (illegal aliens) northward, while *traficantes* and their "mules" (teenagers hired by the traffickers) smuggle cocaine, marijuana, and heroin across the border into the United States. Mexican contraband ranges from relatively innocent items like pharmaceutical drugs, cigarettes, and exotic birds to prostitutes, unregulated liquor and drugs, cattle, and counterfeit currency.[44]

Despite these difficulties, it would appear that the solution for Mexico's problems lies outside of Mexico in the global economy. Unlike the fictionalized Mexamerica of Carlos Fuentes's new novel *Christopher Unborn* (in which Mexamerica is an independent nation thriving on its own), the real Mexamerica is intricately connected with Mexico and the United States, and maybe even all of North America. Recent reforms of the Salinas administration have been designed to win the favor of the Mexican North—especially the reduction of subsidies to industry, privatization of state-owned property, promotion of free trade, and rapprochement with the Catholic church. All of these measures are well received in the north. In addition, in a break with Mexico's traditional policy of economic nationalism, Mr. Salinas is promoting negotiations for a free-trade agreement with the United States in the form of a North American Free Trade Agreement (NAFTA).[45]

The results of economic globalization are in, and global trading blocs are becoming a reality in the form of the multination European Economic Community and the Japanese-led Pacific Rim Alliance of commercial partners. With the unification of Germany absorbing that country's energy and capital, and the decline of communism in eastern Europe presenting Mexico with a whole new set of rivals for global dollars, Mexico has found itself desperate to attract foreign investors. Logic dictates that a North American Common Market of Mexico, Canada, and the United States would enable North America to compete with the other blocs, while allowing Mexico to solve many of its development problems.[46]

In theory, NAFTA would unite a population of over 360 million people in a $7 trillion economy and create a free-trade zone independent of European and Asian competitors. The proposal would unite population-poor and resource-rich Canada with population- and oil-rich Mexico (which is also technology- and investment-poor) with the technology- and investment-rich, but population-poor, United States. Salinas and his team of American-educated (Harvard, Yale, MIT, and Stanford) advisers speculate that U.S. capital would be attracted to Mexico to act as a platform for launching trade to the U.S. market. American capital would also solve the illegal alien problem by creating in Mexico a domestic industrial base that would attract Mexicans to Mexico, not the United States. While Canada and the United States would benefit from cheap labor and oil, Mexico would attract the capital it needs to develop the Mexican economy.[47] Needless to say, the idea of NACM has many critics, mostly intellectuals, labor leaders, and nationalists in Canada, Mexico, and the United States.[48]

So it is in the Gran Chichimeca, a place that integrated trade and people during the pre-Columbian past. In the colonial period, the

Gran Chichimeca evolved as a frontier zone remote from, yet partially dependent on, Mexico City, the viceroyalty of New Spain, and north-western Europe. During the nineteenth century the dependency of the borderlands on the expanding economy of the United States was obvious, and today, perhaps the North American market. The current phenomenon of the *maquiladora* reflects the reality of a global market and that the destiny of Mexamerica, Mexico, and the United States are, for good or ill, interwoven with the ecology of the world and the economy of the globe.

Epilogue: The Rediscovery of Mexico

> "These Gringos are terrible people," says the first Mexican—
> "cheaters, liars, and robbers."
> "Sure, *compadre*," says the second Mexican, "Look what they did
> in 1846. They took half our national territory."
> "Yes, *compadre*," says the first, "and the half with all the paved
> roads."
>
> The compadre story as retold by Américo Paredes

Every half century or so, New Yorkers rediscover Mexico. In 1940, all things Mexican were the rage. The Museum of Modern Art, under the direction of Nelson A. Rockefeller, hosted "Twenty Centuries of Mexican Art," an exhibition of 5,000 selections of ancient and modern Mexican works. A calendar of cultural and social events accompanied the exhibit, from a concert by Carlos Chávez and his orchestra to "Mexico-theme" museum parties featuring such guests as Greta Garbo and Georgia O'Keeffe. Even Macy's got into the act with its own show of contemporary Mexican painting. Much of Europe was already at war, and North Americans, for security reasons, needed the friendship of their hemispheric neighbors. The celebration of Mexican culture by New Yorkers was one token of that friendship.[1]

As in 1940, the early 1990s witnessed another revival of Mexican culture and arts in New York City. On 10 October 1990 the Metropolitan Museum of Art opened an exhibition entitled "Mexico: Splendors of Thirty Centuries," featuring works of Mayan and Aztecan sculpture, early postconquest manuscripts, popular religious and devotional paintings, and modern art ranging from 1000 B.C. to A.D. 1950. During the same period there were exhibits at thirty other New York museums, galleries, and cultural institutions that surveyed three thousand years of Mexican art, including shows at the National Academy, the Americas Society, the Museo del Barrio, and the IBM Gallery of Science and Art.[2]

During the same month as the "Mexico" exhibition, Octavio Paz, a member of the Mexican advisory committee to the Metropolitan (who was in New York City to assist the Metropolitan), received the Nobel Prize in Literature proving that Mexico's high culture was being recognized on all fronts.

The Metropolitan show did indeed exhibit several Mexican splendors. Juxtaposing a *chacmool* from Chichén-Itzá with one from Tenochtitlán strikingly revealed the Mexican tendency to elaborate on previous art forms. Several works from colonial Mexico testified to the blending of Indian and European ideas, materials, and techniques; for example: the atrial cross from Tepeyac, a column base with earth monster relief, the cornstalk-paste sculpture of a crucified Christ, a gilded Virgin of Guadalupe of oil and mother-of-pearl inlays, and the depictions of racial mixtures reflected in Miguel Cabrera's eighteenth-century oil paintings. Modern art reflected the subject of *indigenismo*, as in Diego Rivera's *Tortilla Maker*, as well as the truly dramatic and universal themes of lost salvation and human solitude a la José Clemente Orozco's *Christ Destroying His Cross* and Frida Kahlo's *Self-Portrait with Monkeys*.[3]

Even though Mexico was alive once again in the minds of the literati, one must wonder about the accuracy of the Mexican image that was being portrayed. The Metropolitan exhibit followed a rather safe scheme, not unlike the 1940 show, depicting the grandeur and continuity of the Mexican tradition. Yet, for all of its immensity, the exhibit said nothing about the contemporary world of Mexico, or the contributions of anonymous folk artists over the centuries.[4] A display that was the brainchild of Emilio Azcarraga, the chairman of Mexico's Televisa network, and the Friends of the Arts of Mexico based in Los Angeles that had the backing of president Carlos Salinas of Mexico and the Ministry of Tourism and was produced by the cultural aristocracy of New York City could not help but present the elitist view of Mexico—an honest and apolitical, but partial, view of reality.[5]

Nothing in the show spoke of the current realities of Mexico: the political tragedy of Tlatelolco; the financial crisis of 1982; the governmental corruption of the mid-1980s; the ecological disasters, from the earthquake damage of 1985 to the air pollution of contemporary Mexico City; the deaths of Manuel Buendia and "Kiki" Camarena; or the endless drug wars and vigilante justice of the army and police.

Nowhere could be found the papier-mâché skulls of Jaime Garza from Matamoros, a border craftsman whose surrealistic folk art is not recognized by the Mexico City art community that considers *norteño* culture irretrievably *pocho*. The ceramics of Olivia Domínguez Renteria from Mata Ortiz, Chihuahua, near Casas Grandes, were missing, as was the folk art of potter María Victoria, a Tarahumara woman from Raramuchi, near San Ignacio. And what would be more *típico* than a Judas effigy from Guerrero in which Ronald Reagan was Judas! Of course, that was not in the exhibit.[6]

The American interest in things Mexican was in part a reflection of the United States' need for Mexican oil and closer trade ties with Mexico and Canada. With the U.S.-trained advisers of Salinas advocating a modernization program that glorified the privatization of property and bourgeois democracy, it was natural that the American response would be warm and supportive of Mexico. As for Mexico, the country struggled with an "image problem" in the U.S. due to a notorious history of drugs and corruption, and in 1990 desired a free trade pact and more American capital and tourists as well. It made good diplomatic sense to use the show to help improve Mexico's image and pave the way for a new alliance.[7]

Thus, the Metropolitan exhibit not only celebrated Mexican art history and identity but also testified to the fusion of interests of Reagan-Bush elites in the U.S. with *priista* technocrats in Mexico. Unfortunately, on this level it was Mexican art geared toward American tastes.

These "smiling aspects of Mexican life," so well displayed in the Metropolitan show, were also exhibited by Salinas during the first years of his administration. Salinas-style modernization meant stressing the themes of electoral reform, debt reduction, improved productivity, privatization of property, a larger role for U.S. capital, and realignment with the church. This meant that Mexico was going to continue the neo-*porfirian* directions first started by the de la Madrid government in 1982. This path, now a new secular faith for *priistas*, was also a welcome dose of "old-time religion" for U.S. conservatives.

In his inaugural address after the election of 1988, Salinas called for a revision of the electoral code to bring about honest elections and return government to the people. Attacking corruption on all fronts, he spent his first year in office dispelling any image of ineffectiveness as he dramatically moved against corrupt Pemex officials, dishonest brokerage agents, and well-known drug traffickers.

Until 1988, the PRI had not lost an election for state governor. In July 1989, the right-wing opposition National Action Party (PAN) won the Baja California statehouse, and after the February 1995 election in Jalisco, PAN controlled four state governments and more than one hundred and fifty municipal councils. Although *panista* candidates were not always successful in Michoacán, Chihuahua, or Guanajuato, results there favored private enterprise and a decline in the hopes of the left-leaning, socialist Democratic Revolutionary Party (PRD).

The national election of August 1994 revealed a continuation of this trend, with PRI presidential candidate Ernesto Zedillo Ponce de León receiving only 48.2 percent of the vote, while PAN gathered 29.5 percent. This reflected a major *panista* gain since the previous election of 1988. Equally important, Cuauhtémoc Cárdenas' fortunes fell as the PRD collected a paltry 16.2 percent. A surprise to observers north of the border, the election was relatively honest with only modest irregularities. Because Salinas had spent his years making overtures to businessmen and church leaders, in other words becoming more *panismo* in approach and outlook, this election, while dividing Mexican leftists, supported the developmental policies of the PRI and the private enterprise ethic of PAN, not to mention the U.S. banking community.[8]

The huge foreign debt inherited from the de la Madrid years continued to be a major problem for Salinas. By July 1989, Salinas was able to announce an accord with a committee of international bankers that reduced the debt to commercial banks. By the early 1990s, this strategy effectively reduced Mexico's internal debt. Yet Mexico's foreign debt was still more than $101 billion (U.S.) in 1991. Only foreign private investment allowed Salinas to meet the costs of debt service and imports. If investment stopped, the debt problem would rise to the surface again (which it did in December 1994).[9]

Unabashedly pro-growth, Salinas eagerly sought developmental capital by instituting tax reforms and modifying the regulations of the 1973 investment law to favor foreigners. He also eliminated many government regulations, froze prices, and declared that the reforms of the Mexican Revolution had run their course. Most importantly, he pushed the de la Madrid privatization program, selling off banks (nationalized in 1982), TV networks, Teléfonos de México, and highway construction. CONASUPO warehouses and supermarkets were privatized, and in February 1992, the heretofore sacrosanct *ejido* was attacked by an amendment to the constitution that allowed it to be sold and rented.

Maquiladoras and the auto industry were favored. New Ford plants were established in Chihuahua and Hermosillo, and General Motors became Mexico's largest private employer. IBM received special concessions as Guadalajara became Mexico's Silicon Valley. Not all the development came from foreigners, as Vitro, traditionally Mexico's leading glass manufacturer, and Cemex became international corporations with operations in Florida, Texas, California, Europe, and Japan. By 1994, Salinas could note with some satisfaction that Mexico had the third-largest economy in the Third World (after India and Brazil) and the eleventh-largest in the world.[10]

During the 1992 U.S. presidential elections, it was obvious that Salinas was favoring the reelection of George Bush. When Bill Clinton won the election Salinas made the most of the situation. Soon after, he met with Clinton in Texas. There, Clinton not only backed the North American Free Trade Agreement (NAFTA) but also expressed support of Salinas and Mexico as well.

NAFTA is designed to create a single market in Mexico, Canada, and the United States by eliminating barriers to investment and trade. A NAFTA "common market" services a population of more than 360 million in North America with a gross domestic product of $7 trillion.

The agreement will reduce tariffs and quotas over a ten- to fifteen-year period. While it is usually thought of as a free trade arrangement, it is more of a financial arrangement that protects U.S. investments in Mexico. The idea that access to the U.S. market will create enormous investment opportunities in Mexico has been a driving force in Salinas' public career. It was believed that bankers, consumers, and high-tech industries in the United States would be favored by the NAFTA agreement, while labor-intensive industries, such as textiles, sugar producers, and citrus growers, would be hurt. In Mexico small manufacturing firms as well as general agriculture including corn production could suffer from the accord. Mexico and the United States spent most of 1993 debating the pros and cons of NAFTA. In late 1993, Clinton, using presidential clout and aided by House Republicans, won congressional support for the agreement. Shortly thereafter it was approved by the Mexican Senate. NAFTA became a reality on 1 January 1994.

It is said in Mexico that when Salinas went to bed on New Year's Eve he thought he would wake up a North American. Instead, due to the actions of Tzotzil Maya Indians in Chiapas, he woke up a Guatemalan. On New Year's Day, Subcommandante Marcos and his ski-masked indigenous followers took over San Cristóbal de las Casas and issued their "Declaration of the Lacandón Jungle," a manifesto declaring opposition to the Mexican state, its land policies, and NAFTA. The rebel action was timed to coincide with the enactment of NAFTA and attract the attention of the international press to the plight of the Maya peoples of Chiapas, a place where cattle ranchers and coffee producers have traditionally pushed Indian peasants off their lands. It was feared that massive imports of U.S. corn would force Mexican maize off the market, and that North American capital would buy up "privatized" communal *ejidos* and *campesino* lands.[11]

The rebellion initially led to conflict between the national army and the insurgents, known as the Zapatista National Liberation Army (EZLN). According to most press reports, the first few weeks of fighting led to the death of more than one hundred and fifty men, both Zapatistas and *federales*. The popularity of the subcommandante and his cause, especially in important centers such as Mexico City, soon led Salinas to declare a cease-fire and seek a political solution to the crisis. Unlike their Maya brothers in Guatemala, the Chiapas rebels spent most of the year in a nonviolent dance of threats and negotiations with a government that wanted to avoid bloodshed.[12]

The years 1994 and early 1995 were filled with setbacks for the Mexican people and Zedillo. Nineteen ninety-four produced a series of shocks. First, the assassination of Luis Donaldo Colosio occurred on March 23 in Tijuana. Colosio had been handpicked by Salinas as the PRI's presidential candidate. At the time of Colosio's death Mexico was still mourning the killing of Cardinal Jesús Posadas Ocampo who, along with six others, had been gunned down in front of the Guadalajara airport in May 1993. Then on September 28, a month after the 1994 presidential election, José Francisco Ruiz Massieu, the former governor of Guerrero and PRI's secretary general who was divorced from the younger sister of Carlos Salinas, was assassinated in Mexico City.

Investigations in February and March of 1995 soon led to allegations that these deaths were masterminded by well-known politicians with links to drug traffickers. Complicity with drug traffickers by Jalisco and Mexico City officials was a factor in the death of Cardinal Posadas Ocampo. Individuals involved in the killing of Colosio were linked to the PRI hierarchy in Baja California and drug families in Tijuana. Then on February 24, Raul Salinas, the brother of Carlos Salinas, was arrested and charged with arranging the murder of his former brother-in-law, Ruiz Massieu.

A few days later, the former deputy attorney general, Mario Ruiz Massieu, was charged with impeding the investigation into the death of his own brother. It was alleged that the gulf cartel, headquartered in Tamaulipas, was angry with José Ruiz Massieu who, while governor, jailed a cartel associate and delayed the construction of an Acapulco resort in which Raul Salinas was involved. Similarly, Colosio had vowed to crack down on drug traffickers. The former deputy attorney had been linked to both the gulf and Tijuana cartels and reportedly had refused to arrest wealthy associates who were traffickers. Instead, he received payoffs to provide his drug friends with protection and favors, and impeded any investigations into their illegal behavior. Finally, in early March, Carlos Salinas was forced into exile in the United States and settled in Boston, where he had formerly attended Harvard University.[13] He eventually located in Ireland.

The complicity of high government officials in drug deals and political murders was certain to taint the image of Mexico in the United States. Contrary to U.S. public opinion, the Mexican government has been relatively successful in its drug eradication program since the mid-1970s. Marijuana production in 1981 and 1982 was one-third of what it had been in the late 1970s, and opium production in 1980 was reduced to more than one-third of the 1976 figure as well. Similarly, in 1991 Mexico boasted of the impressive statistics concerning the confiscation of marijuana, cocaine, and firearms. In addition, 45,000 people had been arrested for drug violations. In fact, the prisons of northern Mexico were overcrowded with prisoners who were jailed on drug-related charges.[14]

Yet, even though Mexican marijuana was nearly eliminated from the U.S. market, as of 1981 and 1982, other suppliers in Colombia, Belize, Jamaica, and the United States have filled in the gaps. The same is true for opium and heroin; the southwestern Asian nations of Pakistan, Afghanistan, and Iran supply American markets now that opium from Mexico has been eradicated. The current drug situation has been further complicated by the involvement of the Cali cartel in Mexico, which continues to channel cocaine through the Tijuana and gulf cartels into the United States. By the early 1990s, more than 70 percent of marijuana and cocaine imported into the United States originated in Mexico. Yet burning drug crops and jailing drug offenders has not been entirely successful. Obviously, the U.S. Drug Enforcement Agency's attempts to curtail production of illegal drugs in Mexico has failed to reduce the supply in the United States to date.[15]

By 1995, the most dismaying set back was the financial crisis that the Zedillo administration has faced. The debt crisis resurfaced in late 1994 when foreign investors withdrew capital from the Mexican market. During the last week of December the peso began to fall against the American dollar. This was followed by weeks of indecision that sent the devalued peso plummeting to new lows. Finally, in early March 1995, the Mexican government adopted a tough stabilization plan that presented a bleak picture of recession, unemployment, austerity, and personal hardship as the price of recovery.

The austerity plan of 1995 continues the tradition of belt-tightening that characterized the administrations of de la Madrid and Salinas. Starting with a $20 billion loan package from the United States and advances from the International Monetary Bank, Zedillo hopes to initiate a loan restructuring plan for businesses. Fiscal reforms include an incrase in the consumer sales tax, a rise in the price of gasoline and electricity, restrictions on wage increases, and the reduction of purchasing power for most Mexicans. While Wall Street and the Mexican financial community reacted to the austerity plan with enthusiasm, it is unclear whether the Mexican middle class will react as friendly. If not, a political backlash could cost PRI several state governorships that are to be decided in elections later in 1995.

New economic problems could agitate the illegal immigration problem as well. Since 1990, as job creation in Mexico decreased, the number of illegal immigrants entering the United States has increased. Since most emigrants are better educated than the average Mexican, their loss translates into stunted development for Mexico. Many immigrants also suffer abuse from illegal smugglers called *coyotes* and the U.S. Customs Service.

American public opinion has not been sympathetic to the plight of the Mexican immigrant. In 1986 the Overseas Development Council conducted a telephone poll in which 71 percent of the American public agreed with the statement that "the United States should limit the number of immigrants entering the country because they compete with Americans for jobs."[16] In 1994 the citizens of California voted in favor of an ordinance to limit immigration and halt the flow of "illegals" into the United States.

Zapatista rebels, political assassinations, drug trafficking, austerity programs, financial crises—Zedillo battles the shadow of 1982 as he tries to govern Mexico through the nineties. When he leaves office in the year 2000 will he look back on success or not? Undoubtedly, his administration will not relish the critical eye of U.S. image makers.

Most of the image makers in the United States, especially such prestigious presses as the *New York Times, Washington Post, Los Angeles Times, Christian Science Monitor,* and *Wall Street Journal,* tend to judge Mexico's performance in terms of U.S. values of democracy, that is, honest elections and benign capitalism. As indicated in chapter 1, this is not how Mexicans define democracy. Often, as in the case of the Hollywood film industry, Mexico has remained a stage or backdrop for stories about American valor and superiority.[17]

Mexico's image problem, of course, is not one-sided. The Mexicans have been mistaken and shortsighted in their views of North Americans. And, at times, as in the Metropolitan exhibit, the Mexicans project only a very narrow image of their culture for U.S. consumption. The quandary of ethnocentrism is still with us.

This ethnocentrism has led two writers, Jorge Castañeda, a professor at the National Autonomous University of Mexico, and Robert A. Pastor, an Emory University professor, to publish a book entitled *Limits of Frienship* in which it is argued that even with well-intended attempts at communication Mexicans and Americans often speak across each other—resulting, more often than not, in misunderstanding and confrontation.[18]

But if there are limits to the friendship between Mexico and the U.S., Americans can still learn something about themselves in the image that is reflected back to them from the waters of Lake Texcoco. In curbing their ethnocentrism, they can learn that language, customs, ideas, and habits differ between people, and that one set of values is not necessarily superior to the other. North Americans should realize that U.S. influence in Mexico is one reason for the Mexican's fall from colonial splendor. A sensitivity to their nineteenth-century heritage will make most Americans hesitate to sing the U.S. Marine Corps anthem line "from the halls of Montezuma" when touring Chapultepec Castle. The gradual decline of the American empire should remind *norteamericanos* that there are limits to U.S. military and economic power, and in the best of worlds it is unlikely that gringos can make happy yeoman farmers out of a nation of proud Mexican Indians.

Notes

1. "Gringos" and "Greasers"

1. Yi-Fu Tuan, *Topophilia: A Study of Environmental Perception, Attitudes, and Values* (Englewood Cliffs, N.J., 1974), 30–31.
2. Ibid., 31–33.
3. Evon Z. Vogt and Ethel M. Albert, eds., *People of Rimrock: A Study of Values in Five Cultures* (Cambridge, Mass., 1966), 26–28.
4. Tuan, *Topophilia*, 41–42. See also Denys Hay, *Europe: The Emergence of an Idea* (New York, 1966).
5. Jacques Soustelle, *Daily Life of the Aztecs* (Stanford, Calif., 1961), xv, 1–2, 130–32, 216–22.
6. Robert H. Lister and Florence C. Lister, *Those Who Came Before* (Southwest Parks and Monuments Association, 1983), 19–52.
7. Ibid., 116–21.
8. Tuan, *Topophilia*, 32–34.
9. Vogt and Albert, *People of Rimrock*, 46–52.
10. Tuan, *Topophilia*, 66–67.
11. Ibid., 67. See also Raymund A. Paredes, "The Mexican Image in American Travel Literature, 1831–1869," *New Mexico Historical Review* 52 (January 1977): 6–7; and Walter Prescott Webb, *The Great Plains* (Boston, 1931).
12. Samuel Harman Lowrie, *Culture Conflict in Texas, 1821–1835* (New York, 1967), 80.
13. Quoted in Paredes, "The Mexican Image," 9.
14. Vogt and Albert, *People of Rimrock*, 81. Many nineteenth-century travelers noted that the Zuni were more industrious than the Mexicans. The Doniphan expedition chronicler, John T. Hughes, went so far as to describe the Navajo as "a highly civilized people . . . of a higher order . . . than the mass of their neighbors, the Mexicans" (Paredes, "The Mexican Image," 17).
15. Quoted in Paredes, "The Mexican Image," 10.
16. Quoted in Lowrie, *Culture Conflict in Texas*, 95.
17. Paredes, "The Mexican Image," 24.

18. For *serrano* and *agrarista* rebellions see Alan Knight, *The Mexican Revolution*, 2 vols. (Cambridge, Eng., 1986), 1:78–170.

19. Burt M. McConnell, *Mexico at the Bar of Public Opinion* (New York, 1939), 60, 220, 222.

20. John C. Merrill, *Gringo: The American as Seen by Mexican Journalists* (Gainesville, Fla., 1963).

21. Ibid., 12–19, 22, 35–42.

22. "Gringo" might originally be a corruption of *griego* [Greek]; so a gringo was one who spoke Greek or some other language not intelligible to a Spanish speaker. One can catch a glimpse of this meaning in English when one hears "I don't know what he said, its all Greek to me." Although border Mexicans trace the term to the American occupation of Mexico City in 1846, it is doubtless much older than that. Contemporary references to gringo only allude to North Americans, and usually, but not always, in an unfavorable way.

   More recent studies have looked at other social groups in addition to journalists, including government workers, businessmen, intellectuals, and popular opinion as reflected in *corridos* or ballads. While making allowances for diversity of views and ambivalent attitudes, the general view is that Mexicans are often yankeephobes. At the very least, the United States is not universally esteemed in Mexico. See, for example, the article by Michael C. Meyer, "Mexican Views of the United States," in *Twentieth-Century Mexico*, ed. W. Dirk Raat and William H. Beezley (Lincoln, Nebr., 1986), 286–300.

23. Most white North Americans would use a "Europeanization" scale in determining the status and rank of individuals—with Englishmen rated ahead of Eastern Europeans, and Argentines ranked higher than Mexicans. For this and other stereotypes see Américo Paredes, "The Problem of Identity in a Changing Culture: Popular Expressions of Culture Conflict along the Lower Río Grande Border," in *Views across the Border: The United States and Mexico*, ed. Stanley R. Ross (Albuquerque, N.M., 1978), 69–70, 79–81. For a living example of the all-too-real differences between gringos and *mexicanos* see the exchange that occurs between Robert A. Pastor and Jorge G. Castañeda in *Limits of Friendship: The United States and Mexico* (New York, 1988).

24. Américo Paredes, "Problem of Identity," 72–76.

25. Ibid., 72–75.

26. Juan A. Ortega y Medina, "Race and Democracy," in *Texas Myths*, ed. Robert F. O'Connor (College Station, Tex., 1986), 61–69.

27. Quoted in James LeMoyne, "Can the Contras Go On?" *New York Times Magazine* (4 October 1987): 34, 66.

28. Conversations with Professor Carlos Rico of El Colegio de México, Conference of the International Federation of Latin American and Caribbean Studies, Buffalo, N.Y., 25 September 1987. See also Olga Pellicer de Brody, "National Security in Mexico: Traditional Notions and New Preoccupations," in *U.S.-Mexico Relations: Economic and Social Aspects*, ed. Clark W. Reynolds and Carlos Tello (Stanford, Calif., 1983), 185.

29. Olga Pellicer de Brody, "National Security in Mexico," 188.

30. Immanuel Wallerstein, "Friends as Foes," *Foreign Policy* 40 (Fall 1980): 119.

2. Space/Time in the Tierra de la Mexica

1. See Andrew Hacker, *A Statistical Portrait of the American People* (New York, 1983), 12–13, 23; and Cathryn L. Lombardi and John V. Lombardi, *Latin American History: A Teaching Atlas* (Madison, Wis., 1983), 86–91. An excellent source for bibliography, containing over twelve-hundred entries, is Warren D. Kress, *Publications on the Geography of Mexico by United States Geographers*, Bibliographic Report no. 4 (Fargo, N.D., 1979). See also James B. Pick et al., *Atlas of Mexico* (Boulder, Colo., 1989), 12–13.

2. Hacker, *A Statistical Portrait*, 36–37, 47–48.

3. Mary W. Helms, *Middle America: A Culture History of Heartland and Frontiers* (Englewood Cliffs, N.J., 1975), 7–11.

4. Octavio Paz, "The Other Mexico," in the *Labyrinth of Solitude* [and other essays] (New York, 1985), 293. James J. Parsons is the pioneer of Latin American historical geography. For a sample of his work see William M. Denevan, *Hispanic Lands and Peoples: Selected Writings of James J. Parsons* (Boulder, Colo., 1989).

5. The symbol of the pyramid is also used to describe the geography of Mexico in Eric Wolf, *Sons of the Shaking Earth* (Chicago, 1967), 3.

6. Ibid., 3–6.

7. Ibid., 16–17.

8. Ibid., 17–19.

9. Paz, "The Other Mexico," 315–18.

10. Octavio Paz, *The Labyrinth of Solitude: Life and Thought in Mexico* (New York, 1961), 55.
11. C. Warren Thornthwaite, "The Climates of North America according to a New Classification," *The Geographical Review* 21:4 (October 1931): 634–54.
12. Carl Sauer, *Man in Nature* (Berkeley, Calif., 1975), maps 6, 8.
13. Curtis P. Nettels, *The Roots of American Civilization: A History of American Colonial Life* (New York, 1938), 148–50.
14. Ibid., 147.
15. Ibid., 147–48.
16. Charles C. Di Peso, *Las sociedades no nucleares de Norteamérica: la Gran Chichimeca*, vol. 7 of *Historia general de America, periodo indigena*, ed. Guillermo Moron (Caracas, 1983), 19–20.
17. Alvar W. Carlson, "Environmental Overview," in *Borderlands Sourcebook: A Guide to the Literature on Northern Mexico and the American Southwest*, ed. Ellwyn R. Stoddard et al. (Norman, Okla., 1983), 77. See also Charles C. Di Peso, *The Gran Chichimeca: Casas Grandes and the People of the Southwest* (n.p., 1974), 3.
18. Carlson, "Environmental Overview," 76–77.
19. J. Russell Smith and M. Ogden Phillips, *North America: Its People and the Resources, Development, and Prospects of the Continent as the Home of Man* (New York, 1940), 582.
20. Thornthwaite, "The Climates of North America," 652–53. See also Roger Dunbier, *The Sonoran Desert: Its Geography, Economy, and People* (Tucson, Ariz., 1968), 1. There are also other smaller desert areas in the western United States, such as the southern San Joaquin Valley, the Great Salt Lake Desert of western Utah, and the southeastern Utah desert.
21. Charles C. Cumberland, *Mexico: The Struggle for Modernity* (London, 1968), 11, 14.
22. Harold E. Davis, *The Americas in History* (New York, 1953), 21, 23.
23. Joe B. Frantz, "The Borderlands: Ideas on a Leafless Landscape," in *Views across the Border: The United States and Mexico*, ed. Stanley R. Ross (Albuquerque, N.M., 1978), 45.
24. Moctezuma II was the Aztec emperor at the time of the Spanish conquest. Dona Maria, or Malinche, was the Nahuatl speaking Native American mistress of the conqueror, Hernán Cortés. Benito Juárez, a Zapotec Indian, was the reform president of nineteenth-century Mexico. And Emiliano Zapata, although a mestizo, became the symbol of *indigenismo* for twentieth-century peasants and revolutionaries.

25. For estimates of recent and past Indian populations in the Americas see William M. Denevan, ed., *The Native Population of the Americas in 1492* (Madison, Wis., 1978), esp. 7, 291. From the Denevan work I constructed the figure for the Gran Chichimeca area as follows: 540,000 for the northwest, 100,000 for the northeast, 60,000 for Baja California, 41,000 for the southern plains of the United States, and 72,000 for New Mexico and Arizona—a total of 813,000. The figure of 21 million for Mexico does not include the 113,000 of the southern plains, Arizona, and New Mexico. The 1570 figure comes from Lyle N. McAlister, *Spain and Portugal in the New World* (Minneapolis, Minn., 1984), table 1. For the demographic disaster see Magnus Morner, *Race Mixture in the History of Latin America* (Boston, 1967), 31–33; Alfred W. Crosby, Jr., *The Columbian Exchange: Biological and Cultural Consequences of 1492* (Westport, Conn., 1973), 35–63; or Alfred W. Crosby, *Ecological Imperialism: The Biological Expansion of Europe, 900–1900* (Cambridge, Eng., 1986), 195–216.
26. Robert Claiborne, *The First Americans* (New York, 1973), 11; William T. Hagan, *American Indians* (Chicago, 1979), 3; Wolf, *Sons of the Shaking Earth*, 29.
27. Wolf, *Sons of the Shaking Earth*, 34–47.
28. Hagan, *American Indians*, 3; and Marvin Harris, *Cannibals and Kings: The Origins of Cultures* (New York, 1977), 47, 86, 147–66. The best argument for the ecological basis of Aztec sacrifice and cannibalism is Michael Harner, "The Ecological Basis for Aztec Sacrifice," *American Ethnologist* 4 (February 1977): 117–35; or his article "The Enigma of Aztec Sacrifice" in *Natural History* (April 1977): 47–51. A contrary view can be found in "Aztec Experts Deny as Ridiculous Professor's Charge That They Withheld Data on Extent of Cannibalism," *New York Times*, 3 March 1977. Harris and Harner are critiqued in Geoffrey W. Conrad and Arthur A. Demarest, *Religion and Empire: The Dynamics of Aztec and Inca Expansionism* (Cambridge, Eng., 1988), 167–70, 195–99.
29. James Lockhart and Stuart B. Schwartz, *Early Latin America: A History of Colonial Spanish America and Brazil* (Cambridge, Eng., 1984), 33–52. It must be remembered that most agriculturalists were also hunters and gatherers. Gathering is a low-risk, high-yield subsistence activity, unlike hunting, which is a high-risk, low-yield activity. See Richard B. Lee, "What Hunters Do for a Living, or, How to Make Out on Scarce Resources," in *Man the Hunter*, ed. Richard B. Lee and Irven DeVore (Chicago, 1968), 30–48.

30. Lockhart and Schwartz, *Early Latin America*, 41–43.
31. Ibid., 52–55.
32. Ibid., 55–56, 288.
33. See Thomas C. Patterson, *America's Past: A New World Archaeology* (Glenview, Ill., 1973), 76–89; Helms, *Middle America*, 52–68; and Miguel León-Portilla, "Mesoamerica before 1519," in the *Cambridge History of Latin America*, ed. Leslie Bethell (Cambridge, Eng., 1984), I:7–8, 11. By "urban" I mean a nucleated settlement pattern with a large population in the tens of thousands and a high degree of internal differentiation in political, social, and economic activities. The definition comes from Helms, *Middle America*, 52.
34. León-Portilla, "Mesoamerica," 11–13; and Helms, *Middle America*, 88–98. For an indepth treatment of the Toltecs see Miguel León-Portilla, ed., *Historia de México*, vol. 3 of *Período posclásico* (Mexico, 1978). Mesoamerican culture did have some glaring omissions, such as no domesticated animals (apart from the dog), a lack of the technology of the wheel, and until A.D. 950, no metallurgy.
35. Helms, *Middle America*, 98–99.
36. Ibid., 103–4; and Jacques Soustelle, *Daily Life of the Aztecs* (Stanford, Calif., 1961), 5–9. Helms argues for a conservative estimate of 60,000 to 120,000 inhabitants for Tenochtitlán, while Soustelle contends that the range was from 500,000 to 1 million (Helms, *Middle America*, 101).
37. Soustelle, *Daily Life*, 36–70.
38. Ibid., 70–78, and Lockhart and Schwartz, *Early Latin America*, 71, 91.
39. Soustelle, *Daily Life*, 95–104; and Harris, *Cannibals and Kings*, 148–66.
40. For the early Maya see Boyce Rensberger, "Knowledge of Mayas Greatly Extended," *New York Times*, 13 May 1980. The standard account of the classic Maya remains T. Patrick Culbert, *The Lost Civilization: The Story of the Classic Maya* (New York, 1974).
41. See Linda Schele and Mary Ellen Miller, *The Blood of Kings: Dynasty and Ritual in Maya Art* (Fort Worth, Tex., 1986), esp. chapters 4, 5. An account based on recent interpretation is Linda Schele and David Freidel, *A Forest of Kings: The Untold Story of the Ancient Maya* (New York, 1990).
42. Culbert, *The Lost Civilization*, 105–17.
43. Jeremy A. Sabloff and William L. Rathje, "The Rise of a Maya Merchant Class," *Scientific American* 233 (October 1975): 74–76. Also see Jeremy A. Sabloff and E. Wyllys Andrews V, eds., *Late Lowland Maya Civilization: Classic to Postclassic* (Albuquerque, N.M., 1986).

44. Sabloff and Rathje, "The Rise of a Maya Merchant Class," 73–76.

45. Ibid., 77. See also Inga Clendinnen, *Ambivalent Conquests: Maya and Spaniard in Yucatan, 1517–1577* (Cambridge, Eng., 1988), 3–4.

46. See Nancy M. Farriss, *Maya Society under Colonial Rule* (Princeton, N.J., 1984), esp. 389–95; and E. Bradford Burns, *The Poverty of Progress* (Berkeley, Calif., 1980), 110–13. For the tragic decade since 1976 in which three million Mayas of Guatemala were subjected to a government sponsored "holocaust," see Robert M. Carmack, ed., *Harvest of Violence: The Maya Indians and the Guatemalan Crisis* (Norman, Okla., 1988).

47. Ignacio Bernal, "The Cultural Roots of the Border," in *Views across the Border*, 26–29.

48. Charles C. Di Peso, *Casas Grandes: A Fallen Trading Center of the Gran Chichimeca* (Flagstaff, 1974), 2:299–309.

49. Ibid., 320, 321.

50. Lockhart and Schwartz, *Early Latin America*, 290–93. See also Marc Simmons, "Tlascalans in the Spanish Borderlands," *New Mexico Historical Review* 39 (April 1964): 101–10. It is equally true that the Anglo-Americans enslaved Native Americans; for example, the Puritans sold hundreds of Narragansetts into slavery in the seventeenth century, most of them ending up in the West Indies.

51. Lockhart and Schwartz, *Early Latin America*, 293–96.

52. Edward H. Spicer, *Cycles of Conquest: The Impact of Spain, Mexico, and the United States on the Indians of the Southwest, 1533–1960* (Tucson, Ariz., 1962), 298–306.

53. Lockhart and Schwartz, *Early Latin America*, 298.

54. Ibid., 42, 52–53, 56.

55. Charles Gibson, *The Aztecs under Spanish Rule* (Stanford, Calif., 1964), p. 409; and Nathan Wachtel, "The Indian and the Spanish Conquest," in the *Cambridge History of Latin America*, 1:230–37.

56. Spicer, *Cycles of Conquest*, 281–308. For church–Native American relations see Gibson, *The Aztecs under Spanish Rule*, 98–135. A good history of Spain's northern frontier and Native American–white relations is Oakah L. Jones, Jr., *Nueva Vizcaya: Heartland of the Spanish Frontier* (Albuquerque, N.M., 1988).

57. James Lockhart, "Encomienda and Hacienda: The Evolution of the Great Estate in the Spanish Indies," *Hispanic American Historical Review* 49 (August 1969): 411–29.

58. See the several schemata that appear in Lockhart and Schwartz, *Early*

Latin America. For the structure of Spanish American society and the dynamics of social change, see James Lockhart, "Social Organization and Social Change in Colonial Spanish America," the *Cambridge History of Latin America*, 2:265–319. Also worth reviewing is Charles Gibson's essay in the same volume entitled "Indian Societies under Spanish Rule," 381–419.

59. For a literary analysis of this phenomenon see the chapter "The Sons of La Malinche" in Octavio Paz, *The Labyrinth of Solitude* (New York, 1961), 65–88.

60. Population data from Lyle McAlister, *Spain and Portugal*, tables 1, 6; and Lockhart and Schwartz, *Early Latin America*, tables 4, 5.

61. Quoted in Hagan, *American Indians*, 13.

62. Walter Russell Mead, *Mortal Splendor: The American Empire in Transition* (Boston, 1987), 7. As Mead notes, the policy in America was not as bad as in Tasmania where British misfits were encouraged to practice extermination in an attempt to round up and kill every last native.

63. Spicer, *Cycles of Conquest*, 345–47, 353–57.

64. Thomas W. Dunlay, "Indian Allies in the Armies of New Spain and the United States: A Comparative Study," *New Mexico Historical Review* 56 (July 1981): 239, 253–54.

65. Guillermo Bonfil Batalla, *Mexico profundo: Una civilización negada* (Mexico, 1987), 9–15.

3. Up and Down from Colonialism

1. For the history of this economic gap see W. Dirk Raat, *Spain and England in the New World: A Note on Colonialism and the Global Economy* Occasional Papers in Latin American Studies no. 4 (Storrs, Conn.: University of Connecticut, November 1988), 1–7; and John Coatsworth, "The Economic Historiography of Mexico" (unpublished paper, American Historical Association, 29 December 1986). The gap was created in the period between 1770 and 1870. Mexico's per capita income grew at roughly the same rate as the United States between 1880 and 1950. During the period of the Mexican "miracle," from 1950 to 1970, Mexico made some gains in reducing the gap between the United States and itself.

A comparison of the Gross Domestic Product for the two countries in 1975 indicates that the Mexican GDP was 988 billion pesos, or $67 billion

(U.S.), while the United States had a GDP of $1,518 billion. This averages out to approximately a per capita income of $957 (U.S.) for each Mexican, and $7,590 (U.S.) for each American citizen. While the per capita income for Mexico in 1877 was one-tenth that of the United States, by 1975 it had changed to a little over one-eighth of the U.S. per capita income. A more conservative estimate is given by Daniel Chirot who argues that the Gross Domestic Product per capita of Mexico in 1980 (in 1985 U.S. dollars) would be about one-third to one-fourth the U.S. per capita income. See Daniel Chirot, *Social Change in the Modern Era* (San Diego, Calif., 1986), 204–5. The former comparison was based on information in *International Financial Statistics* [a publication of the International Monetary Fund; English edition] vol. 32, no. 2 (February 1979), 254–57, 386–89. See also chapter 8, n. 18. It should be noted that GDP and GNP only measure productivity, not distribution of income.

2. See C. H. Haring, *The Spanish Empire in America* (New York, 1963), 27–37. Some of Haring's observations need tailoring. For example, the northern colonies of America not only attracted proper middle-class farmers but British misfits, paupers, and dissidents. And, as Eric Wolf has noted, in English North America between 1607 and 1776, only two out of ten indentured servants attained the status of independent farmer or artisan. Most died before their contract was up or joined the pool of day laborers and paupers. Finally, the flip side of British middle-class settlements, for all their positive features, was their hostility toward and exclusion of indigenous populations, whether in North America, Tasmania, or New Zealand. India, which was colonized later, was an exception mostly because the natives were too numerous to exterminate or exclude. For a comparison of indentured servitude with African slavery see Eric R. Wolf, *Europe and the People without History* (Berkeley, Calif., 1982), 201–4.

3. Ibid. Although most farm colonies were English, and exploitation colonies were usually Spanish (or Portuguese), the English plantation colonies of the West Indies were exploitation colonies, while the Spanish communities in Chile were farm colonies. It is also true that the English tried to exploit their farm colonies through restrictive legislation and navigation acts, and that some exploitation colonies, like Virginia for example, started out as farm colonies and did not develop slavery until late in the seventeenth century. As can be seen, Haring's categories are less than precise.

4. The idea of fragmentation patterns is best developed in Louis Hartz, *The Founding of New Societies: Studies in the History of the United States, Latin America, South Africa, Canada, and Australia* (New York, 1964), esp. 3–48.

5. See James Lang, *Conquest and Commerce: Spain and England in the Americas* (New York, 1975), 219–22. See also Richard M. Morse, "The Heritage of Latin America," in *The Founding of New Societies*, 123–59.

6. Lang, *Conquest and Commerce*, 220.

7. See the introduction of H. B. Johnson, Jr., ed., *From Reconquest to Empire: The Iberian Background to Latin American History* (New York, 1970), 3–37.

8. James Lockhart and Stuart B. Schwartz, *Early Latin America* (New York, 1983), 16.

9. Ibid., 16, 26–28, 74–76. See also Charles Verlinden, "Italian Influences in Iberian Colonization," in *From Reconquest to Empire*, 55–67.

10. Lockhart and Schwartz, *Early Latin America*, 79. See also Claudio Sánchez-Albornoz, *España, un enigma histórico*, 2 vols. (Buenos Aires, 1956), 2:500–13.

11. Lockhart and Schwartz, *Early Latin America*, 29–30, 79–80.

12. Ibid., 3–4; Johnson, *From Reconquest to Empire*, 8–9.

13. Lockhart and Schwartz, *Early Latin America*, 65–68, 125–32. It is generally true that cities in Spain were less nucleated than in the Americas, but all the tendencies of the Spanish American city find their antecedent in Spanish cities.

14. Hartz, *The Founding of New Societies*, 139–51.

15. Haring, *The Spanish Empire*, 166–93.

16. Lockhart and Schwartz, *Early Latin America*, 13–15, 157–59.

17. For the importance of the Guadalupe cult see Eric R. Wolf, "The Virgin of Guadalupe: A Mexican National Symbol," *Journal of American Folklore* (January 1958): 34–39. Also see Jacques Lafaye, *Quetzalcoatl and Guadalupe: The Formation of Mexican National Consciousness, 1531–1813* (Chicago, 1974).

18. Lockhart and Schwartz, *Early Latin America*, 129–31. This homogenization process is a major theme of Colin M. MacLachlan and Jaime E. Rodríguez O., *The Forging of the Cosmic Race* (Berkeley, Calif., 1980).

19. MacLachlan and Rodríguez, *Cosmic Race*, 155–56.

20. Ibid., 157–63.

21. Lockhart and Schwartz, *Early Latin America*, 132–42. Debt peonage appears to be a function of demography, with the practice increasing when landowners need to monopolize labor in times of labor shortages and decreasing when the Native American population is increasing. In many

instances, owners owed their workers back wages. Generally speaking, peons were the best-paid and most acculturated segment of the rural work force and seldom retained on the land through debt peonage. Debt peonage was always regional and localized and probably more characteristic of the nineteenth century than of the eighteenth.

22. Eric Van Young, "The Age of Paradox: Mexican Agriculture at the End of the Colonial Period, 1750–1810," in Nils Jacobsen and Hans-Jürgen Puhle, eds., *The Economies of Mexico and Peru during the Late Colonial Period, 1760–1810* (Berlin, 1986), 64–90.

23. MacLachlan and Rodríguez, *Cosmic Race*, 171–72; Lockhart and Schwartz, *Early Latin America*, 149–50.

24. Using official figures for the year 1785, Fernand Braudel estimates that goods and bullion from Latin America to Spain amounted to 63.29 million pesos (of which gold and silver accounted for nearly 70 percent). Adding in Brazil's 6.25 million pesos in exports, he calculates that America sent Europe 69.54 million pesos of goods and bullion in 1785. Exports in the other direction, from Spain to America, were worth 38.3 million pesos. Thus, Europe was taking out of America at least 31 million pesos, or in pounds sterling, at least 6 million pounds. As Braudel notes, "So Latin America (about 19 million inhabitants) was sending back to Europe every year four or five times as much as India (about 100 million inhabitants). This would certainly make it the greatest treasure-store in the world." It was this kind of decapitalization that helped to create the gap between the developed and undeveloped parts of the world today. See Fernand Braudel, *The Perspective of the World*, vol. 3 of *Civilization and Capitalism: 15th–18th Century* (New York, 1984), 405, 421–22, 491. Also see Wolf, *Europe and the People without History*, 151–54.

25. Haring, *The Spanish Empire*, 249–51. See also Stanley J. Stein and Barbara H. Stein, *The Colonial Heritage of Latin America* (New York, 1970), 31, 43. For a study on how states divert resources to military purposes and the imperial cycles that follow, and in this context the relationship of Spain to the New World, see Paul Kennedy, *The Rise and Fall of the Great Powers* (New York, 1987), 31–72. For the escalation of military expenditures under Philip II see William H. McNeil, *The Pursuit of Power* (Chicago, 1982), 109–16.

26. John H. Coatsworth, "The Mexican Mining Industry in the Eighteenth Century," in Jacobsen and Puhle, *The Economies of Mexico and Peru*, 26–45.

27. Curtis P. Nettels, *The Roots of American Civilization* (New York, 1938), 78–

79. In contrast to Spain, after 1700 the English encouraged the migration of non-English Europeans to North America. By 1776 sizeable numbers of Germans, Dutch, Swedes, French, Welsh, Scots, Swiss, Scotch-Irish, Jews, and other non-English Europeans settled Anglo-America from Maine to Georgia. See Robert Detweiler and Ramón Eduardo Ruíz, eds., *Liberation in the Americas: Comparative Aspects of the Independence Movements in Mexico and the United States* (San Diego, Calif., 1978), 5.

28. Anyone disbelieving this claim need only compare the ornamental and glittering interiors of the ultra-Baroque cathedrals that dot Mexico's landscape to the straight lines and unadorned architecture of a New England town meeting hall.

29. Nettels, *The Roots of American Civilization*, 57–59. See also Bernard Bailyn, *The New England Merchants in the Seventeenth Century* (Cambridge, Mass., 1955), 16–44.

30. Lang, *Conquest and Commerce*, 222.

31. Nettels, *The Roots of American Civilization*, 169–71.

32. Braudel, *Civilization and Capitalism*, 3:410–11.

33. Luis Villoro, "Mexican and North American Independence: Parallels and Divergences," in *Liberation in the Americas: Comparative Aspects of the Independence Movements in Mexico and the United States*, ed. Detweiler and Ruíz, 19–42. For the redemption of 1804 see Jan Bazant, *A Concise History of Mexico from Hidalgo to Cárdenas, 1805–1940* (Cambridge, Eng., 1977), 5–7.

34. Stein and Stein, *The Colonial Heritage of Latin America*, 126–30. See also Douglass C. North, *Growth and Welfare in the American Past: A New Economic History* (Englewood Cliffs, N.J., 1966), 75–89.

35. John H. Coatsworth, "Obstacles to Economic Growth in Nineteenth-Century Mexico," *American Historical Review* 83 (February 1978): 91–94. See also Richard Graham, *Independence in Latin America* (New York, 1972), 113–19.

36. Immanuel Wallerstein, *The Modern World-System I: Capitalist Agriculture and the Origins of the European World-Economy in the Sixteenth Century* (New York, 1974), 100–3, 112, 349. *Desagüe* labor was a form of highly exploitative flood-control work in Mexico City that involved thousands of Native Americans working to build dikes, drainage works, and tunnels during the sixteenth and early seventeenth centuries. For Wallerstein, "coerced cash-crop labor" is a system of agricultural labor control wherein peasants are required to work at least part of the time on a large domain producing some product for sale on the world market (Ibid., 91). It is one form of

serfdom. Wallerstein argues that *encomienda* labor, in which Native Americans were used in agriculture, mining, and ranching, was another type of serfdom. The allocation of Native American labor by the state known as the *mita* in Peru and the *repartimiento* or *cuatequil* in New Spain (colonial Mexico) was a form of coercive labor most often used in the mines of Peru and in agriculture in New Spain. It is true, however, that there were some noncoercive forms of labor in New Spain at this time, including the use of *gañanes* (independent Native American laborers), sharecroppers, and wage workers (especially in the mines). Concerning landholding, colonial Mexico had *minifundia,* as well as *latifundia,* smallholders (*rancheros*) as well as *hacendados.*

37. Ibid., 100–2, 112, 116, 355.
38. Ibid., 102–8. The quote is from page 105. As Wallerstein notes, sharecropping was known in other areas but was primary in the semiperiphery. It was not the *only* type of labor. Sharecropping was characteristic of certain regions of New Spain, especially in the late colonial period.
39. Johnson, *From Reconquest to Empire,* 10–11.
40. Fernand Braudel, *Civilization and Capitalism,* 3:40. For a critical review of Braudel see Eric R. Wolf, "Unifying the Vision," *New York Times Book Review* (4 November 1984): 11–12. Also see Keith Thomas, "The Long March," *New York Review* (22 November 1984): 41–44.
41. Immanuel Wallerstein, *Modern World-System II: Mercantilism and the Consolidation of the European World-Economy, 1600–1750* (New York, 1980), 156–57.
42. Ibid., 150–51.
43. Ibid., 179, 237–41. Sweden and Brandenburg-Prussia were also semiperipheral areas that improved their relative status at the same time as the United States (ca. 1600 to 1750). Within the core the Dutch were declining, and England and France were succeeding to the top. For a survey of the North American colonial economy see North, *Growth and Welfare in the American Past,* 35–49.
44. Coatsworth, "Obstacles to Economic Growth," 91, 94–95.
45. Ibid., 81–83.
46. Ibid., 83. See also John H. Coatsworth, "The Decline of the Mexican Economy, 1800–1860," (unpublished paper presented at the Symposium on "The Formation of Latin American National Economies," Ibero-Amerikanisches Institut, Berlin, 23 September 1983), 6–7. A similar but more conventional thesis is argued by Jaime E. Rodríguez, *Down from Colo-*

nialism: Mexico's Nineteenth Century Crisis (Los Angeles, Chicano Studies Research Center, 1983). Rodríguez's estimate of Mexico's population in 1800 is only 4 million (Ibid., 7). Data on American economic growth comes from Stuart Bruchey, *The Roots of American Economic Growth, 1607–1861* (New York, 1965), 74–91.

4. Texas and a Collision of Cultures

1. Because of plagues of smallpox and syphilis, U.S. forces suffered a higher mortality rate during the Mexican War than Northern troops did during the U.S. Civil War. The United States lost 15,000 lives during the war, of which only 1,733 were battle deaths—the rest died of diseases or disappeared.

2. David J. Weber, *The Mexican Frontier, 1821–1846: The American Southwest under Mexico* (Albuquerque, N.M., 1982), 278–80; Stuart F. Voss, *On the Periphery of Nineteenth-Century Mexico: Sonora and Sinaloa, 1810–1877* (Tucson, Ariz., 1982), 24–32.

3. Ralph H. Brown, *Historical Geography of the United States* (New York, 1948), 429, 435–37. See also Charles Julian Bishko, "The Inheritance of the Plainsman," in *From Reconquest to Empire: The Iberian Background to Latin American History*, ed. H. B. Johnson, Jr. (New York, 1970), 106–8; and Terry G. Jordan, *Trails to Texas: Southern Roots of Western Cattle Ranching* (Lincoln, Nebr., 1981), 1–24.

4. Jordan, *Trails to Texas*, 1–24; D. W. Meinig, *Imperial Texas: An Interpretive Essay in Cultural Geography* (Austin, Tex., 1969), 66–68.

5. According to Terry Jordan, "buckaroo" may be derived from the African *buckra;* the South Carolinian variant of the African word was *bockorau*. See Jordan, *Trails to Texas*, 6, 14–16. Also see Jack Jackson, *Los Mesteños: Spanish Ranching in Texas, 1721–1821* (College Station, Tex., 1986), 9–10; David Montejano, *Anglos and Mexicans in the Making of Texas, 1836–1986* (Austin, Tex., 1987), 44.

6. Meinig, *Imperial Texas*, 23–28. La Bahía was renamed Goliad after 1828 as an anagram for one of the heroes of the Mexican wars of independence, Miguel Hidalgo.

7. Jackson, *Los Mesteños*, 7.

8. For the migration of Canary Islanders to the Americas, especially Florida,

Louisiana, and Texas, see James J. Parsons, "The Migration of Canary Islanders to the Americas: An Unbroken Current since Columbus," in *Hispanic Lands and Peoples, Selected Writings of James J. Parsons*, ed. William M. Denevan (Boulder, Colo., 1989), 389–427.

9. Meinig, *Imperial Texas*, 23–28; and Jackson, *Los Mesteños*, 117–23.

10. David J. Weber, *"From Hell Itself": The Americanization of Mexico's Northern Frontier, 1821–1846*, Center for Inter-American and Border Studies no. 5 (El Paso, 1983), 3–6.

11. Ibid., 6–8.

12. David J. Weber, "American Westward Expansion and the Breakdown of Relations between Pobladores and 'Indios Bárbaros' on Mexico's Far Northern Frontier, 1821–1846," *New Mexico Historical Review* 56 (July 1981): 221–38. See also Ralph A. Smith, "Indians in American-Mexican Relations before the War of 1846," *Hispanic American Historical Review* 43 (February 1963): 34–64.

13. Weber, "American Westward Expansion," 224; Ralph A. Smith, "Indians in American-Mexican Relations," 34.

14. Weber, *The Mexican Frontier*, 125–30.

15. Ibid., 130–41.

16. Weber, *"From Hell Itself"*, 10.

17. Norman A. Graebner, *Empire on the Pacific* (New York, 1955), 217–28. See also Norman A. Graebner, "The Mexican War: A Study in Causation," *Pacific Historical Review* 49 (August 1980): 405–26.

18. Josefina Vázquez de Knauth, *Mexicanos y Norteamericanos ante la Guerra del 47* (Mexico, 1972), 12–13; Brown, *Historical Geography*, 434–35.

19. David Montejano, *Anglos and Mexicans in the Making of Texas* (Austin, Tex., 1987), 15–19. See also Josefina Zoraida Vázquez, "The Texas Question in Mexican Politics, 1836–1845," *Southwestern Historical Quarterly* 89 (January 1986): 309–44.

20. The best study on Manifest Destiny remains Albert K. Weinberg, *Manifest Destiny: A Study of Nationalist Expansion in American History* (Chicago, 1963). The quote is from p. 90. Another study worth consulting is Frederick Merk, *Manifest Destiny and Mission in American History: A Reinterpretation* (New York, 1963). See also Gene M. Brack, *Mexico Views Manifest Destiny, 1821–1846: An Essay on the Origins of the Mexican War* (Albuquerque, N.M., 1975).

21. Merk, *Manifest Destiny and Mission*, 265. For a good treatment of the popu-

lar American image of Mexican weaknesses see Robert W. Johannsen, *To the Halls of Montezuma: The Mexican War in the American Imagination* (New York, 1985).

22. Josefina Zoraida Vázquez and Lorenzo Meyer, *México frente a Estados Unidos: un ensayo histórico, 1776–1980* (Mexico, 1982), 25–31. This book appears in English translation as *The United States and Mexico* (Chicago, 1985).

23. Vázquez and Meyer, *México frente a Estados Unidos*, 31–32; Meinig, *Imperial Texas*, 28–32.

24. Meinig, *Imperial Texas*, 29–31; Michael C. Meyer and William L. Sherman, *The Course of Mexican History* (New York, 1987), 336.

25. Quoted in David J. Weber, ed., *Foreigners in Their Native Land: Historical Roots of the Mexican Americans* (Albuquerque, N.M., 1973), 102. See also Vázquez and Meyer, *México frente a Estados Unidos*, 33.

26. Vázquez and Meyer, *México frente a Estados Unidos*, 33–34.

27. Ibid., 34–36; Meinig, *Imperial Texas*, 30, 32–37. The events leading up to the outbreak of the Texas battles are narrated in Samuel Harman Lowrie, *Cultural Conflict in Texas, 1821–1835* (New York, 1967).

28. James A. Michener, *Texas* (New York, 1985), 431–32. Although a novel, Michener's description of the Monclova blizzard strives to depict historical fact.

29. Walter Lord, "Myths and Realities of the Alamo," *The American West* 5:3 (May 1968): 21. Santa Anna's own "official" account underestimates the size of the Mexican force (1,400 soldiers) and inflates the number of enemy dead (600 rebels). See Michael P. Costeloe, "The Mexican Press of 1836 and the Battle of the Alamo," *Southwestern Historical Quarterly* 91 (April 1988): 533–43.

30. Lord, "Myths and Realities," 20–21, 23–24. Among those who surrendered and were executed was David Crockett. David Weber talks about the myths and realities of the Alamo in his *Myth and the History of the Hispanic Southwest* (Albuquerque, N.M., 1988), 133–51.

31. Meyer and Sherman, *The Course of Mexican History*, 339–40; Lord, "Myths and Realities," 24–25. A good survey of the military phase of the Texas Revolution is James W. Pohl and Stephen L. Hardin, "The Military History of the Texas Revolution: An Overview," *Southwestern Historical Quarterly* 89 (January 1986): 269–308.

32. Vázquez and Meyer, *México frente a Estados Unidos*, 36–37.

33. Raymund A. Paredes, "The Mexican Image in American Travel Literature, 1831–1869," *New Mexico Historical Review* 52 (January 1977): 10.

34. Vázquez and Meyer, *México frente a Estados Unidos*, 38–41. For the Texas expedition into New Mexico see either Noel M. Loomis, *The Texan-Santa Fe Pioneers* (Norman, Okla., 1958); or Rodolfo Acuña, *Occupied America: A History of Chicanos* (New York, 1988), 56–58. Joseph Milton Nance narrates the story of Mexico's reconquering attempts in two massive volumes, *After San Jacinto: The Texas-Mexican Frontier, 1836–1841* and *Attack and Counterattack: The Texas-Mexican Frontier, 1842* (Austin, Tex., 1963 and 1964). For the annexation of Texas see Carlos Bosch García, *Historia de las relaciones entre México y los Estados Unidos, 1819–1848* (Mexico, 1974), 58–96. Also see David M. Pletcher, *The Diplomacy of Annexation: Texas, Oregon, and the Mexican War* (Columbia, Mo., 1973).

35. Meyer and Sherman, *The Course of Mexican History*, 342–46.

36. Ibid., 346. For the naval role see K. Jack Bauer, *Surfboats and Horse Marines: U.S. Naval Operations in the Mexican War, 1846–48* (Annapolis, Md., 1969), 235–40; and, K. Jack Bauer, *The Mexican War* (New York, 1974), 106–26. The quote and comparative military data is from Robert Leckie, *The Wars of America* (New York, 1981), 328, 338.

37. Meyer and Sherman, *The Course of Mexican History*, 347–48; Leckie, *The Wars of America*, 341–43.

38. John D. Eisenhower, "Polk and His Generals," in *Essays on the Mexican War*, ed. Douglas W. Richmond (College Station, Tex., 1986) 56; Meyer and Sherman, *The Course of Mexican History*, 348–51; Vázquez and Meyer, *México frente a Estados Unidos*, 47.

39. Meyer and Sherman, *The Course of Mexican History*, 351–53; Vázquez and Meyer, *México frente a Estados Unidos*, 47–50. During the nineteenth century, the Mexican peso and the American dollar were equivalent. After 1895, the price of silver fell, and by 1905 the peso was worth half the U.S. dollar.

The Mexican view of the Mexican-American War can be found in Cecil Robinson, ed., *The View from Chapultepec* (Tucson, Ariz., 1989), esp. xii–lvi. See also Thomas Benjamin, "Recent Historiography of the Origins of the Mexican War," *New Mexico Historical Review* 54 (July 1979): 169–81. For the Mexican historiography of the Treaty of Guadalupe Hidalgo see Richard Griswold del Castillo, "Mexican Views of 1848: The Treaty of Guadalupe Hidalgo through Mexican History," *Journal of Borderlands Studies* 1 (Fall 1986): 24–40. Surprisingly, for the North American who might expect pages of vindictive analysis, Mexican historians are very self-critical and reserve their harshest comments for their own countrymen.

40. Oscar J. Martínez, *Troublesome Border* (Tucson, Ariz., 1988), 16–19; Donald H. Bufkin, "The Making of a Boundary between the United States and Mexico: A Study in Political Geography," *The Cochise Quarterly* 13: 1 and 2 (Spring/Summer 1983): 3–29; Harry P. Hewitt, "The Treaty of Guadalupe Hidalgo Revisited: Myths and Realities of the Mexican Boundary Survey" (unpublished paper presented to the American Historical Association, Washington, D.C., December 1987). The story of the boundary commissions is told in Leon C. Metz, *Border: The U.S.-Mexico Line* (El Paso, Tex., 1989), 3–68.

41. Weber, *Foreigners in Their Native Land*, 140; Montejano, *Anglos and Mexicans*, 30–31.

Other migrations involved the movement of Mexican peons who escaped the cotton fields of Matamoros to live in Texas, and the arrival in Coahuila of Seminoles and Kickapoos who, as "civilized Native Americans," were hired to fight "barbaric Native Americans" like the Apaches and Comanches. For this latter topic see Edward H. Moseley, "Indians from the Eastern United States and the Defense of Northeastern Mexico: 1855–1864," *Southwestern Social Science Quarterly* 46 (December 1965): 273–80.

42. Weber, *Foreigners in Their Native Land*, 145, 148.

43. Montejano, *Anglos and Mexicans*, 20–21, 50; Iris Wilson Engstrand, "Land Grant Problems in the Southwest: The Spanish and Mexican Heritage," *New Mexico Historical Review* 53:4 (October 1978): 330–33. In 1856 the U.S. Supreme Court ruled in McKinney *v.* Saviego that the Treaty of Guadalupe Hidalgo did not apply to Mexicans in Texas.

44. Montejano, *Anglos and Mexicans*, 34–51.

45. Américo Paredes, *With His Pistol in His Hand* (Austin, Tex., 1958), 15–23.

46. Walter Prescott Webb, *The Texas Rangers: A Century of Frontier Defense* (Austin, Tex., 1965), 14.

47. Paredes, *With His Pistol in His Hand*, 23–32. See also Miles W. Williams, "Border Corrido and Ranger Lore: A Contrast in Written and Oral Traditions," *Journal of Borderlands Studies* 2 (Fall 1987): 33–46.

48. Jan Bazant, *A Concise History of Mexico* (London, 1977), 58–61; James D. Cockcroft, *Mexico: Class Formation, Capital Accumulation, and the State* (New York, 1983), 71–74.

49. Charles Hale, "The War with the United States and the Crisis in Mexican Thought," *The Americas* 14 (October 1957): 153–73.

50. Eduardo Galeano, *Memory of Fire: Faces & Masks* (New York, 1987), 148.

51. Michener, *Texas*, 674; Bauer, *Surfboats and Horse Marines*, 238–40.
52. Michael H. Hunt, *Ideology and U.S. Foreign Policy* (New Haven, Conn., 1987), 32–36. For the role of the British, Trist, and the treaty process, see George Baker, "Percy Doyle and the Treaty of Guadalupe Hidalgo," in *Proceedings from the 37th Annual Meeting of the Rocky Mountain Council on Latin American Studies* (Las Cruces, N.M., 2–4 Feb. 1989), 1–11.
53. Stuart Bruchey, *The Roots of American Economic Growth, 1607–1861: An Essay in Social Causation* (New York, 1965), 75, 90–91, 162–64; Robert Higgs, *The Transformation of the American Economy, 1865–1914: An Essay in Interpretation* (New York, 1971), 24.
54. Higgs, *The Transformation of the American Economy*, 24–47.
55. John H. Coatsworth, "The Decline of the Mexican Economy, 1800–1860" (paper presented at symposium, The Formation of Latin American National Economies, Ibero-Amerikanisches Institut, Berlin, 23 September 1983), 7, 9; John H. Coatsworth, "The Economic Historiography of Mexico" (paper presented at American Historical Association, 29 December 1986), 9.

5. From Pueblo to Global Village

1. Eric Hobsbawm, *The Age of Empire 1875–1914* (New York, 1987), 8–9. Contrary to Hobsbawm's view, Immanuel Wallerstein argues that the industrial revolution and the French Revolution were not the important events of this period, since industrialization had taken place in sixteenth- and seventeenth-century England, and the transition from feudalism to bourgeois capitalism had long since occurred. See the review by Stephen S. Gosch of Immanuel Wallerstein's *The Modern World–System III: The Second Era of Great Expansion of the Capitalist World-Economy, 1730–1840s* (San Diego, Calif., 1989) in the *Journal of World History* 1 (Fall 1990): 274–76.
2. Hobsbawm, *The Age of Empire*, 50–52, 56–57, 66.
3. Paul Kennedy, *The Rise and Fall of the Great Powers* (New York, 1987), 198–202; Hobsbawm, *The Age of Empire*, 51, 338.
4. Kennedy, *The Rise and Fall of the Great Powers*, 148–49; Fernand Braudel, *The Perspective of the World*, vol. 3 of *Civilization and Capitalism: 15th–18th Century* (New York, 1984), 534–35.
5. Braudel, *Civilization and Capitalism*, 3:556–88.
6. Hobsbawm, *The Age of Empire*, 39–40, 74.

7. Ibid., 74; Marvin D. Bernstein, *Foreign Investment in Latin America* (New York, 1966), 6–7.

8. For a listing of 170 major foreign companies in Mexico during the *porfiriato* see José Luis Ceceña, *México en la órbita imperial* (Mexico, 1975), 868–94. Some major British businesses in Mexico at the time of Porfirio Díaz's administration were: Compañia Ferrocarrilera Mexicana Ltd.; Mexican Light & Power Co.; Monterrey Railway Light & Power Co.; Banco de Londres y México; Banco de Montreal; The Mexican Tramways Co.; El Oro Mining & Railway; San Francisco del Oro Mining Co.; The Mazapil Copper Co., Ltd.; Michoacán Railways & Mining Co., Ltd.; Guayule Rubber Co., Ltd.; Lower California Development Co., Ltd.; Land Company of Chiapas Ltd.; Mexico Cotton Estates of Tlahualilo, Ltd.; Soconusco Rubber Plantations; Mexican Mahogany and Rubber Corp., Ltd.; Veracruz Land & Cattle Co.

The Real del Monte-Pachuca silver mining company of Hidalgo was, perhaps, the most impressive British mining venture in nineteenth-century Mexico. Although it was declared a financial failure in 1849, its heritage of steam-engine drainage proved profitable for later mining operations. In 1906, the Real del Monte mines came under American ownership. See Robert W. Randall, *Real del Monte: A British Mining Venture in Mexico* (Austin, Tex., 1972).

9. Allen Weinstein and R. Jackson Wilson, *Freedom and Crisis* (New York, 1978), 2:533; Kennedy, *The Rise and Fall of the Great Powers*, 242.

10. Kennedy, *The Rise and Fall of the Great Powers*, 199–201, 243.

11. Ibid., 244.

12. Bernstein, *Foreign Investment in Latin America*, 7–8. For Mexican government statistics see Montgomery Schuyler (Mexico) to the Secretary of State, 9 December 1912, Records of the Department of State Relating to the Internal Affairs of Mexico, Microfilm Publication, Record Group 59, file 812.60, microcopy 274. Also see Josefina Zoraida Vázquez and Lorenzo Meyer, *México frente a Estados Unidos: un ensayo histórico, 1776–1980* (Mexico, 1982), 109. Data supplied by the U.S. consulate were slightly higher, estimating a total of $642.2 million for U.S. investments in Mexico in 1911.

13. Ceceña, *México en la órbita imperial*, 86. In addition to those mentioned, some major U.S. interests were: Intercontinental Rubber Co.; Ferrocarril Sud Pacífico; Pan American Co.; Batopilas Mining Co.; Moctezuma Copper Co. (Phelps Dodge); Yaqui Land and Water Co.; Guanajuato Amalgamated Gold Mines; Río Plata Mining Co. (Chihuahua); Pacific Smelting &

Mining Co.; Michoacan Power Co.; Aguila Sugar Refining Co.; American Bank (Mexico City); American Bank of Torreón.

14. James D. Cockcroft, *Mexico: Class Formation, Capital Accumulation, and the State* (New York, 1983), 93; Vázquez and Meyer, *México frente a Estados Unidos*, 100, 109; Luis Nicolau d'Olwer, "Las inversiones extranjeras," in *Historia moderna de México, El Porfiriato, La vida económica*, vol. 7, pt. 2, ed. Daniel Cosío Villegas (Mexico, 1965), 1166–67.

15. Oscar J. Martínez, *Troublesome Border* (Tucson, Ariz., 1988), 32–52.

16. For an excellent discussion of the Tuxtepec uprising in which Díaz seized power and the American role in backing Díaz see John Mason Hart, *Revolutionary Mexico: The Coming and Process of the Mexican Revolution* (Berkeley, Calif., 1987), 105–31. Other influential individuals who worked for U.S. recognition of Díaz were National City Bank's James Stillman; railroad tycoon Colis Huntington; Edward Lee Plumb, secretary to the U.S. Legation in Mexico (who eventually controlled the Mexican National route from Laredo to Mexico City); and Senator Roscoe Conkling of New York.

17. Hart, *Revolutionary Mexico*, 127; Cockcroft, *Mexico*, 85–86; Vázquez and Meyer, *México frente a Estados Unidos*, 88–91. A good study on the first administration of Díaz and the problems of recognition is that of Daniel Cosío Villegas, *The United States Versus Porfirio Diaz* (Lincoln, Nebr., 1963).

18. Steven Topik, "Entrepreneurs or Lumpenbourgeoisie?" *Mexican Studies/ Estudios Mexicanos* 4 (Summer 1988): 332–33.

19. Barbara Tenenbaum, *The Politics of Penury; Debts and Taxes in Mexico, 1821– 1856* (Albuquerque, N.M., 1986), 164. The Ley Lerdo of 1856, drafted by secretary of the treasury Miguel Lerdo de Tejada, prohibited ecclesiastical and civil institutions from owning or administering real property not used in daily operations.

20. David Bushnell and Neill Macaulay, *The Emergence of Latin America in the Nineteenth Century* (New York, 1988), 193–97.

21. Ibid., 197–99. See also Richard N. Sinkin, "The Mexican Constitutional Congress, 1856–1857: A Statistical Analysis," *Hispanic American Historical Review* 53 (1973): 1–26.

22. Bushnell and Macaulay, *The Emergence of Latin America*, 200–202. Favorable relations between Juárez and the United States had begun earlier during the era of La Reforma when the U.S. Navy assisted Juárez in his struggle against enemy warships and when the United States and Juárez agreed to the Ocampo-McLane Treaty that would have, had it been ratified, provided the United States with a right of transit across the isthmus

of Tehuantepec. See Vázquez and Meyer, *México frente a Estados Unidos,* 69–70; and A. B. Belenki, *La intervención extranjera de 1861–1867 en México* (Mexico, 1972), 174–76.

An interesting sidelight of the Juárez era was the activity of Matías Romero, the Mexican ambassador to the United States. Not unlike the first U.S. minister to Mexico, Joel R. Poinsett (who was notorious for intervening in the domestic affairs of Mexico between 1824 and 1830), Romero tried to oust Secretary of State William Seward and unseat Abraham Lincoln. He also played a peripheral role in the impeachment of President Andrew Johnson. See Thomas D. Schoonover, ed., *Mexican Lobby: Matías Romero in Washington 1861–67* (Lexington, Ky., 1986), 31–49, 114–15.

23. Thomas David Schoonover, *Dollars over Dominion: The Triumph of Liberalism in Mexican-United States Relations, 1861–1867* (Baton Rouge, La., 1978), 251–53, 275–76.

24. Hart, *Revolutionary Mexico,* 112–13; Ronnie C. Tyler, *Santiago Vidaurri and the Southern Confederacy* (Fort Worth, Texas State Historical Association, 1973), 135–56.

25. Bushnell and Macaulay, *The Emergence of Latin America,* 201.

26. Friedrich Katz, "Mexico: Restored Republic and Porfiriato, 1867–1910," in the *Cambridge History of Latin America,* ed. Leslie Bethell (Cambridge, Eng., 1986), 5:29.

27. For Santa Anna's connections with chicle and the chewing gum business in the United States see Alvin Morland, "Chewing-Gum Chronicles," *American Way* (18 March 1986): 49–53.

28. For the railroads and the usurpation of Native American village lands see John H. Coatsworth, *Growth against Development: The Economic Impact of Railroads in Porfirian Mexico* (De Kalb, Ill., 1981), 149–74.

29. William H. Beezley, *Judas at the Jockey Club and Other Episodes of Porfirian Mexico* (Lincoln, Nebr., 1987), 103–4.

30. Hart, *Revolutionary Mexico,* 131–34; Francisco R. Calderón, "Los ferrocarriles," *Historia moderna de México, El Porfiriato, La vida económica,* vol. 7, pt. 1, ed. Daniel Cosío Villegas (Mexico, 1965), 483–634.

31. Charles C. Cumberland, *Mexico: The Struggle for Modernity* (New York, 1968), 217–20.

32. John Tutino, *From Insurrection to Revolution in Mexico* (Princeton, N.J., 1986), 285–86.

33. Marvin D. Bernstein, *The Mexican Mining Industry, 1890–1950* (Albany, N.Y., 1964), 18–19.

34. Ibid., 21. See also Hart, *Revolutionary Mexico*, 141–42. For Cananea see W. Dirk Raat, *Revoltosos: Mexico's Rebels in the United States, 1903–1923* (College Station, Tex., 1981), 68–69. The latter appears in Spanish as *Los revoltosos: Rebeldes mexicanos en los Estados Unidos 1903–1923* (Mexico, 1988).

Two large mining operations of the 1880s and 1890s in which railroads were not a major factor were the French-owned copper works of El Boleo at Santa Rosalia, Lower California, where the mines and town were serviced by sea by a small company-owned fleet, and the silver mines of Batopilas developed by Alexander R. Shepard, ex-governor of Washington, D.C. From Batopilas, mules were used to transport the silver ore 120 miles from the rugged canyonlands to wagons and carriages in the upland country. From there they would cross the foothills and plains another 115 miles to Chihuahua City. By the mid-1930s a line ran from the U.S. border to the Sierra Madre Occidental within 105 miles from Batopilas. In 1961 the route from Chihuahua to Los Mochis was completed with the Chihuahua al Pacífico Railway going from Chihuahua City through Creel and the Copper Canyon country of Chihuahua to Sinaloa.

35. Bernstein, *The Mexican Mining Industry*, 37–39; Hart, *Revolutionary Mexico*, 142–43.

36. William Glade, "Latin America and the International Economy, 1870–1914," in the *Cambridge History of Latin America*, 4:21.

37. Katz, "Mexico: Restored Republic and Porfiriato," 29–30.

38. Stephen H. Haber, *Industry and Underdevelopment: The Industrialization of Mexico, 1890–1940* (Stanford, Calif., 1989), 27–102, 122–49.

39. Ibid., 63–102.

40. Katz, "Mexico: Restored Republic and Porfiriato," 48; Coatsworth, *Growth against Development*, 149–74.

41. Hart, *Revolutionary Mexico*, 157–62. The quote is from p. 158.

42. Tutino, *From Insurrection to Revolution*, 287.

43. Katz, "Mexico: Restored Republic and Porfiriato," 30–31.

44. The complexity of the countryside is excellently surveyed in Tutino, *From Insurrection to Revolution*, 288–325.

45. See Friedrich Katz, "The Transformation of the Northern Frontier into 'the Border,'" in his *The Secret War in Mexico* (Chicago, 1981), 7–27.

46. Katz, "Mexico: Restored Republic and Porfiriato," 42–43.

47. Ibid., 43–44. For Alexander Shepherd's innovations see David M. Pletcher, *Rails, Mines, & Progress: Seven American Promoters in Mexico, 1867–1911* (Ithaca, N.Y., 1958), 193–206.

48. James R. Scobie, "The Growth of Latin American Cities, 1870–1930," in the *Cambridge History of Latin America*, 4:253. For the Fundidora and the Cervecería of Monterrey see Alex M. Saragoza, *The Monterrey Elite and the Mexican State, 1880–1940* (Austin, Tex., 1988), 31–71.

49. Katz, "Mexico: Restored Republic and Porfiriato," 43; Saragoza, *The Monterrey Elite*, 72–95; Ramón Eduardo Ruíz, *The People of Sonora and Yankee Capitalists* (Tucson, Ariz., 1988), 7–10, 117–33, 212–27.

50. Political "modernization" under Díaz involved extending national authority over the church, regional oligarchs, and state and municipal politicians. The *porfiriato* witnessed the growth of the state bureaucracy, an expansion of the police and army, the development of a spy system, an extension of the tax powers of the government, and state involvement in the economy. To be sure, these measures were partial and did not amount to the kind of political modernization that characterized Mexico after 1920; nor was political participation broad enough to include the newly emerging social groups that accompanied the growth of the economy. These groups of workers, peons, and petty bourgeoisie were blocked from political participation by Díaz, and as a result civil war and violence soon followed his departure from government. For a discussion of the theory of modernization and its application to the Mexican Revolution see the classic work by Samuel P. Huntington, *Political Order in Changing Societies* (New Haven, Conn., 1968), 1–92, 264–324.

51. W. Dirk Raat, ed., *Mexico: From Independence to Revolution, 1810–1910* (Lincoln, Nebr., 1982), 189.

52. Wilfrid Hardy Callcott, *Liberalism in Mexico, 1857–1929* (Hamden, Conn., 1965), 129.

53. For the *científicos* see William D. Raat, *El positivismo durante el Porfiriato* (Mexico, 1975), 107–42.

54. Raat, *Mexico: From Independence to Revolution*, 189; Katz, "Mexico: Restored Republic and Porfiriato," 32, 39. For the importance of electric telegraphs and railways to the technology of warfare see Martin van Creveld, *Technology and War* (New York, 1989), 155–66. For the Rural Police Force see Paul J. Vanderwood, *Disorder and Progress: Bandits, Police, and Mexican Development* (Lincoln, Nebr., 1981), 107–38.

55. Raat, *Revoltosos*, 175–99; W. Dirk Raat, "US Intelligence Operations and Covert Action in Mexico, 1900–1947," *Journal of Contemporary History* 22 (1987): 618–20.

56. Raat, "US Intelligence Operations," 619.

57. Katz, "Mexico: Restored Republic and Porfiriato," 37; Ruíz, *The People of Sonora and Yankee Capitalists*, 197–211; William H. Beezley, *Insurgent Governor: Abraham González and the Mexican Revolution in Chihuahua* (Lincoln, Nebr., 1973), 1–12.
58. Katz, "Mexico: Restored Republic and Porfiriato," 46–47. See also Francisco Almada, *La rebelión de Tomochi* (Chihuahua, 1938).
59. Ruíz, *The People of Sonora and Yankee Capitalists*, 162–82.
60. David R. Mares, "Mexico's Foreign Policy as a Middle Power: The Nicaragua Connection, 1884–1986," *Latin American Research Review* 23:3 (1988): 81–107.
61. W. Dirk Raat, "Synthesizing the Mexican Experience," *Latin American Research Review* 15:3 (1980): 266–72. The quote comes from Raat, *Revoltosos*, 176.
62. Longevity data from an interview of the author with Michael Meyer, Los Cruces, New Mexico, 2 February 1989.

6. The Mexican Revolution in the United States

1. For Abner Doubleday in the Halls of Montezuma see William H. Beezley, *Judas at the Jockey Club and Other Episodes of Porfirian Mexico* (Lincoln, Nebr., 1987), 17–26. For the story of the Doubleday myth see R. Brasch, *How did Sports Begin?* (New York, 1970), 29–45.
2. Martin Van Creveld, *Technology and War* (New York, 1989), 177–78, 185–89, 207–11.
3. Paul Kennedy, *The Rise and Fall of the Great Powers* (New York, 1987), 200–203, 248.
4. Ibid., 257–74, 280–82.
5. John H. Coatsworth, "Comment on 'The United States and the Mexican Peasantry'," in *Rural Revolt in Mexico and U.S. Intervention*, ed. Daniel Nugent (San Diego, Calif., 1988), 65–68.
6. John M. Hart, *Revolutionary Mexico: The Coming and Process of the Mexican Revolution* (Los Angeles, 1987), 349–52. See also John Mason Hart, "U.S. Economic Hegemony, Nationalism, and Violence in the Mexican Countryside, 1876–1920," in *Rural Revolt in Mexico and U.S. Intervention*, 73–78.
7. Ramón Eduardo Ruíz profiles the revolutionaries in *The Great Rebellion, Mexico 1905–1924* (New York, 1980), 213–38.

8. John Womack, Jr., "The Mexican Revolution, 1910–1920," in the *Cambridge History of Latin America*, ed. Leslie Bethell (Cambridge, Eng., 1986), 5:82–87; Hart, "U.S. Economic Hegemony," 77–78.

9. W. Dirk Raat, *Revoltosos: Mexico's Rebels in the United States, 1903–1923* (College Station, Tex., 1981), 203–50.

10. Womack, "The Mexican Revolution," 85–88.

11. Martin J. Sklar, "Woodrow Wilson and the Political Economy of Modern United States Liberalism," *Studies on the Left* 1:3 (1960): 17–47. For Wilson's Mexican policy see Mark T. Gilderhus, *Diplomacy and Revolution: U.S.-Mexican Relations under Wilson and Carranza* (Tucson, Ariz., 1977). Also see Berta Ulloa, *La Revolución intervenida: Relaciones diplomáticas entre México y Estados Unidos, 1910–1914* (Mexico, 1971).

12. Friedrich Katz, *The Secret War in Mexico: Europe, the United States and the Mexican Revolution* (Chicago, 1981): 156–58.

13. Womack, "The Mexican Revolution," 93–97.

14. Ibid., 97–107; Katz, *The Secret War in Mexico*, 135, 161, 165.

15. Womack, "The Mexican Revolution," 107–13.

16. Ibid., 110–15.

17. Friedrich Katz, "From Alliance to Dependency: The Formation and Deformation of an Alliance between Francisco Villa and the United States," in *Rural Revolt in Mexico and U.S. Intervention*, 231–36.

18. Ibid., 237–39. For the American retreat from Veracruz see Hart, *Revolutionary Mexico*, 299–302.

19. For the motives behind Villa's attack on Columbus, see Friedrich Katz, "Pancho Villa and the Attack on Columbus, New Mexico," *American Historical Review* 83 (Feb. 1978): 101–30. Villa's motivation is also treated by Charles Harris III and Louis R. Sadler in an essay entitled "Pancho Villa and the Columbus Raid: The Missing Documents," in *Border Revolution* (Las Cruces, N.M., 1988), 101–12. For a colorful regional account of the event that contains interesting photographs see Bill Rakocy, *Villa Raids Columbus, N. Mex. Mar. 9, 1916* (El Paso, n.d.). Explanations range from the simple story of Villa wishing to settle a score with townsman Sam Ravel for his alleged lack of delivery of war supplies to a conspiracy theory that alleges that the U.S. government paid Villa to have the raid take place so that complacent Americans would be willing to arm for war in Europe.

20. Womack, "The Mexican Revolution," 119–25.

21. Robert Freeman Smith, *The United States and Revolutionary Nationalism in Mexico, 1916–1932* (Chicago, 1972), 47–62.

22. Gilderhus, *Diplomacy and Revolution*, 53–54.
23. Ibid., 54–56; Womack, "The Mexican Revolution," 129; Josefina Zoraida Vázquez and Lorenzo Meyer, *México frente a Estados Unidos: un ensayo histórico, 1776–1980* (Mexico, 1982), 135–36.
24. Vázquez and Meyer, *México frente a Estados Unidos*, 138–41.
25. "Death of General Francisco Villa," 21 July 1924, *U.S. Military Intelligence Reports, 1919–1941* (Frederick, Md., 1984), microfilm.
26. Vázquez and Meyer, *México frente a Estados Unidos*, 149–51. U.S. military aid to Obregón (including eleven airplanes) is documented in the J. W. F. Dulles Mexican Papers, Nettie Lee Benson Latin American Collection, University of Texas at Austin. See especially Dulles, interview of Jorge Prieto Laurens, 9 Nov. 1955, Dulles Mexican Papers, vol. 4, no. 21. For de la Huerta's view see Dulles, interview of Adolfo de la Huerta, 6 June 1955, Dulles Mexican Papers, vol. 4, no. 49.
27. Hart, *Revolutionary Mexico*, 367–69.
28. Raat, *Revoltosos*, 289–90.
29. Hart, *Revolutionary Mexico*, 369; Womack, "The Mexican Revolution," 152–53; John Womack, "The Mexican Economy during the Revolution, 1910–1920," in *Twentieth-Century Mexico*, ed. W. Dirk Raat and William Beezley (Lincoln, Nebr., 1986), 81.
30. Stephen H. Haber, *Industry and Underdevelopment: The Industrialization of Mexico, 1890–1940* (Stanford, Calif., 1989), 124.
31. Womack, "The Mexican Revolution," 82.
32. Thomas E. Skidmore and Peter H. Smith, *Modern Latin America* (New York, 1989), 76–78.
33. Ibid., 76; Katz, *The Secret War in Mexico*, 5–7.
34. Katz, "From Alliance to Dependency," 249.
35. This is not to say that the question of the extent and nature of U.S. influence during the Mexican Revolution is not being debated. A major issue is the question of economic nationalism in the countryside and the extent of anti-Americanism associated with it. The foremost advocate of the limited anti-Americanism view is Alan Knight who argues that "foreign interests did not figure as victims of the Revolution to anything like the extent argued or assumed in many studies. . . . To put it at its simplest, the idea of a virulently nationalist popular revolution was largely a myth." John Mason Hart says that the "crisis of the Mexican countryside that erupted in violence during the Revolution of 1910 was rooted in peasant and local elite groups . . . who were resisting the intrusive growth

of foreign-controlled (mostly American) commercial agricultural estates."
Much of the debate centers around the idea of nationalism and the con-
fusion between nationalism and xenophobia. Knight correctly points out
that much of the popular resistance was directed against Spaniards and
not Americans. Hart, for his part, has documented hundreds of anti-
American land seizures. It is obvious that at least in the Mexican North
anti-Americanism was virulent.

Knight's views can be found in several places, including his two-volume
work *The Mexican Revolution* (Cambridge, Eng., 1986). Also see Alan
Knight, "Interpreting the Mexican Revolution," in *Texas Papers on Mexico*
(Mexican Center, Institute of Latin American Studies, University of Texas
at Austin, Paper No. 88-02), 26 pp.; and his *U.S.-Mexican Relations, 1910–
1940: An Interpretation*, Center for U.S.-Mexican Studies (San Diego, Calif.,
1987). Hart's argument can be found in his *Revolutionary Mexico*. For the
best expression of both points of view plus those of other critics see *Rural
Revolt in Mexico and U.S. Intervention*. Anyone doubting anti-Americanism
in Chihuahua need only look at the chronology in Eugenia Meyer et al.,
Museo Histórico de la Revolución en el estado de Chihuahua (Mexico, 1982).

36. Linda B. Hall and Don M. Coerver, *Revolution on the Border* (Albuquerque,
N.M., 1988), 7. For the impact of immigration on U.S. border policy see
Douglas W. Richmond, "Mexican Immigration and Border Strategy during
the Revolution, 1910–1920," *New Mexico Historical Review* 57 (July 1982):
269–88.

37. Hall and Coerver, *Revolution on the Border*, 24–25, 40. See also Charles
Harris III and Louis R. Sadler, "The Plan of San Diego and the Mexican-
United States War Crisis of 1916: A Reexamination," *Hispanic American
Historical Review* 58 (August 1978): 381–408. For a vivid recreation of the
Bisbee strike see Robert Houston, *Bisbee '17: A Novel* (New York, 1979).

38. Hall and Coerver, *Revolution on the Border*, 31, 43.

39. The complete story of the *revoltosos* can be found in Raat, *Revoltosos*.

40. Hall and Coerver, *Revolution on the Border*, 44–77.

41. W. Dirk Raat, "US Intelligence Operations and Covert Action in Mexico,
1900–47," *Journal of Contemporary History* 22 (1987): 623. For the Army Air
Service see Stacy C. Hinkle, *Wings over the Border*, Southwestern Studies
Monograph no. 26 (El Paso, Tex., 1970).

42. Hall and Coerver, *Revolution on the Border*, 93–125.

43. Ibid., 93–95; Lorenzo Meyer, *Mexico and the United States in the Oil Controversy, 1917–1942* (Austin, Tex., 1977), 7, 10.

44. Hall and Coerver, *Revolution on the Border*, 96.
45. Ibid., 97. For evidence of Buckley's covert activity, see the reports from agent "no. 16" (who was probably a private investigator for the Fall Committee) during October and November of 1919, folder 164 of the William F. Buckley Papers, Nettie Lee Benson Latin American Collection, University of Texas at Austin.
46. Hall and Coerver, *Revolution on the Border*, 142–43, 157–58.
47. Ibid., 152–57.
48. Public opinion and the popular press had a positive effect on the campaign for diplomatic recognition of the Obregón government. For this dimension see C. Dennis Ignasias, "Propaganda and Public Opinion in Harding's Foreign Affairs: The Case for Mexican Recognition," *Journalism Quarterly* 48 (Spring 1971): 41–52.

7. Soldiers, Priests, and Lords of Land and Industry

1. In Latin America this nationalistic assertion of equal sovereignty is known as the Calvo Doctrine, named for the Argentine diplomat Carlos Calvo. For the Calvo Doctrine see Robert Freeman Smith, *The United States and Revolutionary Nationalism in Mexico, 1916–1932* (Chicago, 1972), 27–29.
2. Paul Kennedy, *The Rise and Fall of the Great Powers* (New York, 1987), 282–91, 327–33. The 1940 authorization alone doubled the navy's combat fleet, created seven thousand combat aircraft for the Army Air Corps, and resulted in an army of over a million men.
3. Jean Meyer, "Mexico: Revolution and Reconstruction in the 1920s," in the *Cambridge History of Latin America*, ed. Leslie Bethell (Cambridge, Eng., 1986), 5:176–79.
4. Ibid., 179. See also Stephen H. Haber, *Industry and Underdevelopment: The Industrialization of Mexico, 1890–1940* (Stanford, Calif., 1989), 150–52; and Jonathan C. Brown, "Why Foreign Oil Companies Shifted Their Production from Mexico to Venezuela during the 1920s," *American Historical Review* 2 (April 1985): 362–85.
5. Meyer, "Mexico in the 1920s," 179–81; Haber, *Industry and Underdevelopment*, 153–70. Peculiarly enough, the manufacturing of producer goods by Mexican firms did relatively well during the depression. This was partly due to government spending on construction projects that increased the demand for steel and cement.

6. James W. Wilkie constructs an index of poverty for the period between 1910 and 1960 in his *The Mexican Revolution: Federal Expenditure and Social Change since 1910* (Berkeley, Calif., 1967), 204–45. For the recovery of 1933–40 see Haber, *Industry and Underdevelopment*, 171–89.

7. James D. Cockcroft, *Mexico: Class Formation, Capital Accumulation, and the State* (New York, 1983), 125.

8. Wilkie, *The Mexican Revolution*, 60–81; Haber, *Industry and Underdevelopment*, 173–77, 187–89.

9. For the Good Neighbor Policy see Lloyd Gardner, *Economic Aspects of New Deal Diplomacy* (Madison, Wis., 1964), 47–63, 109–32. See also David Green, *The Containment of Latin America* (Chicago, 1971), 3–35; and Josefina Zoraida Vázquez and Lorenzo Meyer, *México frente a Estados Unidos: un ensayo histórico, 1776–1980* (Mexico, 1982), 166–72.

10. Vázquez and Meyer, *México frente a Estados Unidos*, 164.

11. See the novel by Carlos Fuentes, *El Gringo Viejo* (Mexico, 1985), translated by Margaret Sayers Peden as *The Old Gringo* (New York, 1985).

12. Masha Zakheim Jewett, *Coit Tower, San Francisco: Its History and Art* (San Francisco, 1983), 27–30. See also Laurance P. Hulburt, *The Mexican Muralists in the United States* (Albuquerque, N.M., 1989). Hulburt argues that America's first great national school of art, that of abstract expressionism, grew out of the Mexican mural movement. As for the PWAP, it should not be confused with the Federal Art Project (FAP). The FAP was under the Works Progress Administration (WPA) and was characterized as a "relief project for starving artists." The PWAP, however, solicited the works of artists by regional committees.

13. By "corporativism" I mean a state that, through the apparatus of the official party, creates a political machine that manipulates class organizations (e.g., workers, peasants, or corporations) through populist slogans, concessions, coaptation, and if necessary, repression. In Mexico, state-supported corporations were favored in their struggle with traditional groups such as military and religious oligarchs and private landholders. See Cockcroft, *Mexico*, 139–41; or Lyle C. Brown, "The Calles-Cárdenas Connection," in *Twentieth-Century Mexico*, ed. W. Dirk Raat and William H. Beezley (Lincoln, Nebr., 1986), 146–58. For the special theme of soldier, priest, and landlord see Donald Hodges and Ross Gandy, *Mexico, 1910–1982: Reform or Revolution?* (London, 1983), 28–44.

14. W. Dirk Raat, "US Intelligence Operations and Covert Action in Mexico, 1900–1947," *Journal of Contemporary History* 22 (1987): 619; James D.

Rudolph, ed., *Mexico: A Country Study* (Washington, D.C., 1985), 439; John Child, *Unequal Alliance: The Inter-American Military System, 1938–1978* (Boulder, Colo., 1980), 13–14, 56–59; Cockcroft, *Mexico*, 117.

15. Raat, "Covert Action in Mexico," 624. For the ONI in Mexico see the Records of the Office of Chief of Naval Operations, ONI, Record Group 38, assorted records; and Naval Records Collection of the Office of Naval Records and Library, Record Group 45, W-E-5, ONI, 1900–21, National Archives, Washington, D.C. A general history of the ONI is Jeffrey M. Dorwart, *The Office of Naval Intelligence* (Annapolis, Md., 1979).

16. Raat, "Covert Action in Mexico," 624–31. For the MID in Mexico see *US Military Intelligence Reports, 1919–1941*, ed. Dale Reynolds (Frederick, Md., 1984), 9 reels (hereafter cited as *MIR*). These are microfilmed copies of documents from the National Archives and Records Service, Washington, D.C., Record Group 165; and Records of the War Department General and Special Staffs, MID, Files, Mexico. For a general study see Bruce W. Bidwell, *History of the Military Intelligence Division, Department of the Army General Staff, 1775–1941* (Frederick, Md., 1985).

17. John W. F. Dulles, *Yesterday in Mexico: A Chronicle of the Revolution, 1919–1936* (Austin, Tex., 1961), 228–30, 259.

18. Ibid., 443. See also Vázquez and Meyer, *México frente a Estados Unidos*, 158.

19. Rudolph, *Mexico: A Country Study*, 327.

20. Edwin Lieuwen, *Mexican Militarism: The Political Rise and Fall of the Revolutionary Army* (Albuquerque, N.M., 1968), 64–65.

21. Ibid., 67–72.

22. Ibid., 85–95. See also Edwin Lieuwen, "Depoliticization of the Mexican Army, 1915–1940," in *The Modern Mexican Military: A Reassessment*, ed. David Ronfeldt, Center for U.S.-Mexican Studies, University of California, Monograph Series 15 (San Diego and La Jolla, Calif., 1984), 55–57; and Carleton Beals, "The Indian Who Sways Mexico's Destiny," *New York Times* 7 December 1930, in James W. Wilkie and Albert L. Michaels, *Revolution in Mexico: Years of Upheaval, 1910–1940* (New York, 1969), 170–173.

23. Lieuwen, *Mexican Militarism*, 118–21. By 1946, the military share of the federal budget was 10 percent; by 1952, 7 percent. For an excellent study of the Cárdenas era, especially the army, see Alicia Hernández Chávez, *La mecánica cardenista*, vol. 16 of *Historia de la Revolución Mexicana* (Mexico, 1980).

24. Lieuwen, "Depoliticization of the Mexican Revolutionary Army," 55–58.

25. Ibid., 59–60. The drug ring information came from G-2 Report No. 3394,

Military Attaché, Mexico City, 12 June 1931, *MIR*. The end of Almazán and the triumph of Camacho in 1940 eventually led to the dissolution of *sector militar* influence in the party.

26. The best studies of the Cristeros are Jean A. Meyer, *The Cristero Rebellion: The Mexican People between Church and State, 1926–1929*, abridged and translated by Richard Southern from the three volume *La Cristiada* (New York, 1976); and David C. Bailey, *Víva Crísto Rey!: The Cristero Rebellion and the Church-State Conflict in Mexico* (Austin, Tex., 1974).

27. Meyer, *The Cristero Rebellion*, 49–59; Meyer, "Mexico in the 1920s," 190.

28. Bailey, *Víva Crísto Rey!* 287, 303–4. The fatality figures come from "Armed Revolutionary Movements: Cristero Activities in 1928 and 1929 in Jalisco," G-2 Report by Gordon Johnston, Military Attaché, 15 April 1930, *MIR*.

29. The Nicaraguan issue is treated by Richard V. Salisbury in his article "Mexico, the United States, and the 1926–1927 Nicaraguan Crisis," *Hispanic American Historical Review* 66 (May 1986): 319–39.

30. Vázquez and Meyer, *México frente a Estados Unidos*, 154–55.

31. Quoted in Robert H. Vinca, "The American Catholic Reaction to the Persecution of the Church in Mexico, 1926–1929," *Records of the American Catholic Historical Society of Philadelphia* 79 (March 1968): 14. See also the unpublished manuscript by Jeffrey Vogt, "The Mexican Cristero Rebellion: The American Catholic Reaction," Senior thesis, State University of New York at Fredonia, January 1987.

32. Luis González, *San José de Gracia: Mexican Village in Transition* (Austin, Tex., 1974), 152.

33. Bailey, *Víva Crísto Rey!* 308.

34. *America: A Catholic Review of the Week*, 35 (21 August 1926): 433.

35. Bailey, *Víva Crísto Rey!* 307–8.

36. Wilkie and Michaels, *Revolution in Mexico*, 199–203. See also "Religion: Freedom of Religious Belief and Practice, the Church Situation in Mexico," G-2 Report No. 3083, 26 September 1930, *MIR*.

37. For the role of Daniels in seeking a solution to the church-state controversy see E. David Cronon, *Josephus Daniels in Mexico* (Madison, Wis., 1960), 82–111.

38. Jan Bazant, *A Concise History of Mexico from Hidalgo to Cárdenas, 1805–1940* (Cambridge, Eng., 1977), 191.

39. For a general analysis of Mexico's agrarian reform program see Rodolfo Stavenhagen, "Collective Agriculture and Capitalism in Mexico: A Way Out or a Dead End?" *Latin American Perspectives* 2 (Summer 1975): 145–

63. See also Hodges and Gandy, *Mexico, 1910–1982*, 42; and Cockcroft, *Mexico*, 133.

40. See table on land distribution in Mexico in John Womack, Jr., "The Mexican Economy during the Revolution, 1910–20," in *Twentieth-Century Mexico*, 81.

41. Vázquez and Meyer, *México frente a Estados Unidos*, 167. Cockcroft, *Mexico*, 133–34.

42. Hodges and Gandy, *Mexico, 1910–1982*, 43; Meyer, "Mexico in the 1920s," 191.

43. Manuel R. Millor, *Mexico's Oil: Catalyst for a New Relationship with the U.S.?* (Boulder, Colo., 1982), 19–24.

44. Quoted in Lorenzo Meyer, *Mexico and the United States in the Oil Controversy, 1917–1942* (Austin, Tex., 1977), 167–168.

45. Some writers, like Lorenzo Meyer (ibid., 169), refer to the act of 1938 as nationalization, rather than expropriation. Expropriation is an act directed at a particular firm usually followed by some effort at compensation. Nationalization is a generalized action by the state to bring about a basic change in the economy. Confiscation, however, is a seizure of property without effective compensation. Expropriation is acceptable international practice; confiscation is a violation of international law. Throughout the controversy the Mexican government spoke of "expropriation," while the oil companies and the U.S. State Department called it "confiscation."

46. Millor, *Mexico's Oil*, 25–27; George W. Grayson, *The Politics of Mexican Oil* (Pittsburgh, Pa., 1980), 14–15.

47. Quoted in "All Property of Oil Companies Expropriated by President Cardenas," G-2 Report, no. 8373, Military Attaché, Mexico City, 22 March 1938.

48. For the role of PEMEX after 1940 see Michael Tanzer, *The Political Economy of International Oil and the Underdeveloped Countries* (Boston, 1969), 288–303.

49. Grayson, *The Politics of Mexican Oil*, 16–17.

50. For Roosevelt's U.S. critics see Cronon, *Josephus Daniels in Mexico*, pp. 232–33.

51. Karl M. Schmitt, *Communism in Mexico: A Study in Political Frustration* (Austin, Tex., 1965), 14–15.

52. "Nazi-Communist Influence in Mexico," in Roscoe B. Gaither (New York City) to War Department, 1 October 1940, *MIR*.

53. Grayson, *The Politics of Mexican Oil*, 17–18. For Josephus Daniels's role in the oil controversy see Cronon, *Josephus Daniels in Mexico*, 185–271.

Daniels gives his own account in his autobiography, *Shirt-Sleeve Diplomat* (Chapel Hill, N.C., 1947).

54. For the global settlement that brought the oil crisis to an end see David S. Painter, *Oil and the American Century: The Political Economy of U.S. Foreign Oil Policy, 1941–1954* (Baltimore, Md., 1986), 22–31.

55. Many of these ideas were suggested to me in correspondence from John Womack, Jr., 29 January 1990.

56. The congruence of Mexican and U.S. history in the early twentieth century is the theme of Alan Knight's work, *U.S.-Mexican Relations, 1910–1940: An Interpretation*, Center for U.S.-Mexican Studies (San Diego, Calif., 1987), esp. 1–20.

8. Preening and Ruffling the Serpent's Plumage

1. Immanuel Wallerstein, "Friends as Foes," *Foreign Policy* 40 (Fall 1980): 121–22.

2. Ibid., 122. Interview of Irwin L. Kellner, "Federal Deficit Problems," *Boardroom Reports* (1 May 1990): 8. See also Paul Kennedy, *The Rise and Fall of the Great Powers* (New York, 1987), 526–27. Most of the literature debunking the decline of the American power thesis has taken aim at Paul Kennedy's book. See, for example, Daniel Patrick Moynihan, "Debunking the Myth of Decline," *New York Times Magazine* (19 June 1988): 34, 52–53; Peter Schmeisser, "Is America on the Rocks?" *Buffalo News*, 1 May 1988; and Joseph S. Nye, Jr., "Still in the Game," *World Monitor* 3 (March 1990): 42–47. See also Susan Strange, "The Future of the American Empire," *Journal of International Affairs* 42 (Fall 1988): 1–17.

3. The Tlatelolco and Corpus Christi incidents are studied in Judith Adler Hellman, *Mexico in Crisis* (New York, 1983), 173–186, 202–4. See also Elena Poniatowska, *La Noche de Tlatelolco* (Mexico, 1971).

4. An excellent general overview of contemporary Mexican history can be found in Peter H. Smith, "Mexico since 1946," in the *Cambridge History of Latin America*, ed. Leslie Bethell (Cambridge, Eng., 1990), 6:83–157.

5. James B. Pick et al., *Atlas of Mexico* (Boulder, Colo., 1989), 11–54; Peter M. Ward, "Mexico City" (paper presented at Megacities of the Americas Conference, Lewis Mumford Center, SUNY, Albany, New York, 5–7 April 1990), 3. For a history of Mexico City, see Jonathan Kandell, *La Capital: The Biography of Mexico City* (New York, 1988).

The preliminary findings of the 1990 U.S. census indicated that the United States had a total population of 245,837,683, up nearly 20 million from the 1980 figure but less than originally projected. Likewise, Mexico, calculated to be 85 million in 1990, was less than expected, but how much less was yet to be determined at the time of this writing.

6. For the triangular relationship between Germany, Mexico, and the United States see Friedrich Schuler, "Germany, Mexico and the United States during the Second World War," *Jahrbuch fur Geschichte von Staat, Wirtschaft und Gesallschaft Lateinamerika* 22 (1985): 457–76.

7. The history of Mexico-U.S. relations during World War II is recounted in Josefina Zoraida Vázquez and Lorenzo Meyer, *México frente a Estados Unidos un ensayo histórico, 1776–1980* (Mexico, 1982), 180–88.

8. Ibid., 182–84. The military's share of the national budget continued to decline during this period. From 30 percent in 1930, the military's share had been reduced to 7 percent in 1952 and was only 1 percent of the 1980 budget. See James W. Wilkie, *The Mexican Revolution: Federal Expenditures and Social Change since 1910* (Berkeley, Calif., 1967), 102–3, and Francisco Carrada Bravo, *Oil, Money, and the Mexican Economy: A Macroeconomic Analysis* (Boulder, Colo., 1982), 43.

9. W. Dirk Raat, "Gus T. Jones and the FBI in Mexico, 1900–1947," (paper presented at the American Historical Association, San Francisco, 29 December 1989). Much of the material in this paper was taken from FBI files and also the unpublished manuscript by Gus T. Jones, "The Nazi Failure in Mexico," Hoover Institution Archives, Stanford University, Stanford, California.

10. Ibid. See also Leslie B. Rout and John F. Bratzel, *The Shadow War: German Espionage and United States Counterespionage in Latin America during World War II* (Frederick, Md., 1986), esp. 79.

11. Vázquez and Meyer, *México frente a Estados Unidos*, 185. For the legalized production of opium in Mexico during the war see Elaine Shannon, *Desperados: Latin Drug Lords, U.S. Lawmen, and the War America Can't Win* (New York, 1989), 34, 63.

12. Richard B. Craig, *The Bracero Program* (Austin, Tex., 1971), 38; Peter Brown and Henry Shue, *The Border that Joins* (Potowar, N.J., 1983), 57–59; James D. Cockcroft, *Outlaws in the Promised Land* (New York, 1986), 69.

13. Vázquez and Meyer, *México frente a Estados Unidos*, 185–86.

14. Michael C. Meyer and William L. Sherman, *The Course of Mexican History* (New York, 1987), 633–37.

15. For the PEMEX story see Michael Tanzer, *The Political Economy of International Oil and the Underdeveloped Countries* (Boston, 1969), 288–303.
16. Thomas E. Skidmore and Peter H. Smith, *Modern Latin America* (New York, 1989), 235.
17. Vázquez and Meyer, *México frente a Estados Unidos*, 197–98, 201, 206; Meyer and Sherman, *The Course of Mexican History*, 646; José Luis Ceceña, *México en la órbita imperial* (Mexico, 1970), 210–12.
18. Kennedy, *The Rise and Fall of the Great Powers*, 413–16; Daniel Chirot, *Social Change in the Modern Era* (New York, 1986), 204–5.
19. Chirot, *Social Change in the Modern Era*, 206–7.
20. Skidmore and Smith, *Modern Latin America*, 239.
21. Hellman, *Mexico in Crisis*, 192–93. See also Richard R. Fagan, "The Realities of U.S.-Mexican Relations," *Foreign Affairs* 55 (July 1977): 692–93.
22. Hellman, *Mexico in Crisis*, 193–94; Vázquez and Meyer, *México frente a Estados Unidos*, 218.
23. Hellman, *Mexico in Crisis*, 195.
24. Kennedy, *The Rise and Fall of the Great Powers*, 404–9, 413–37.
25. U.S. Congress, Senate Committee to Study Governmental Operations with respect to Intelligence Activities, *Covert Action in Chile 1963–1973*, 93rd Cong., 2nd Sess., 18 December 1975. Also see Errol D. Jones and David LaFrance, "Mexico's Foreign Affairs under President Echeverria: The Special Case of Chile," *Inter-American Economic Affairs* 30 (Summer 1976): 45–78.

    Consistently inconsistent, Echeverría, to appease the Right, quietly sent his minister to Santiago that next year (May 1974) to pursue trade relations with the government of General Augusto Pinochet.
26. Kennedy, *The Rise and Fall of the Great Powers*, 357–72.
27. Vázquez and Meyer, *México frente a Estados Unidos*, 202, 205–6; Hellman, *Mexico in Crisis*, 207–8.
28. Jones and LaFrance, "Mexico's Foreign Affairs," 77–78.
29. Ibid.; Fagen, "The Realities of U.S.-Mexican Relations," 692–95.
30. Lorenzo Meyer, "Oil Booms and the Mexican Historical Experience: Past Problems—Future Prospects," in *Mexico-U.S. Relations: Conflict and Convergence*, ed. Carlos Vásquez and Manuel García Griego (Los Angeles, 1983), 182; Fagen, "The Realities of U.S.-Mexican Relations," 696–97. For an early account of the oil discovery by a U.S. analyst see Richard B. Mancke, *Mexican Oil and Natural Gas: Political, Strategic, and Economic Implications* (New York, 1979), 59–75.

31. Meyer, "Oil Booms and the Mexican Historical Experience," 186–92.
32. Manuel R. Millor, *Mexico's Oil: Catalyst for a New Relationship with the U.S.?* (Boulder, Colo., 1982), 218, 220.
33. Ibid., 221.
34. Farhad Simyar, "Winners and Losers of the Oil Price Roller-Coaster," in *U.S.-Mexican Economic Relations: Prospects and Problems*, ed. Khosrow Fatemi (New York, 1988), 187–201.
35. Hellman, *Mexico in Crisis*, 218–28; *New York Times*, 19 October 1988.
36. Miguel D. Ramírez, *The IMF Austerity Program, 1983–87: Miguel de la Madrid's Legacy*, Occasional Papers in Latin American Studies no. 7 (Storrs, Conn.: University of Connecticut, July 1989), 2–3. See also Ramírez's "Mexico's Development Experience, 1950–85: Lessons and Future Prospects," *Journal of Interamerican Studies and World Affairs* 28 (Summer 1986): 39–65.
37. Ramírez, *The IMF Austerity Program*, 7. For the political fallout from the earthquakes, see Steve Frazier's article "Nation in Jeopardy: Aftermath of the Earthquake Points up the Weaknesses of Mexico's Leadership," in the *Wall Street Journal*, 15 October 1985. Not helping the administration's public image was the discovery of eight bodies of tortured victims in the ruins of the basement of the Judicial Police building.
38. Alan Riding, "Beleaguered Mexico Cedes Role as Central America Power Broker," *New York Times*, 24 October 1986; Olga Pellicer, "Mexico in Central America: The Difficult Exercise of Regional Power," in *The Future of Central America: Policy Choices for the U.S. and Mexico*, ed. Richard R. Fagen and Olga Pellicer (Stanford, Calif., 1983), 119–33; Mario Ojeda, "Mexican Policy toward Central America in the Context of U.S.-Mexico Relations," in *The Future of Central America*, 135–60.
39. John Naisbitt and Patricia Aburdene, *Megatrends 2000* (New York, 1990), 160; *New York Times*, 17 June 1988.
40. Jackie Roddick, *The Dance of the Millions: Latin America and the Debt Crisis* (London, 1988), 114–18. The CIA report and the $3.5 billion bridge loan are noted in the 19 October 1986 issue of the *New York Times*. See also the report by Peter Kilborn on world debt in the 23 October 1988 issue of the *New York Times*. James W. Wilkie comments on the Brady Plan in his report "Refocusing Interpretation on the Mexican Political Economy," in *Mexico Policy News* 4 (Spring 1990): 18.

    Patrick Buchanan suggests that James Baker's plan to help the beleagured banks is motivated by his personal fortune that is tied up in the

Chemical Banking Corp. of New York, an institution holding $5.7 billion in Third World debt. See Patrick Buchanan, "Baker's hanky panky with bankers," *Buffalo News*, 24 February 1989.

41. Ramírez, *The IMF Austerity Program*, 8–12.

42. Roddick, *The Dance of the Millions*, 116; *New York Times*, 29 March 1990. For the classic statement on the IMF and the World Bank and imperialism, see Teresa Hayter, *Aid as Imperialism* (Middlesex, Eng., 1971).

43. Jeffrey Bortz, "Long Waves, Postwar Industrialization, and the Origins of Mexico's Economic Crisis," paper presented at the University of Connecticut and Brown University-sponsored conference on 'Mexico in Crisis: Past, Present, Future' held at the Bishop Center, University of Connecticut, Storrs, 22–23 April 1988, 39–40. Bortz places the Mexican crisis of 1982 in a global historical perspective, noting from GNP data that, for the entire period from the late nineteenth century to the present, Mexican and U.S. growth phases have tended to coincide.

44. Robert A. Rankin, "How the Latin debt crisis affects Americans directly," *Buffalo News*, 10 April 1989.

45. Shannon, *Desperados*, 70, 73–75, 122, 412–13. See also Scott B. MacDonald, *Dancing on a Volcano: The Latin American Drug Trade* (New York, 1988), 69–87.

    Allegations have been made that U.S. equipment was sent to Mexico not only to fight the drug war, but that the drug war was actually a cover to allow the United States to equip the Mexican army.

46. Ibid., 64–68.

47. Ibid., 67–68.

48. Paul Salopek, "Harvest of Violence: Narcotics pistoleros seize land of Indians," *El Paso Times*, 26 February 1989; John J. Fialka, "Death of U.S. Agent in Mexico Drug Case Uncovers Grid of Graft," *Wall Street Journal*, 19 November 1986.

49. Jeff Gerth, "C.I.A. Shedding Its Reluctance to Aid in Fight against Drugs," *New York Times*, 25 March 1990; Robert S. Greenberger and John E. Yang, "Congressional Mexico-Bashing, Despite Criticism, Becomes Core of a Way to Fight U.S. Drug Problem," *Wall Street Journal*, 4 May 1988.

50. Shannon, *Desperados*, 284–91, 513; "Former Mexican police head indicted," *Buffalo News*, 1 February 1990.

51. The Buendía affair is discussed in Robert A. Pastor and Jorge G. Castañeda, *Limits to Friendship: The United States and Mexico* (New York, 1988),

66–67. See also Timothy Stirton, "Mexican journalist slain—a grim saga continues," *In These Times* 12 (4–10 May 1988), 4, and "Identifican al Asesino de Buendía," *El Heraldo*, 12 June 1989. For the connection between the DFS and the CIA in this incident, see Jack Anderson, "Mexico Slow to Act on Death," *Evening Observer* (Dunkirk, N.Y.), 21 August 1990. Since the Buendía incident, and because of its tarnished image, the DFS has been abolished.

52. For the accusations against Ibarra-Herrera, see "Former Mexican police head indicted," *Buffalo News*, 1 February 1990. An analysis of Mexico's internal security forces, including the MFJP and the DFS, is found in James D. Rudolph, ed., *Mexico: A Country Study* (Washington, D.C., 1985), 360–70. Corruption continues to characterize the Salinas era. On 21 May 1990 the president of the Sinaloa state bar and head of the Commission on Human Rights, Norma Corona Sapiens, was killed in Culiacán. It was hinted that federal judicial police were involved in her assassination. Also in May, the former governor of Jalisco and current attorney general was implicated in drug trafficking while governor of Jalisco. See "Mil Policias Tras el Asesino de la Dra." in *Excelsior*, 23 May 1990; and "Testifica Agente de la DEA que el Procurador Alvarez del Castillo Estuvo Ligado al Narco Cuando Gobernó Jalisco," *Diario de Chihuahua*, 31 May 1990. The general issue of police corruption is treated in an entertaining fashion in Dick J. Reavis, *Conversations with Moctezuma* (New York, 1990), 83–89.

The issue of corruption is two-edged. Certainly the U.S. government had a variety of forms of corruption under the Reagan administration— for example, the corrupt public officials who ran the Housing and Urban Development agency (HUD), the Iran-Contra secret warriors, the bankers (and their congressional friends) of the savings and loan industry, and the Deaver-Meese-Nofziger scandals. For both sides of the story see William Branigin, "A Stinging Indictment of High-Level Mexican Corruption," *Washington Post*, 13–19 February 1989; and William F. Weld, "We Greatly Underrate the Power of Corruption in U.S.," *Buffalo News*, 1 May 1988.

53. Joseph Contreras, "Low Blow in Chihuahua?" *Newsweek*, 21 July 1986. For a profile of a "typical" panista see Patrick Oster, *The Mexicans: A Personal Portrait of a People* (New York, 1989), 110–19.

54. *Wall Street Journal*, 11 July 1988.

55. Jonathan Kandell and Matt Moffett, "As Mexico Vote Count Remains

in Limbo, Rumors Center on Left Wing's Cardenas," *Wall Street Journal*, 12 July 1988; Oster, *The Mexicans*, 93–109.

56. *Wall Street Journal*, 15 July 1988; Ward, "Mexico City," 8.

9. Mexamerica

1. For a discussion on terminology see Paul Kutsche, "Borders and Frontiers," in *Borderlands Sourcebook: A Guide to the Literature on Northern Mexico and the American Southwest*, ed. Ellwyn R. Stoddard, et al. (Norman, Okla., 1983), 18. The idea of border culture, that is, an area of Anglo-Latin cultural transition, is examined in Richard Nostrand, "A Changing Cultural Region," in *Borderlands Sourcebook*, 13.

2. Lester D. Langley, *MexAmerica: Two Countries, One Future* (New York, 1988), 4–5.

3. For popular culture on the frontier see Américo Paredes, "The Problem of Identity in a Changing Culture: Popular Expressions of Culture Conflict among the Low Rio Grande Border," in *Views across the Border: The United States and Mexico*, ed. Stanley R. Ross (Albuquerque, N.M., 1978), 68–94. For several studies on the popular culture in the United States and Mexico see *Mexico and the United States: Intercultural Relations in the Humanities*, ed. Juanita Luna Lawhn et al. (San Antonio, Tex., 1984), 67–126. See also Merle E. Simmons, *The Mexican Corrido as a Source for Interpretive Study of Modern Mexico (1870–1950)* (Bloomington, Ind., 1957), 419–60.

4. Raúl A. Fernández, *The Mexican-American Border Region: Issues and Trends* (Notre Dame, Ind., 1989), 16–17, 31. On the U.S. side Niles Hanson identifies seven subregions in the borderlands: the San Diego metropolitan area; the Imperial Valley; the Arizona borderlands; the El Paso economic region; the middle Río Grande region of Texas; the south Texas region; and the lower Rio Grande valley. See Niles Hanson, *The Border Economy: Regional Development in the Southwest* (Austin, Tex., 1981), 35–52.

5. This Mexamericana scenario is derived from a factual base with some embellishments that are imaginary but plausible. The facts have been taken from the following: John M. Crewdson, "Border Region Is almost a Country unto Itself, Neither Mexican Nor American," *New York Times*, 14 February 1979; John Hurst, "Proud Mixtec Indians Face Exploitation," *Los Angeles Times*, 5 January 1987; Matt Moffett, "Winter Texans," *Wall*

Street Journal, 9 March 1987; "Town mourns for 7 lost under Texas sun," *El Paso Times*, 5 July 1987.

6. Jack D. Forbes, *Apache, Navaho and Spaniard* (1960; reprint, Westport, Conn., 1980); xi–xxiii, 281–85. See also Elizabeth A. H. John, *Storms Brewed in Other Men's Worlds* (Lincoln, Nebr., 1975), 57–64, 114–17.

7. The history and theory of incorporation is the subject of Thomas D. Hall, *Social Change in the Southwest, 1350–1880* (Lawrence, Kans., 1989). My account is very dependent on Hall's work. Richard Nostrand surveys several post-Columbian images of Mexamerica in "A Changing Culture Region," *Borderlands Sourcebook*, 6–15. For the turquoise trade see Garman Harbottle and Phil C. Weigand, "Turquoise in Pre-Columbian America," *Scientific American* 266 (February 1992), 78–85.

8. The 1990 census data did not appear in its final form as of this writing. The best source for statistics of the border area is David E. Lorey, ed., *United States-Mexico Border Statistics since 1900*, UCLA Latin American Center, Los Angeles, 1990. See esp. the first section on demography, 5–46. All of the Lorey materials are derived from the 1980 census. For the limitations of available border data and problems inherent in their use see David E. Lorey, "The Emergence of the U.S.-Mexico Border Region in the Twentieth Century: A Brief Overview of Social and Economic Trends," paper presented for the UCLA Program on Mexico, Los Angeles, 1–5.

Additional data for these Mexamerican groups were taken from Andrew Hacker, ed., *A Statistical Portrait of the American People* (New York, 1983), 15, 33–43; James B. Pick et al., *Atlas of Mexico* (Boulder, Colo., 1989), 48–50, 157–58; and "Hispanics log population rise," *Buffalo News*, 7 September 1988. The figure of forty million for the borderlands is cited by J. Lawrence McConville, "Society and Culture," in *Borderlands Sourcebook*, 246. For recent population growth see Lay James Gibson and Alfonso Corona Rentería, eds., *The U.S. and Mexico: Borderland Development and the National Economies* (Boulder, Colo., 1985), 20–21.

There are a variety of Spanish-speaking foreign nationals in Mexamerica besides those of Mexican descent, from Colombian drug traffickers in Dublan and Casas Grandes, Chihuahua, to Salvadoran political exiles outside Brownsville, Texas.

9. Oscar J. Martínez, *Troublesome Border* (Tucson, Ariz., 1988), 71–76.

10. See Evelyn Hu-DeHart, *Missionaries, Miners and Spaniards: Spanish Contact with the Yaqui Nation of Northwestern New Spain, 1533–1820* (Tucson, Ariz.,

1981); or her other work, *Yaqui Resistance and Survival: The Struggle for Land and Autonomy, 1821–1910* (Madison, Wis., 1984), esp. 3–12.

11. Hu-Dehart, *Yaqui Resistance and Survival*, 6–8.

12. Ibid., 9–12.

13. Felipe A. Latorre and Dolores L. Latorre, *The Mexican Kickapoo Indians* (Austin, Tex., 1976), 3–8.

14. Ibid., 8–20.

15. Ibid., 20–25.

16. Tom Miller, *On the Border* (New York, 1981), 65. As a personal note, when I traveled to Piedras Negras during the summer of 1987, the Kickapoos were nowhere to be found, having been relocated by the Mexican government.

17. Cambell W. Pennington, *The Tarahumar of Mexico* (Salt Lake City, Utah, 1963), 13–18.

18. Martínez, *Troublesome Border*, 78; William L. Merrill, *Rarámuri Souls* (Washington, D.C., 1988), 30–43. The herbal medicine and peyote cults of the Tarahumara are celebrated in the poem by Alfonso Reyes, "Yerbas del Tarahumara" in *An Anthology of Mexican Poetry*, ed. Octavio Paz (Bloomington, Ind., 1973), 188–90.

19. See, for example, David J. Weber, ed., *Foreigners in Their Native Land* (Albuquerque, N.M., 1973). See also Martínez, *Troublesome Border*, 80–98.

20. Martínez, *Troublesome Border*, 97.

21. Bill Bryson, *The Mother Tongue: English & How It Got That Way* (New York, 1990), 239–41. The quotation by Fuentes is found in Bill Moyers, *A World of Ideas: Conversations with Thoughtful Men and Women about American Life Today and the Ideas Shaping Our Future*, ed. Betty Sue Flowers (New York, 1989), 506.

22. Martínez, *Troublesome Border*, 101–2.

23. Ibid., 99–101; Mario García, "La Frontera: The Border as Symbol and Reality in Mexican-American Thought," *Mexican Studies/Estudios Mexicanos* 1:2 (Summer 1985): 224–25. For Chicanos and U.S.-Mexico relations see James D. Cockcroft, *Outlaws in the Promised Land* (New York, 1986), 152–74, and Rodolfo O. de la Garza, "Chicanos and U.S. Foreign Policy: The Future of Chicano-Mexican Relations," in *Mexican-U.S. Relations: Conflict and Convergence*, ed. Carlos Vásquez and Manuel García y Griego (Los Angeles, UCLA Chicano Studies Research Center, 1983), 399–416.

24. Paredes, "The Problem of Identity," 93; Richard L. Nostrand, "A Changing Culture Region," in *Borderlands Sourcebook*, 12–13. The disdain goes

both ways, of course, with *norteños* disliking *chilangos* (residents of Mexico City). In Chihuahua I recently saw a bumper sticker that read "Chilangos . . . Bievenidos a Chihuahua. Pero, Ya Se Van?," which roughly translates into "Chilangos . . . welcome to Chihuahua. But, when are you leaving?"

25. See Edward J. Williams, "The Resurgent North and Contemporary Mexican Regionalism," in *Mexican Studies/Estudios Mexicanos* 6:2 (Summer 1990): 299–323.

26. Martínez, *Troublesome Border*, 108–9.

27. Ibid., 114–19; Williams, "The Resurgent North," 313, 318.

28. Hansen, *The Border Economy*, 16.

29. Ibid., 15, 33; Gibson and Rentería, *The U.S. and Mexico*, 11; Pick, *Atlas of Mexico*, 47; Richard Reeves, "The facts are in—the rich got richer," *Buffalo News*, 31 August 1990; Stanley Meisler, "Gap widens between income of rich, poor," *Buffalo News*, 24 July 1990; Leslie Sklair, *Assembling for Development: The Maquila Industry in Mexico and the United States* (London, 1989), 218–23.

30. Mario Ojeda, *The Northern Border as a National Concern* (Center for Inter-American and Border Studies, University of Texas at El Paso, No. 4, 1983), 1; Steven E. Sanderson, *The Transformation of Mexican Agriculture* (Princeton, N.J., 1986), 44–45.

31. Sklair, *Assembling for Development*, 17; Gibson and Rentería, *The U.S. and Mexico*, 9.

32. Fernández, *The Mexican-American Border Region*, 16–18.

33. William Stockton, "Mexico's Grand 'Maquiladora' Plan," *New York Times*, 19 January 1986; "Mother, Teen work long hours to pay for food, Keep hopes alive," *Buffalo News*, 11 March 1987; "Toy plants here bucking trend to go overseas," *Buffalo News*, 2 March 1990; "Buffalo China completes plant in Mexico," *Buffalo News*, 8 May 1989.

34. "San Diego finds itself in sea of social change," *Buffalo News*, 20 August 1989; C. Richard Scott et al., "Japanese Reach into the U.S. Marketplace," paper presented at the Rocky Mountain Council on Latin American Studies, Las Cruces, N.M., 3 February 1989.

35. Sklair, *Assembling for Development*, 238.

36. Ellwyn R. Stoddard, *Maquila: Assembly Plants in Northern Mexico* (El Paso, Tex., 1987), 70–71.

37. Interview of B. W. Wolfe, President of Trico Corp. in Texas and Mexico, by W. Dirk Raat, Brownsville, Texas, 1 July 1987.

38. Susan Tiano, "Maquiladoras, Women's Work, and Unemployment in Northern Mexico," *Aztlán* 15:2 (Fall 1984): 341–78; Gay Young, *Women, Border Industrialization Program, and Human Rights* (Center for Inter-American and Border Studies, University of Texas at El Paso, No. 14, September 1984), 1–33; Wilkie English, Susan Williams, and Santiago Ibarreche, "Employee Turnover in the Maquiladoras," *Journal of Borderlands Studies* 4 (Fall 1989): 70–99; "In Health there Are No Borders," *Newsweek*, 1 August 1988; Sarah Henry, "The Poison Trail," *Los Angeles Times Magazine*, 23 September 1990; "Trico cuts 405 jobs as part of Texas-Mexico move," *Buffalo News*, 1 September 1987; John J. LaFalce, " 'Maquiladoras' Cost American Jobs," *New York Times*, 13 December 1987; Michael Beebe, "U.S. firms leave stain on Mexico," *Buffalo News*, 28 April 1991. The vast literature of the *maquiladora* industry is surveyed by Leslie Sklair in *Maquiladoras: Annotated Bibliography and Research Guide to Mexico's In-Bond Industry, 1980–1988* (Monograph No. 24, San Diego, Center for U.S.-Mexican Studies, 1988.)
39. Pick, *Atlas of Mexico*, 47, 49.
40. A catalog of border problems can be found in Stanley R. Ross, ed., *Views across the Border*, and César Sepúlveda and Albert E. Utton, eds., *The U.S.-Mexico Border Region: Anticipating Resource Needs and Issues to the Year 2000* (El Paso, Tex., 1984). For a case study of the needs of one border community see Gay Young, ed., *The Social Ecology and Economic Development of Ciudad Juárez* (Boulder, Colo., 1986). For demographic and economic aspects of U.S.-Mexican relations see Paul Ganster and Alan Sweedler, "The United States-Mexican Border Region: Security and Interdependence," in *United States-Mexico Border Statistics*, ed. David E. Lorey, 432–41.
41. Peter A. Lupsha, "The Border Underworld," in *Teaching about International Boundaries*, ed. Garth M. Hansen (Las Cruces, N.M. Joint Border Research Institute, New Mexico State University, vol. 1, *Borders and Frontiers*, 1985), 57–59.
42. Ibid., 64–65.
43. Ibid., 59, 64–66. A recent example of underworld and upperworld ties can be seen in the story of the tunnel that was discovered in 1990 connecting Agua Prieta, Sonora, with Douglas, Arizona, and was used for smuggling cocaine. Francisco Rafael Camarena, who claimed to be an attorney and investor from Guadalajara, was a drug runner who needed an outlet for a cocaine-smuggling tunnel in Mexico. He arranged to purchase two parcels of land in Douglas from Cochise County Justice of the Peace Ronald J. "Joe" Barone. The U.S. end of the tunnel was found to be

on property Barone had sold to Camarena. Barone made a huge profit on the deal, netting a profit of 472 percent on his investment. Incidentally, Barone was godfather to Camarena's son and thus a *compadre* of Camarena. See Paul Brinkley-Rogers and Keoki Skinner, "Land deal staining JP's life," *Arizona Republic*, 24 June 1990.

44. Lupsha, "The Border Underworld," 61.
45. Williams, "Resurgent North," 318; Larry Rohter, "Free-Trade Talks with U.S. Set Off Debate in Mexico," *New York Times*, 29 March 1990.
46. The literature of NAFTA is vast, but an excellent analysis is found in Larry Rohter, "Stop the World, Mexico is Getting on," *New York Times*, 3 June 1990 (reproduced in Spanish in *Diario de Juarez*, 4 June 1990). See also "Comercio Libre con EU y Canadá," *Excelsior* (Mexico City), 22 May 1990. On oil and the common market see Manuel R. Millor, *Mexico's Oil: Catalyst for a New Relationship with the U.S.?* (Boulder, Colo., 1982), 189–91. A number of professional groups in the United States have held meetings on the topic, including the League of Women Voters of Connecticut meeting in cooperation with Yale University at New Haven on 15 March 1989. Even the National Football League was talking in 1990 about a World League of Football that would include Montreal, Mexico City, and several U.S. cities.
47. Rohter, "Stop the World, Mexico is Getting on"; Robert Pear, "Centralized Immigration Control Urged," *New York Times*, 3 June 1990; *Bottom Line*, 30 December 1989, 1, 2; Robert J. Samuelson, "Mexican Standoff," *Newsweek*, 25 June 1990; John N. MacLean, "Mexico ending its siesta to enter the big economic league," *Buffalo News*, 21 April 1991.
48. Canadian Liberals, New Democrats, and labor leaders fear an exodus of manufacturers seeking low-cost labor and a flood of cheap Mexican goods inundating Canada. They oppose the U.S.-Canada free-trade pact as well. U.S. labor leaders also dislike the NAFTA idea too, usually arguing against any moves that would lead to a loss of jobs in the United States. U.S. leaders in the environmental movement also oppose the idea of a NAFTA. Mexican intellectuals and politicans generally argue that since the relationship between the overdeveloped United States and underdeveloped Mexico is asymmetrical, a NAFTA will simply reinforce an unequal relationship with the United States. The U.S. will get the economic reforms that a creditor nation like the United States needs and will use its power to maintain the existing Mexican political system (allegedly undemocratic and corrupt), while Mexico will continue to stay under-

developed and dependent on the United States. Before you can have inter-dependence between the U.S. and Mexico, argues Carlos Fuentes, Mexico must be independent (which it is not). See the following: Barbara O'Brien, "Envoy calls Canadians sour on free trade," *Buffalo News*, 29 March 1990; James T. Madore, "Mexico could ruin city's [Buffalo's] free-trade boom," *Buffalo News*, 6 May 1990; Cuauhtémoc Cárdenas, "For Mexico, Freedom Before Free Trade," *New York Times*, 1 April 1990; Interview by Bill Moyers of Carlos Fuentes, *A World of Ideas*, 4; and Charles F. Bonser, ed., *Toward a North American Common Market* (Boulder, Colo., 1991).

Epilogue: The Rediscovery of Mexico

1. John Phillip Santos, "In 1940, All Things Mexican Were All the Rage," *Los Angeles Times/Calendar*, 30 September 1990.
2. *Vogue* (New York City), October 1990. See also Jack Flam, "Mexican Art over Three Millennia," *Wall Street Journal*, 9 October 1990; and "Sending New York 30 Centuries of Splendor," *World Monitor* (November 1990): 10.

    Also scheduled for this time in New York City were a symposium on pre-Columbian Mexican culture that accompanied the Metropolitan exhibit, as well as an ongoing series of lectures on U.S.-Mexico relations at the Bildner Center, City University of New York graduate school. In addition, there were related exhibitions throughout the city on Mexican scientific research, engineering, architecture, literature, film, and coinage. There were also performing arts, such as rarely heard sixteenth-to eighteenth-century music, under the heading "Mexico, A Work of Art: Music."
3. *Mexico: Splendors of Thirty Centuries*, introduction by Octavio Paz (Boston, 1990) was published in conjunction with the Metropolitan exhibition. See also Octavio Paz, "The Power of Ancient Mexican Art," trans. Anthony Stanton, the *New York Review of Books*, 6 December 1990: 18–21.
4. The Museo del Barrio's exhibit, entitled "Through the Path of Echoes: Contemporary Art in Mexico," did focus on paintings, prints, photographs, and sculptures created in the 1980s by young Mexican artists. See *The Chronicle of Higher Education*, 17 October 1990, B64. Popular culture, unlike folk art, was represented in the exhibit with colonial *retablos*, the prints of José Guadalupe Posada, and the populist works of Frida Kahlo and Diego Rivera. When the Metropolitan show traveled to San Antonio,

Texas, for its 6 April 1991 opening, the exhibit was appended by the San Antonio Museum of Art's own collection of folk art. Obviously, someone was listening to the New York show's critics. See "Mexico: Splendors of Thirty Centuries," *San Antonio Express-News*, 31 March 1991.

5. When asked why the 1990 show stopped in the 1950s, William S. Lieberman, chairman of the Metropolitan's department of twentieth-century art, explained that "some of the Mexican advisers were opposed to showing the contemporary work." See Carlos Monsivais, "The Splendors of Mexico," *Artnews* 89 (October 1990): 151. See also John Phillip Santos, "3000 Years of Mexican Art," *Los Angeles Times/Calendar*, 30 September 1990; and "Mexico on Five Galleries a Day," *Newsweek* (29 October 1990): 70–71, 74.

6. For the art of Jaime Garza, see Alan Weisman, *La Frontera: The United States Border with Mexico*, with photographs by Jay Dusard (San Diego, Calif., 1986), 11–12, plate 1 (following p. 30). For the Reagan effigy see either "Quemaron al *contra* Reagan en la Guerrero," *El Día*, 30 March 1986; or "En la casa de los tres 'trono' Reagan," *Metrópoli*, 30 March 1986.

7. Robert Hughes, "Onward From Olmec," *Time*, 15 October 1990; and William Dirk Raat, "New York rediscovers the elitist view of Mexican art," *Buffalo News*, 25 November 1990. For U.S. interest in Mexican oil see Katherine Ellison, "Mexicans' anxiety grows over giving U.S. a role in oil industry," *Buffalo News*, 4 December 1990. For the Salinas years see Philip L. Russell, *Mexico under Salinas* (Austin, 1994). See also Peter Smith, "Mexico since 1946," in *The Cambridge History of Latin America*, ed. Leslie Bethell (Cambridge, Eng., 1990), 7:156.

8. See three articles by Tim Golden that appeared in the *New York Times*: "Mexicans Cast Votes in Large Numbers," 22 August 1994; "An Uncertain Mandate," 23 August 1994; "Winner in Mexico Calls for 'Dialogue' with Other Parties," 24 August 1994.

9. Russell, *Mexico under Salinas*, 160–76.

10. Ibid., 177–229.

11. See several articles in *Akwe:kon: A Journal of Indigenous Issues* (Summer 1994).

12. Alma Guillermoprieto, "The Shadow War," *New York Review of Books*, 2 March 1995: 34–43.

13. *Mexico News Pak* (Feb. 27–Mar. 9, 1995): 1–6.

14. Miguel Ruiz-Cabañas, "Mexico's Changing Illicit Drug Supply Role," in *The Drug Connection in U.S.-Mexican Relations*, ed. Guadalupe González

and Marta Tienda (Center for U.S.-Mexican Studies, University of California, San Diego, 1989), 43–68. See also Russell, *Mexico under Salinas,* 319–24.

15. Ruiz-Cabañas, "Mexico's Changing Illicit Drug Supply Role," 43–68.
16. Christine E. Contee, "U.S. Perceptions of United States-Mexican Relations," in *Images of Mexico in the United States,* ed. John H. Coatsworth and Carlos Rico (Center for U.S.-Mexican Studies, University of California, San Diego, 1989), 40–41. The relationship of disease and public health concerns to illegal immigration and "thirdworldization" is discussed by Richard Horton in "Infection: The Global Threat," the *New York Review of Books* (April 6, 1995): 24–28.
17. John Bailey, "Mexico in the U.S. Media, 1979–88: Implications for the Bilateral Relation," in *Images of Mexico in the United States,* 58; Carlos E. Cortés, "To View a Neighbor: The Hollywood Textbook on Mexico," in *Images of Mexico in the United States,* 94–95.
18. Pastor and Castañeda, *Limits to Friendship: The United States and Mexico* (New York, 1988), 63–69, 79.

Bibliographical Essay

This essay does not consider works that are general histories of Mexico. Its main concern is the history of the relationship of Mexico and the United States within the context of the world-economy. Individuals seeking specific items, archival and other primary works, should consult the notes.

Sources for the history of Mexico's relationship with the United States since 1810 can be found in the multivolume works published annually since 1982 by El Colegio de Mexico, *Relaciones México-Estados Unidos*, compiled by Marie Claire Fischer de Figueroa, and the various "Mexico" sections of *A Bibliography of United States-Latin American Relations since 1810*, edited by David F. Trask, Michael C. Meyer and Roger R. Trask (Lincoln, Nebr., 1968; *Supplement*, 1979). Assorted bibliographical essays relating to Mexican history are found throughout the *Cambridge History of Latin America*, edited by Leslie Bethell, especially volumes 1, 2, 3, 5, and 6 (Cambridge, Eng., 1984–1986, 1990). Also see *Guide to American Foreign Relations Since 1700*, edited by Richard Dean Burns (Santa Barbara, Calif., 1983). For recent history see the foreign relations section of W. Dirk Raat, *The Mexican Revolution: An Annotated Guide to Recent Scholarship* (Boston, 1982). For U.S.-Mexican affairs and border studies, refer to the *International Guide to Research on Mexico*, edited by Sandra del Castillo and Carlos Martín Gutiérrez (San Diego, Calif., 1987).

Aids for the study of the Greater Southwest are plentiful. A very recent and thorough aid is *Borderline: A Bibliography of the United States-Mexico Borderlands*, edited by Barbara G. Valk (Los Angeles, 1988). See especially "Archaeology" and "History," pages 49–145. Also see Ellwyn R. Stoddard, Richard L. Nostrand, and Jonathan P. West, *Borderlands Sourcebook: A Guide to the Literature on Northern Mexico and the American Southwest* (Norman, Okla., 1983). The sundry bibliographies found in the monumental twenty-seven volume set, *The Spanish Borderlands Sourcebooks*, edited by David Hurst Thomas (New York, 1991), provide an excellent source of materials for Native American history and the Spanish Southwest. Peter Gerhard's *Guide to the Historical Geography of New Spain* (Cambridge, Eng., 1972) is central for the history of *encomiendas*, *corregimientos*, *cabildos*, and local events. Still useful, though somewhat dated, is Charles Cumberland, "The United States-Mexican Border," *Rural Sociology*

25 (1960). See also Jorge A. Bustamante and Francisco Malagamba, *México-Estados Unidos: Bibliografía general sobre estudios fronterizos* (Mexico, 1980). For recent literature on the *maquila* industry see Leslie Sklair, *Maquiladoras: Annotated Bibliography and Research Guide to Mexico's In-Bond Industry, 1980–1988* (San Diego, Calif., 1988).

World-systems models have been best developed by sociologist Immanuel Wallerstein. Three of his projected four volumes have been published: *The Modern World–System I: Capitalist Agriculture and the Origins of the European World-Economy in the Sixteenth Century* (New York, 1974); *II: Mercantilism and the Consolidation of the European World-Economy, 1600–1750* (New York, 1980); and *III: The Second Era of Great Expansion of the Capitalist World-Economy, 1730–1840s* (San Diego, Calif., 1989). The best historical work that applies the world-economy model is the third volume of Fernand Braudel's *Civilization and Capitalism: 15th–18th Century* entitled *The Perspective of the World* (New York, 1984). For an ethnohistorical analysis that uses modes of production theory see Eric R. Wolf, *Europe and the People without History* (Berkeley, Calif., 1982). The history and theory of dependency and incorporation in the American Southwest is the subject of Thomas D. Hall's excellent book *Social Change in the Southwest, 1350–1880* (Lawrence, Kans., 1989). Two recent works of imperial history are Paul Kennedy, *The Rise and Fall of the Great Powers* (New York, 1987); and Walter Russell Mead, *Mortal Splendor: The American Empire in Transition* (Boston, 1987).

Cultural and anthropological studies that compare the civilizations of the Americas have become the concern of a few writers. A general interpretive work by Edmund Stephen Urbanski has been translated from Spanish by Frances Kellam Hendricks and Beatrice Berler and is entitled *Hispanic America and Its Civilizations: Spanish Americans and Anglo-Americans* (Norman, Okla., 1978). The classic essay remains Octavio Paz's "Mexico and the United States," which was originally published in the *New Yorker* (17 September 1979) and was reproduced in the 1985 Grove Press edition of Paz's *The Labyrinth of Solitude* (New York, 1961), 357–76. For comparisons of pre-Columbian Mesoamerican cultures with those of the Gran Chichimeca, see Elsie Clews Parsons, "Some Aztec and Pueblo Parallels," in *The Mesoamerican Southwest*, edited by Basil C. Henrick, J. Charles Kelly, and Carroll L. Riley (Carbondale, Ill., 1974). Comparative studies of colonial empires include James Lang, *Conquest and Commerce: Spain and England in the Americas* (New York, 1975); and Louis Hartz, *The Founding of New Societies: Studies in the History of the United States, Latin America, South Africa, Canada, and Australia* (New York, 1964). For the independence era see *Liberation in the Americas: Comparative Aspects of the Independence Movements in Mexico and the United States*, edited by Robert Detweiler and Ramon Eduardo Ruíz (San Diego, Calif., 1978). A specific study of Spanish and American Indian military relations is Thomas William Dunlay, "Indian Allies in the Armies of New Spain and the United States: A Comparative Study," *New Mexico Historical Review* 56 (July 1981): 239–58. For comparative cultural studies in recent history see Juanita Luna Lawhn, Juan Bruce-Novoa, Guillermo Campos, and Ramón Saldívar, *Mexico and the United States: Intercultural Relations in the Humanities* (San Antonio, Tex., 1984). Finally, a comparative view of the borderlands can be found in John A. Price, "Mexican and Canadian Border Comparisons," in *Borderlands Sourcebook*, edited by Ellwyn R. Stoddard et al. (Norman, Okla., 1983): 20–23.

There are several good surveys of the general history of Mexico-United States relations. A recent study by two competent Mexican historians is Josefina Zoraida Vázquez and Lorenzo Meyer, *México frente a Estados Unidos: un ensayo histórico, 1776–1980* (Mexico, 1982). It appears in English as *The United States and Mexico* (Chicago, 1985). Two earlier standard works are Howard F. Cline, *The United States and Mexico* (New York, 1963); and Luis G. Zorrilla, *Historia de las relaciones entre México y los Estados Unidos de América, 1800–1958*, 2 vols. (Mexico, 1965–66). A brief case study of U.S.-Mexican relations is the essay by Lorenzo Meyer entitled "Mexico: The Exception and the Rule," in *Exporting Democracy. The United States and Latin America: Case Studies*, edited by Abraham F. Lowenthal (Baltimore, Md., 1991), 93–110. For a study of economic dependency and neocolonialism see Karl M. Schmitt, *Mexico and the United States, 1821–1973: Conflict and Coexistence* (New York, 1974). For North American intervention since 1800 see Gaston García Cantu, *Las invasiones norteamericanas en México* (Mexico, 1971). Early nineteenth-century diplomatic relations is narrated by Carlos Bosch García, *Historia de las relaciones entre México y los Estados Unidos, 1819–1848* (Mexico, 1974).

Concerning the topic of contrasting values, ethnocentrism, and national perceptions, see the following: Yi-Fu Tuan, *Topophilia: A Study of Environmental Perception, Attitudes and Values* (Englewood Cliffs, N.J., 1974), in which Spanish, Anglo, and Pueblo world views and attitudes are examined; Evon Z. Vogt and Ethel M. Albert, *People of Rimrock: A Study of Values in Five Cultures* (Cambridge, Mass., 1966), a historical study of Mexicans, Mormons, Texans, Navajos, and Zunis in New Mexico; Arnoldo De León, *They Called Them Greasers: Anglo Attitudes toward Mexicans in Texas, 1821–1900* (Austin, Tex., 1983); David Montejano, *Anglos and Mexicans in the Making of Texas, 1836–1986*

(Austin, Tex., 1987); Raymund A. Paredes, "The Mexican Image in American Travel Literature, 1831–1869," *New Mexico Historical Review* 52 (January 1977): 5–29; John C. Merrill, *Mexico at the Bar of Public Opinion* (New York, 1939); John C. Merrill, *Gringo: The American as Seen by Mexican Journalists* (Gainesville, Fla., 1963); and Michael C. Meyer, "Mexican Views of the United States," in *Twentieth-Century Mexico*, edited by W. Dirk Raat and William H. Beezley (Lincoln, Nebr., 1986), 286–300. For the collision between Anglo-American myths and Hispanic (Mexican) legends see Juan A. Ortega Y Medina, "Race and Democracy," in *Texas Myths*, edited by Robert F. O'Connor (College Station, Tex., 1986), 61–69. Finally, for identity problems see Américo Paredes, "The Problem of Identity in a Changing Culture: Popular Expressions of Culture Conflict along the Lower Río Grande Border," in *Views across the Border: The United States and Mexico*, edited by Stanley R. Ross (Albuquerque, N.M., 1978), 68–94.

An analysis of the biological bases of changing historical ecosystems and their relationship to European expansion in America is Alfred W. Crosby, *Ecological Imperialism: The Biological Expansion of Europe, 900–1900* (Cambridge, Eng., 1986). A general cultural geography is George F. Carter, *Man and the Land: A Cultural Geography* (New York, 1968). For the American Southwest, especially Texas, see D. W. Meinig, *Imperial Texas: An Interpretive Essay in Cultural Geography* (Austin, Tex., 1969). Replacing the classical work of historical geography by Ralph H. Brown (*Historical Geography of the United States*, New York, 1948) is Ronald E. Grim's *Historical Geography of the United States* (Detroit, Mich., 1982). For a list of sources on Mexican geography see Warren D. Kress, *Publications on the Geography of Mexico by United States Geographers* (Fargo, N.D., 1979). A comparative study is Ben F. and Rose V. Lemert, "The United States and Mexico," *The Journal of Geography* 34 (October 1935): 261–66. The geography and historical geography of the American Southwest can be found in two studies by Carl Sauer, "Historical Geography and the Western Frontier," in *Land and Life*, edited by John Leighly (Berkeley, Calif., 1963), 45–52; and in his pioneer study, *Man in Nature* (Berkeley, Calif., 1975), 233–52.

Native American studies has attracted the attention of several competent investigators. The foremost work that contains basic materials on prehistory, linguistics, physical anthropology, ethnohistory, ethnography, and ethnology of Native American communities of Middle America, past and present, is the fifteen volume series called the *Handbook of Middle American Indians*, edited by Robert Wauchope (Austin, Tex., 1964–75). For the American Indian's contributions to world history see the very readable book by Jack Weatherford, *Indian*

Givers: How the Indians of the Americas Transformed the World (New York, 1988). A good introduction to the topic of American Indian history is William T. Hagan, *American Indians* (Chicago, 1979). For the most current estimates of recent and past Native American populations in the Americas see *The Native Population of the Americas in 1492*, edited by William M. Denevan (Madison, Wis., 1978). An excellent survey of the prehistory and history of Mesoamerica and the Gran Chichimeca is Mary W. Helms, *Middle America: A Culture History of Heartland and Frontiers* (Englewood Cliffs, N.J., 1982). A popular overview of the culture history of Mexico and Guatemala is Eric R. Wolf, *Sons of the Shaking Earth* (Chicago, 1959). Jacques Soustelle, *Daily Life of the Aztecs* (Stanford, Calif., 1970) is a historical sociology of the Aztecs, while the most recent "revisionist" study of the classic Maya is Linda Schele and David Freidel, *A Forest of Kings: The Untold Story of the Ancient Maya* (New York, 1990).

The topic of the Native Americans and the Spanish conquest, as well as the history of Indian-European relations, has been developed in a number of competent studies. For the conquest see Nathan Wachtel, "The Indian and the Spanish Conquest," in the *Cambridge History of Latin America*, vol. 1, edited by Leslie Bethell (Cambridge, Eng., 1984), 230–37. The best study of Aztec-Spanish relations remains Charles Gibson, *The Aztecs under Spanish Rule* (Stanford, Calif., 1964). In the Gibson tradition is the study by Nancy M. Farriss, *Maya Society under Colonial Rule* (Princeton, N.J., 1984). On the northern frontier two comparative studies are worth noting, that of Edward H. Spicer, *Cycles of Conquest: The Impact of Spain, Mexico, and the United States on the Indians of the Southwest, 1533–1960* (Tucson, Ariz., 1962); and Elizabeth A. H. John, *Storms Brewed in Other Men's Worlds* (Lincoln, Nebr., 1975). See also Jack D. Forbes, *Apache, Navaho, and Spaniard* (Norman, Okla., 1960), and Oakah L. Jones, Jr., *Nueva Vizcaya: Heartland of the Spanish Frontier* (Albuquerque, N.M., 1988).

There is extensive literature on the topic of Spain and colonial Mexico (New Spain). Fernand Braudel's *The Mediterranean and the Mediterranean World in the Age of Philip II*, 2 vols. (London, 1972–73) traces the shift in the center of gravity of Spanish power from the Mediterranean to the Atlantic during the era of Philip II. John Lynch's *Spain under the Hapsburgs*, 2 vols. (Oxford, Eng., 1981) relates the history of seventeenth-century Spain to that of Spanish America, as does the anthology by H. B. Johnson, Jr., *From Reconquest to Empire* (New York, 1970). The second volume of José Miranda's *España y Nueva España en la época de Felipe II* (Mexico, 1962) is an excellent essay on colonial Mexico, as is Colin M. MacLachlan and Jaime E. Rodríguez O., *The Forging of the Cosmic Race* (Berkeley, Calif., 1980). For the early period see Peggy K. Liss, *Mexico under*

Spain, 1521–1556 (Chicago, 1975), in which Spanish authority is imposed on the *conquistador* society. The seventeenth-century history of New Spain can be found in Woodrow Borah, *New Spain's Century of Depression* (Berkeley, Calif., 1951); J. I. Israel, *Race, Class and Politics in Colonial Mexico, 1610–1670* (Oxford, 1975); and Irving A. Leonard, *Baroque Times in Old Mexico* (Ann Arbor, Mich., 1959). The formation of nationalism is the theme of Jacques Lafaye, *Quetzal-cóatl and Guadalupe: The Formation of Mexican National Consciousness, 1531–1813* (Chicago, 1976). Finally, for the economic history of the late colonial era see both John H. Coatsworth, "The Mexican Mining Industry in the Eighteenth Century," pages 26–45; and Eric Van Young, "The Age of Paradox: Mexican Agriculture at the End of the Colonial Period, 1750–1810," pages 64–90, in *The Economics of Mexico and Peru during the Late Colonial Period, 1760–1810*, edited by Nils Jacobsen and Hans-Jürgen Puhle (Berlin, 1986).

Jaime E. Rodríguez O., in his essay *Down from Colonialism: Mexico's Nineteenth Century Crisis* (Los Angeles, 1983), compares Mexico's society and economy with its North American neighbor during and after the era of independence. A revisionist work of Mexico's independence is Timothy E. Anna, *Spain and the Loss of America* (Lincoln, Nebr., 1983). See also Romeo Flores Caballero, *La contrarevolución en la independencia: los españoles en la vida política, social y económica de México 1804–1838* (Mexico, 1969). For a Soviet historian's point of view see M. S. Alperovich, *Historia de la independencia de México, 1810–1824* (Mexico, 1967). For the specific treatment of Mexico's nineteenth-century social and economic problems see John H. Coatsworth, "Obstacles to Economic Growth in Nineteenth Century Mexico," *American Historical Review* 83 (February 1978): 80–100. A general study of the idea of progress and its role in nineteenth-century Latin America is E. Bradford Burns, *The Poverty of Progress* (Berkeley, Calif., 1980). The intellectual history of nineteenth-century Mexico is narrated in two studies by Charles A. Hale—his earlier work entitled *Mexican Liberalism in the Age of Mora 1821–1853* (New Haven, Conn., 1968) and his later study *The Transformation of Liberalism in the Late Nineteenth-Century Mexico* (Princeton, N.J., 1989).

The Texas revolt and the Mexican war have received a great deal of attention from both Mexican and U.S. scholars. The Mexican background is best told by David J. Weber in *The Mexican Frontier, 1821–1846: The American Southwest under Mexico* (Albuquerque, N.M., 1982). See also Weber, *"From Hell Itself": The Americanization of Mexico's Northern Frontier, 1821–1846* (El Paso, Tex., 1983); and Stuart F. Voss, *On the Periphery of Nineteenth-Century Mexico: Sonora and*

Sinaloa, 1810–1877 (Tucson, Ariz., 1982). For the Texas Revolution see again D. W. Meinig, *Imperial Texas: An Interpretive Essay in Cultural Geography* (Austin, Tex., 1969); and Samuel Harman Lowrie, *Cultural Conflict in Texas, 1821–1835* (New York, 1967).

The Mexican view of the Mexico-U.S. war can be found in *The View from Chapultepec*, edited by Cecil Robinson (Tucson, Ariz., 1989), or the accounts of five Mexican participants, including Santa Anna, that are found in *The Mexican Side of the Texan Revolution 1836*, edited and translated by Carlos E. Castañeda (Washington, D.C., 1971). For Mexican and American historiography of the war see Josefina Vázquez de Knauth, *Mexicanos y Norteamericanos ante la Guerra del 47* (Mexico, 1972). An analysis of the causes of the war is found in Norman A. Graebner, "The Mexican War: A Study in Causation," *Pacific Historical Review* 49 (August 1980): 405–26. Some of the better and more recent studies of the war include G. M. Brack, *Mexico Views Manifest Destiny 1821–1846: An Essay on the Origins of the Mexican War* (Albuquerque, N.M., 1975), a well documented account that uses Mexican newspapers and pamphlets; and Robert W. Johannsen, *To the Halls of Montezuma: The Mexican War in the American Imagination* (New York, 1985), a good treatment of the popular American images of Mexican weaknesses. Standard works remain Norman A. Graebner, *Empire on the Pacific* (New York, 1955); David M. Pletcher, *The Diplomacy of Annexation: Texas, Oregon, and the Mexican War* (Columbia, Mo., 1973); Albert K. Weinberg, *Manifest Destiny: A Study of Nationalist Expansion in American History* (Chicago, 1963); and Frederick Merk, *Manifest Destiny and Mission in American History: A Reinterpretation* (New York, 1963). Finally, an interesting dimension unexplored by other historians is the work by Charles Hale, "The War with the United States and the Crisis in Mexican Thought," *The Americas* 14 (October 1957): 153–73.

The most comprehensive work on the entire period from 1867 to 1910 is the monumental thirteen-volume work edited by Daniel Cosío Villegas, *Historia moderna de México* (Mexico, 1958–72). The best survey of the period is Friedrich Katz, "Mexico: Restored Republic and Porfiriato, 1867–1910," in the *Cambridge History of Latin America*, vol. 5, edited by Leslie Bethell (Cambridge, Eng., 1986): 3–78. Mexico's relations with the United States during the Juárista era are documented in *Mexican Lobby: Matías Romero in Washington 1861–67*, edited by Thomas D. Schoonover (Lexington, Ky., 1986), while U.S. investments during the French intervention are narrated in his book *Dollars over Dominion: The Triumph of Liberalism in Mexican-United States Relations, 1861–1867* (Baton

Rouge, La., 1978). A detailed analysis of U.S.-Mexico relations between 1867 and 1910 is Daniel Cosío Villegas, *The United States versus Porfirio Díaz* (Lincoln, Nebr., 1963).

Discussions of the *porfirian* origins of Mexico's economic underdevelopment are found in the following: John Coatsworth, *Growth against Development: The Economic Impact of Railroads in Porfirian Mexico* (DeKalb, 1980); Sergio de la Peña, *La formación del capitalismo en México* (Mexico, 1976); and *México bajo la dictadura porfiriana*, edited by Enrique Semo (Mexico, 1983). José Luis Ceceña studies the impact of international business and global capitalism on Mexico's economy from 1821 to 1969, with emphasis on the *porfiriato*, in *México en la órbita imperial: Las empresas transacionales* (Mexico, 1970). An excellent discussion of the Tuxtepec uprising and the role of American investors in Díaz's Mexico can be found in John Mason Hart, *Revolutionary Mexico: The Coming and Process of the Mexican Revolution* (Berkeley, Calif., 1987). For specific studies on American investments in Mexico during the turn of the century see David M. Pletcher, *Rails, Mines, & Progress: Seven American Promoters in Mexico, 1867–1911* (Ithaca, N.Y., 1958); Ramón Eduardo Ruíz, *The People of Sonora and Yankee Capitalists* (Tucson, Ariz., 1988); Alex M. Saragoza, *The Monterrey Elite and the Mexican State, 1880–1940* (Austin, Tex., 1988); and Mark Wasserman, *Capitalists, Caciques, and Revolution: Elite and Foreign Enterprise in Chihuahua, 1854–1911* (Chapel Hill, N.C., 1984). For manufacturing during and after the *porfiriato* see Stephen H. Haber, *Industry and Underdevelopment: The Industrialization of Mexico, 1890–1940* (Stanford, Calif., 1989).

Literature on the Mexican Revolution (or rebellion) is unending. What follows is a small sample of what is available. A good survey essay is John Womack, Jr., "The Mexican Revolution, 1910–1920," in the *Cambridge History of Latin America*, vol. 5, edited by Leslie Bethell (Cambridge, Eng., 1986), 79–153. An important historiographical essay with analysis of main historical themes is John Womack, Jr., "The Mexican Economy during the Revolution, 1910–1920: Historiography and Analysis," *Marxist Perspectives* 1, no. 4 (1978): 80–123. General histories include the monumental two-volume *The Mexican Revolution* (Cambridge, Eng., 1986) by Alan Knight; the revisionist work of James D. Cockcroft, *Mexico: Class Formation, Capital Accumulation, and the State* (New York, 1983); and the aforementioned *Revolutionary Mexico* by John M. Hart. An outstanding treatment of foreign relations, politics, and war is Friedrich Katz, *The Secret War in Mexico: Europe, the United States and the Mexican Revolution* (Chicago, 1981). For an introduction to the topic of U.S. relations with Mexico see Arthur S. Link, *Wilson*, 4 vols. (Princeton, N.J.,

1956–65). Two very comprehensive works from opposite perspectives are P. E. Haley, *Revolution and Intervention: The Diplomacy of Taft and Wilson with Mexico, 1910–1917* (Cambridge, 1970); and M. S. Alperovich and B. T. Rudenko, *La revolución mexicana de 1910–1917 y la política de los Estados Unidos* (Mexico, 1960). Less comprehensive but worth consulting are Mark T. Gilderhus, *Diplomacy and Revolution: U. S.-Mexican Relations under Wilson and Carranza* (Tucson, Ariz., 1977); Berta Ulloa, *La Revolución intervenida: Relaciones diplomáticas entre México y Estados Unidos, 1910–1914* (Mexico, 1971); Robert Freeman Smith, *The United States and Revolutionary Nationalism in Mexico, 1916–1932* (Chicago, 1972); Gregg Andrews, *Shoulder to Shoulder: The American Federation of Labor, the United States, and the Mexican Revolution, 1910–1924* (Berkeley, Calif., 1991); and W. Dirk Raat, *Revoltosos: Mexico's Rebels in the United States, 1903–1923* (College Station, Tex., 1981). For U.S. involvement in the Mexican countryside see the various essays in *Rural Revolt in Mexico and U.S. Intervention*, edited by Daniel Nugent (San Diego, Calif., 1988). Finally, for the frontier area see Linda B. Hall and Don M. Coerver, *Revolution on the Border* (Albuquerque, N.M., 1988).

A general survey of the 1920s is that of Jean Meyer, "Mexico: Revolution and Reconstruction in the 1920s," the *Cambridge History of Latin America*, vol. 5, edited by Leslie Bethell (Cambridge, Eng., 1986), 155–94. For the Cárdenas period of the 1930s see Alicia Hernández Chávez, *La mecánica cardenista*, vol. 16 of *Historia de la Revolución Mexicana* (Mexico, 1980). The congruence of Mexican and U.S. history during this era is the theme of Alan Knight's *U.S.-Mexican Relations, 1910–1940: An Interpretation* (San Diego, Calif., 1987). A detailed narrative account of the period is John W. F. Dulles, *Yesterday in Mexico: A Chronicle of the Revolution 1919–36* (Austin, Tex., 1961). For intelligence activities see W. Dirk Raat, "US Intelligence Operations and Covert Action in Mexico, 1900–1947," *Journal of Contemporary History* 22 (1987): 615–38, while military history is covered in Edwin Lieuwen, *Mexican Militarism: The Political Rise and Fall of the Revolutionary Army* (Albuquerque, N.M., 1968); and *The Modern Mexican Military: A Reassessment*, edited by David Ronfeldt (San Diego, Calif., 1984). The religious struggle is dealt with in Elizabeth Ann Rice, *The Diplomatic Relations between the United States and Mexico, as affected by the struggle for religious liberty in Mexico, 1925–1929* (Washington, D.C., 1959). The oil dispute is detailed in Lorenzo Meyer, *Mexico and the United States in the Oil Controversy 1917–42* (Austin, Tex., 1977). A recent study is George W. Grayson, *The Politics of Mexican Oil* (Pittsburgh, Pa., 1980).

An excellent general overview of contemporary Mexican history can be found in Peter H. Smith, "Mexico since 1946," in the *Cambridge History of*

Latin America, vol. 6, edited by Leslie Bethell (Cambridge, Eng., 1990), 83–157. Another current history is Judith Adler Hellman, *Mexico in Crisis* (New York, 1983). A standard source on Mexican foreign policy is Mario Ojeda, *México: El surgimiento de una política exterior activa* (Mexico, 1986). The topics of economic and social interdependence, trade and energy, national security, rural development, migration, and future U.S.-Mexico relations are developed by several writers in *U.S.-Mexico Relations: Economic and Social Aspects*, edited by Clark W. Reynolds and Carlos Tello (Stanford, Calif., 1983). North American and Mexican perspectives of contemporary relations are found in *Mexico-United States Relations*, edited by Susan Kaufman Purcell, vol. 34, no. 1 of *Proceedings of the Academy of Political Science* (New York, 1981). U.S. and Mexican Central American policies are dealt with in *The Future of Central America: Policy Choices for the U.S. and Mexico*, edited by Richard R. Fagen and Olga Pellicer (Stanford, Calif., 1983). For more current affairs see Philip L. Russell, *Mexico under Salinas* (Austin, 1994).

The impact of U.S. policy on the Chicano community is the topic of Rodolfo de la Garza, "Chicanos and U.S. Foreign Policy: The Future of Chicano-Mexican Relations," in *Mexico-U.S. Relations: Conflict and Convergence*, edited by Carlos Vásquez and Manuel García y Griego (Los Angeles, 1983), 399–416. Finally, the issues of conflicting images, economic interdependence, Mexican migration to the United States, the drug trade, and foreign policy are treated in *Dimensions of United States-Mexican Relations*, 5 vols., edited by Rosario Green and Peter H. Smith, (La Jolla, Calif., 1989).

An excellent interpretive history of the American Southwest is the aforementioned Thomas D. Hall, *Social Change in the Southwest, 1350–1880* (Lawrence, Kans., 1989). It should be complemented by Oscar J. Martínez, *Troublesome Border* (Tucson, Ariz., 1988), an account that emphasizes nineteenth- and twentieth-century history. Other general studies include Lester D. Langley, *MexAmerica: Two Countries, One Future* (New York, 1988); *Views across the Border*, edited by Stanley R. Ross (Albuquerque, N.M., 1978); and Raúl A. Fernández, *The Mexican-American Border Region: Issues and Trends* (Notre Dame, Ind., 1989). For economic issues see Niles Hanson, *The Border Economy: Regional Development in the Southwest* (Austin, Tex., 1981). Concerning *maquiladoras*, an analytical study is Leslie Sklair, *Assembling for Development: The Maquila Industry in Mexico and the United States* (London, 1989). Anyone who enjoys leisure reading should peruse the chapters of Tom Miller, *On the Border: Portraits of America's Southwestern Frontier* (Tucson, Ariz., 1985).

The photographs by Jay Dusard that are found in Alan Weisman's *La Fron-*

tera: The United States Border with Mexico (San Diego, Calif., 1986) provide visual delights for the interested reader. Southwestern photographer Otis Aultman is featured in Mary Sarber's *Photographs from the Border* (El Paso, Tex., 1977). A photographic work of contemporary Mexico that integrates historical photographs with an explanatory text is the published collection of Gustavo Casasola, *Historia gráfica de la Revolución Mexicana, 1900–1970*, 5 vols. (Mexico, 1965–1971). Those who wish the rare experience of viewing Mexico from the air will do well to pick up *Mexico, A Higher Vision: An Aerial Journal from Past to Present* (La Jolla, Calif., 1990). The photography of Michael Calderwood is accompanied by an introduction by Carlos Fuentes and text by Michael Calderwood and Gabriel Breña.

Index